Global Child Welfare and Well-Being

Global Child Welfare and Well-Being

Susan C. Mapp

2011

Oxford University Press, Inc., publishes works that further
Oxford University's objective of excellence
in research, scholarship, and education.

Oxford New York
Auckland Cape Town Dar es Salaam Hong Kong Karachi
Kuala Lumpur Madrid Melbourne Mexico City Nairobi
New Delhi Shanghai Taipei Toronto

With offices in
Argentina Austria Brazil Chile Czech Republic France Greece
Guatemala Hungary Italy Japan Poland Portugal Singapore
South Korea Switzerland Thailand Turkey Ukraine Vietnam

Published by Oxford University Press, Inc.
198 Madison Avenue, New York, New York 10016
www.oup.com

Library of Congress Cataloging-in-Publication Data
Mapp, Susan C.
Global child welfare and well-being / Susan C. Mapp.
p. cm.
Includes bibliographical references and index.
ISBN 978-0-19-533971-0
1. Child welfare—International cooperation. 2. Children's rights. I. Title.
HV713.M35 2010
362.7—dc22
2009044506

9 8 7 6 5 4 3 2 1
Printed in the United States of America
on acid-free paper

Contents

Introduction

While most people around the world agree that childhood is a special time of life, many barriers keep children from reaching their full potential—or even from growing up at all. There are 158 million child laborers, including 250,000 child soldiers and 1.2 million children who have been trafficked. As a result of armed conflict, 20 million children have fled their homes and millions more have died or been permanently disabled. Eighty-five percent of all children experience violent discipline from their parents. Ninety-three million children who should be attending primary school are not, while others who do attend receive a substandard education. Members of oppressed groups, especially girls, are even more vulnerable to experiencing these threats to welfare and well-being.

This text will examine these threats in countries around the world, in both the Global North and Global South. While the widespread poverty in the Global South increases threats to children, wealthier nations have not eliminated them, especially for children who live in poor families or who belong to a minority race or ethnicity. This book is based on the concepts detailed in the Convention on the Rights of the Child (CRC): that children require certain things in order to reach their full potential. And it is only when children reach their full potential that communities, nations, and the world can move forward. Chapter One explores the CRC, its background, history, and provisions.

Chapter Two begins to explore the issue of child labor, which continues in Chapter Three on child trafficking and Chapter Four on child soldiers. Chapter Five continues the theme of the impact of war and conflict on children by exploring the impact on noncombatants. Chapter Six explores the threat of child maltreatment and its accompanying topic of adoption, particularly international adoption. Chapter Seven examines the area of education, and Chapter Eight focuses on threats to well-being faced especially by girls. Chapter Nine summarizes the material and explores potential paths forward. While many more topics could have been included, these were selected to give an overview of some of the most common threats to child well-being around the world.

No book is truly authored by one person. Like most authors, I have many people to thank for their assistance. I want to thank Elizabethtown College for granting me leave to focus on writing this book, and my department for covering my classes in my absence as well as offering their support. Many thanks go to the administration at Elizabethtown for funding our research on the impact of war on Palestinian children, my co-researcher Gene Behrens, and our students Kerri Socha and Lore Herzer. An additional thank you to my former students Sara Oglesby and Ashley Huttenstine for their research assistance. Thank you to my friends (bhls and jbts alike), who have offered many words of support. I want to especially thank my husband, who put up with hours of me working on the computer and even with me taking work with us on vacations. Thank you to my mother, who read every chapter as I wrote it and offered suggestions. And thank you to the readers of this book, who care about the children of the world and want to learn about the problems they face. Hopefully, the readers of this book will try to make their world better. Together we can move mountains.

Global Child Welfare and Well-Being

1

The Convention on the Rights of the Child

While the very idea of children having rights can give some people pause, the United Nations states that they do have a set of rights to which they are entitled, regardless of nationality, religion, sex, ethnicity, or any other category of potential difference. All children need certain things in order to reach their full adult potential. These necessities start with the basics of sufficient food, water, shelter, and medical care and progress to the right to have a family, the right to be safe from maltreatment, the right to an education, the right to have their voices heard in matters that concern them, and the right to play. The Convention on the Rights of the Child (CRC), ratified by all but two nations, making it the most widely adopted convention, states that children have these rights and more.

The CRC was developed by the United Nations in recognition of the fact that people under 18 years of age are especially vulnerable to violations of human rights. Children are entitled to the same rights as all people under the Universal Declaration of Human Rights of 1948, but they have the additional protection of the CRC in recognition of the special barriers and threats that they may face. The CRC helps focus the commitment of society toward its children and the necessary conditions for them to flourish so that all parents can raise their children to reach their full potential development (Roose & De Bie, 2008).

The concept of children and children's rights has evolved in recent human history. Childhood itself is a cultural and sociological construct that has changed over time. Children were traditionally regarded as the property of their parents and had no legal rights of their own. Walker, Brooks, and Wrightsman (1999) note that children were treated as chattel—bought, sold, or abandoned as one might treat a pair of shoes. Childhood in early and medieval Europe, while recognized as separate from adulthood, was not accorded special protections, and adulthood was seen as coming much earlier than we today recognize it. This began to change in Europe between the sixteenth and eighteenth centuries as children's status gradually improved. In the eighteenth century, people began to perceive childhood as a stage of life important in its own right (Cunningham, 1995). Books especially for children appeared as well as children's furniture, clothing, and games (King, 2007). Children were still not accorded legal personhood, but their contributions were acknowledged and some protections were afforded to them. These protections tended to be differentiated by class, however, as the labor of children was desired for the economy of the nation and few working class children attended school. In England in 1840, only 20% of children had attended school. It was not until 1870 that the Education Act was passed requiring children between 5 and 10 years of age to attend school (Rios-Kohn, 2007). Boys were also accorded special differentiation before girls; thus, both class and sex affected the notion of a special time of life that deserved protection (Gittins, 2004).

The idea of childhood as a vulnerable stage of life led to the concept of child protection that became prevalent in the nineteenth century through the work of the child-saving movement. This conception of childhood also helped to develop the doctrine of *parens patriae*, under which the state had the right to interfere in private family life under certain circumstances, such as maltreatment of the child or incompetence of the parent (Pardeck, 2006; Walker et al., 1999). Concurrently, the late nineteenth century saw the evolution of children as legal persons in a number of nations in areas such as juvenile justice and education (Walker et al., 1999). It was around this time that governments began to develop the concept that children needed special protections due to their vulnerable position in society (Fuchs, 2007). In the United States the beginnings of these protections could be seen through the work of the Children's Aid Society on child maltreatment (beginning in New York in 1853), the work of the Progressive Movement on child labor in the 1880s and 1890s, and Hull House advocates for juvenile delinquents in the late nineteenth century in Chicago (Edmonds &

Fernekes, 1996). In Europe, international congresses were held beginning in the mid-nineteenth century on juvenile justice, child welfare, and child labor. However, these international efforts lacked a coordinating body until the formation of the League of Nations in 1919, which enabled the development of international declarations regarding children (Fuchs, 2007).

In 1924, the first document to incorporate the rights later included in the CRC was adopted by the League of Nations: the Declaration on the Rights of the Child. Although only five paragraphs long, it included such rights as food, health care, and shelter. The League of Nations was superseded by the United Nations, which developed its own Declaration on the Rights of the Child in 1959. As noted by Ensalaco (2005), the United Nations version contained significant evolution in the area of two distinct sets of rights: education and work. While the League of Nations version did not mention education, the United Nations noted it twice in two separate principles. The evolution of the concept of children's work is clear in examining the two documents. While the 1924 Declaration addressed vocational training in order for the child to be able to earn a livelihood, the 1959 version addressed the concepts of work that interfered with a child's development as well as a minimum age for work (Ensalaco, 2005).

The subject of work clearly illustrates how the changing view of childhood is reflected in the Declarations and Convention. The cultural concept of childhood, which varies considerably from one culture to another, affects whether children work, as well as the type of work they perform. At the end of the nineteenth century, some in the United States began to see childhood as a separate time of life that should be protected; thus, they began to move away from the acceptance of child labor. However, in other nations, especially impoverished ones, this role may still be widely accepted for children. Work performed by children can be important for their social and moral growth (Omokhodion, Omokhodion, & Odusote, 2006). However, it must be evaluated how child work may have been altered by the changing society; economic development has increased the risks of a number of types of child labor, including the introduction of mechanical equipment in agriculture that can transform work to become hazardous (Groves, 2004). In addition, children are now more likely to work away from home, out of the safety of the family (Omokhodion et al., 2006). Therefore, it became important for these international documents to provide for work that benefited children and their families, while protecting them from harmful work and exploitation.

In 1979, it was decided to update the declaration for its thirtieth anniversary in 1989. The 10-year process of drafting the new document was an intensive procedure and saw an unprecedented involvement of nongovernmental organizations (NGOs) in its development. The resulting document was renamed the Convention on the Rights of the Child (CRC). Conventions are considered to have the force of international law; by ratifying them, countries are legally bound to uphold their principles. One of the most important differences between the CRC and other human rights treaties is the requirement that the rights must be actively promoted. Ratifying governments have a responsibility to make the rights contained in the CRC known to their citizens—both adults and children (Amnesty International, 1999). This new document deviated from the previous documents in its view of the child. The Convention operates from the point of view that children are neither the property of their parents nor "helpless objects of charity" (UNICEF, n.d., ¶2). UNICEF states that "the Convention offers a vision of the child as an individual *and* as a member of a family and community, with rights and responsibilities appropriate to his or her age and stage of development. By recognizing children's rights in this way, the Convention firmly sets the focus on the whole child" (¶2).

The Convention is guided by four primary principles: nondiscrimination (Article 2); the best interests of the child (Article 3); the child's right to life, survival, and development (Article 6); and the right of the child to have his or her views heard on matters that pertain to the child (Article 12) (Office of High Commissioner for Human Rights, 1993). The CRC was the first international human rights document to declare that a child's viewpoint should be heard and considered in matters affecting the child, that victims of maltreatment need assistance in healing from the trauma incurred, and that a child's cultural heritage should be considered when arranging alternative care for him or her (Walker et al., 1999).

The rights accorded to children in the CRC have been broken into four broad categories: subsistence rights, protection rights, development rights, and participation rights (Amnesty International, 1999). Subsistence and development rights are also combined and referred to as provision rights (McTernan & Godfrey, 2006). Provision rights are those rights necessary to the basic survival of the child, including the rights to food, shelter, and health care, while protection rights protect the bodily integrity of the children, including the right to life and to be free from maltreatment and exploitation. Development rights are those that allow children to reach their full adult potential, including the right to education, as well of freedom of thought and religion, while participation rights allow children to take an active role in the life of their community. See Table 1.1 for a summarized version of the rights granted to children in the CRC.

TABLE 1.1 Rights Granted in the Convention on the Rights of the Child

1. Definition of Child	Every person under 18 years, unless national law grants majority at an earlier age
2. Freedom from Discrimination	Rights in the UN Convention apply to all children without exception; the state is to protect children from any form of discrimination or punishment based on family's status, activities, or beliefs.
3. Best Interests of Child	The best interests of the child are to prevail in all legal and administrative decisions; the state is to ensure the establishment of standards for the care and protection of children.
4. Implementation of Rights	The state is to translate the rights in this Convention into actuality.
5. Respect for Parental Responsibility	The state is to respect the rights of parents or guardians to provide direction to the child in the exercise of the rights in this Convention.
6. Survival and Development	The child has a right to life; the state is to ensure the survival and optimal development of the child.
7. Name and Nationality	The child has a right to a name and to acquire a nationality and to know and be cared for by parents.
8. Preservation of Identity	The child has a right to preserve or reestablish the child's identity (name, nationality, and family ties).
9. Parental Care and Nonseparation	The child has a right to live with parents, unless this is deemed incompatible with the child's best interests, and a right to maintain contact with both parents; the state is to provide information when separation results from state action.
10. Family Reunification	The child has a right to leave or enter any country for family reunification and to maintain contact with both parents.
11. Illicit Transfer and Nonreturn	The state is to combat the illicit transfer and holding of children abroad.

Continued

TABLE 1.1 continued

12. Free Expression of Opinion	The child has a right to express an opinion in matters affecting that child and to have that opinion heard.
13. Freedom of Information	The child has a right to seek, receive, and impart information through any media.
14. Freedom of Thought, Conscience, and Religion	The child has a right to determine and practice any belief; the state is to respect the rights of parents or guardians to provide direction in the exercise of this right.
15. Freedom of Association	The child has a right to freedom of association and freedom of peaceful assembly.
16. Protection of Privacy	The child has a right to protection from arbitrary or unlawful interference with privacy, family, home, or correspondence, or attacks on honor and reputation.
17. Media and Information	The state is to ensure access to information and material from a diversity of national and international sources.
18. Parental Responsibilities	The state is to recognize the principle that both parents are responsible for the upbringing of the children and that parents or guardians have primary responsibility; the state is to assist parents or guardians in this responsibility and to ensure the provision of child care for eligible working parents.
19. Abuse and Neglect	The state is to protect children from all forms of abuse, neglect, and exploitation by parents or others and to undertake preventative and treatment programs in this regard.
20. Children without Families	The child has a right to receive special protection and assistance from the state when deprived of a family environment and to be provided with alternative care, such as foster placement or Kafala of Islamic Law, adoption, or suitable institutional placement.
21. Adoption	The state is to regulate the process of adoption (including intercountry adoption), where it is permitted.
22. Refugee Children	The state is to ensure protection and assistance to children who are refugees or seeking refugee status and is to cooperate with competent organizations providing such protection and assistance.
23. Disabled Children	Disabled children have a right to special care and training designed to help them achieve self-reliance and a full and decent life in society.
24. Health Care	The child has a right to the highest attainable standard of health and access to medical services; the state is to attempt to diminish infant and child mortality, combat childhood disease and malnutrition, ensure health care for expectant mothers, provide access to health education, develop preventive health care, and abolish harmful traditional practices.

TABLE 1.1 continued

25. Periodic Review	Children placed by the state for reasons of care, protection, or treatment have a right to have all aspects of that placement reviewed regularly.
26. Social Security	The child has a right, where appropriate, to benefit from social security or insurance.
27. Standard of Living	The child has a right to an adequate standard of living; the state is to assist parents who cannot meet this responsibility and to try to recover maintenance for the child from persons having financial responsibility, both within the state and abroad.
28. Education	The child has a right to education; the state is to provide free and compulsory primary education, ensure equal access to secondary and higher education, and ensure that school discipline does not threaten the child's human dignity.
29. Aims of Education	The states parties agree that education is to be directed at developing the child's personality and talents; to prepare the child for responsible life in a free society; to develop respect for the child's parents, basic human rights, the natural environment, and the child's own cultural and national values and those of others.
30. Children of Minorities	Children of minority communities and indigenous populations have a right to enjoy their own culture, practice their own religion, and use their own language.
31. Leisure and Recreation	The child has a right to leisure, play, and participation in cultural and artistic activities.
32. Child Labor	The child has a right to be protected from economic exploitation and from engaging in work that constitutes a threat to health, education, and development; the state is to set minimum ages for employment, regulate conditions of employment, and provide sanctions for effective enforcement.
33. Narcotics	The state is to protect children from illegal narcotic and psychotropic drugs and from involvement in their production or distribution.
34. Sexual Exploitation	The state is to protect children from sexual exploitation and abuse, including prostitution and involvement in pornography.
35. Sale and Trafficking	The state is to prevent the abduction, sale, and trafficking of children.
36. Other Exploitation	The state is to protect children from all other forms of exploitation.
37. Torture, Capital Punishment, and Deprivation of Liberty	The state is to protect children from torture or other cruel, inhuman, or degrading treatment; capital punishment or life imprisonment for offenses committed by persons below the age of 18 years; and unlawful or arbitrary deprivation of liberty. Children deprived of liberty have a right to be treated with humanity and respect, to be separated from adults, to maintain contact with family members, and to have prompt access to legal assistance.

Continued

TABLE 1.1 continued

38. Armed Conflict	The state is to respect international humanitarian law, ensure that no child under 15 years of age takes a direct part in hostilities, refrain from recruiting any child under age 15 into the armed forces, and ensure that all children affected by armed conflict benefit from protection and care.
39. Rehabilitative Care	The state is to promote the physical and psychological recovery and social reintegration of child victims of abuse, neglect, exploitation, torture, or armed conflicts and to do so in an environment that fosters the health, self-respect, and dignity of the child.
40. Juvenile Justice	Accused children have a right to be treated with dignity. The state is to ensure that no child is accused by reason of acts or omissions not prohibited by law at the time committed; that every accused child is informed promptly of the charges, presumed innocent until proven guilty in a prompt and fair trial, receives legal assistance, and is not compelled to give testimony or confess guilt; and that alternatives to institutional care are available.
41. Supremacy of Higher Standards	The standards contained in this Convention do not supersede higher standards contained in national law or other international instruments.

Source: From Walker et al., 1999, with permission.

However, while the CRC requires that the child's best interests, as well as his or her opinions, be considered when making decisions, it does not require decisions to be made based on them (McAdam, 2006). Thus, the CRC still holds to an orientation of nurturance of children and their rights as opposed to self-determination. A nurturance orientation holds that children have the right to certain things, while a self-determination orientation grants them the right to make decisions in matters that concern them. For example, a nurturance orientation to education would grant them the right to quality education, whereas self-determination would grant them the decision of whether to attend. With regard to work, a nurturance orientation would grant them the right to protection from child labor, whereas self-determination gives them the right to enter into binding contracts (Walker et al., 1999).

Since the Convention, two additional optional protocols have entered into force, both in 2002. The Optional Protocol on the involvement of children in armed conflicts broadens the protections given to children from those allotted under the CRC (for a more detailed discussion, see Chapter Four). The Optional Protocol on the sale of children, child prostitution, and child pornography was developed to further strengthen the protections already given in the CRC due to the increasing international sexual exploitation of children (see Chapter Three).

The CRC came into force in 1990. It is the most widely adopted human rights document and was the quickest to be ratified and come into force (Tang, 2003). When it was opened for signature, 61 states signed it immediately, and by September 1990, 40 had ratified it. Only 20 nations needed to ratify it for it to come into force; thus, it quickly had more than double the number needed (Ensalaco, 2005). Currently, every nation in the world except two have ratified the Convention - Somalia and the United States. Somalia has not had a functioning national government for years and is thus unable to consider any international documents. The United States signed the document in 1995, but never submitted it to Congress for ratification.

Some who oppose ratification in the United States have stated that the Convention would undermine parental authority by interfering with parents' rights to raise their children as they see fit and by elevating the rights of children over those of their parents (Walker et al., 1999). However, the rights of children in the CRC are limited to those necessary for them to develop to their adult potential. Even the right for a child's voice to be heard in matters that concern him or her is limited according to the child's level of maturity, and it does not guarantee that the child's opinion will be followed. Thus, children do not have a higher level of rights than their parents; in fact, their voice is not given equal weight. As stated by Smith (2007), allowing children to have a voice does not mean always taking their opinions at face value, as it must be moderated by level of maturity, nor necessarily allowing their views to overrule those of adults. It means that they should be allowed the opportunity to express their views and that adults should attempt to understand their positions. Rather than threatening the family, the importance of the family is continually emphasized in the document.

One of the biggest stumbling blocks to ratification by the United States was the Convention's prohibition against capital punishment for juveniles, which the United States allowed until its Supreme Court declared it unconstitutional in 2005. In addition, the CRC provides for economic, social, and cultural rights of children. The U.S. government does not protect this group of rights it has not ratified the Convention on Economic, Social, and Cultural Rights. The Bush administration noted this as a reason for nonratification when it stated that the human rights approach used in the CRC was problematic and "goes too far when it asserts entitlements based on the economic, social, and cultural rights" (Southwick, 2001, ¶20). For example, the U.S. Supreme Court has held that children do not have a fundamental right to education (Walker et al., 1999). During the presidential campaign, Barack Obama indicated a willingness to review the treaty, but he did not commit to pressing for ratification (Obama, 2008).

While all other nations have ratified the CRC, a number have also posted reservations to some or all of it, noting that some provisions may clash with their specific national culture. For example, Hashemi (2007) explored the status of the CRC in relationship to posted reservations by Muslim nations. Centuries-old Islamic law had developed specific arrangements for the care of children, and 22 of the 57 Islamic nations have posted reservations to alert the United Nations that there may be conflicts between Islamic law and the CRC. Some of these were general reservations to the document, while others specifically addressed the concepts of freedom of religion, nondiscrimination, and adoption. Adoption is not recognized under Islamic law, which has developed another path known as Kafalah, which is recognized and named in the CRC. The difference relates to the basis for the reservation on nondiscrimination: children born out of wedlock are not entitled to the same rights as children born within a marriage. As for freedom of religion, children are born to the religion of their fathers, and, in some Muslim traditions, may not choose another religion. However, in other Muslim laws, conversion is freely permitted and no child has ever been punished for conversion (Hashemi, 2007). Ali (2007) also notes that different interpretations can be made of Islamic tradition and that if countries were to review their reservations, they would withdraw them as Pakistan, Egypt, and Bangladesh have done.

While the rights contained in the CRC are intended to cover all children, regardless of any demographic category, this is not actually so. As Grover (2004) notes, the first article of the Convention defines children as persons under the age of 18 years, unless adulthood is achieved sooner under national law. Thus, the protections can vary by nationality under the very first article of the CRC. The African Children's Charter, the only regional charter on children's rights, does not make this qualification (Njungwe, 2001).

In countries where birth registration is not widespread, people often do not know their exact ages, thus inhibiting the protection afforded to those under 18 years old. This lack of registration also encourages violations of these children's rights; they may be recruited for military service or treated as adult criminals because the government can state that the child is an adult and the government cannot be disproved (Banks, 2007). Banks also notes that in Bangladesh, maturity is viewed as contextual and varies depending on the socioeconomic class of the child and the situation in which he or she is being assessed. For example, middle class children are expected to develop educationally sooner than children from poorer families, but conversely they are expected to remain innocent regarding sexuality for a longer time.

Another criticism is that the CRC holds a Western ideal of childhood as its standard, and nations in Asia and Africa and their cultures were not included in its development. The notion of participation rights and allowing children to have their voices heard is often seen as contrary to the hierarchical nature of some of these societies, with their emphasis on honor, respect, and deference. Western societies tend to focus on developing children as individuals, while other cultures focus on developing them as members of society and emphasize the communal over the individual. Collectivist cultures value not only community cohesion and reciprocal relationships but also a respect for tradition, honoring one's parents, and deference to authority (Rogers, 2004). For countries influenced by Confucianism, the focus is on the family as opposed to the individual, and rather than focusing on the individual child, they focus on the family system (Burr, 2004). Therefore, the socialization of children to become appropriate members of society would be quite different depending on the cultural context.

While nations from the West were the early primary contributors, participation broadened as the process continued and Articles 5 and 20, in particular, were developed to reflect the views of other regions of the world (Goonesekere, 2007). However, as Harris-Short (2003) notes, although the governments of non-Western nations have ratified the CRC, the elites in a society tend to be more "Westernized" even when the majority of their populations have not been exposed to the same value systems. Thus, even when a nation has ratified the CRC, this should not be assumed to mean that the majority of the people have accepted these ideals as their own. Due to the emphasis on politeness and deference, citizens who disagreed with the orientations of the CRC would be unlikely to state so plainly (Burr, 2004). Locally developed charters and laws may give a better understanding of traditional beliefs of childhood. For example, some African nations have stated that the African Charter on the Rights and Welfare of the Child is more in alignment with African cultural norms and traditions because it includes not only rights but also responsibilities and duties. In Vietnam, one of the articles in the national law regarding children states that children have the obligation to show respect toward adults and solidarity with their friends (Burr, 2004).

Due to these cultural differences both between and within nations, achieving the ideals within the CRC may take time. These cultural traditions have developed over centuries and cannot be eliminated within a decade even with laws regarding them. In addition, nations can use the cultural differences as an excuse not to examine their own policies that impede realization of the CRC. China states that the prejudice against girls is rooted in centuries of tradition and thus is difficult to eradicate. However, this provides a dodge for the government in which they then feel they do not need to examine how their fertility control policy impacts the feticide and infanticide of females. In addition, those who state that implementation is slow due to cultural difficulties tend to be those who benefit from the current power structure, typically male urban elites (Harris-Short, 2003). As noted by Ali (2007), a right only becomes a right if people are aware of it and the right can pose a threat to the existing power structure.

Implementing the Convention on the Rights of the Child

Although almost every nation has ratified the CRC, the very fact that this book exists is testimony to the fact that children worldwide still face threats to their well-being and that not all children are able to grow to reach their potential as promised by the CRC. These threats vary from nation to nation, with children in poverty-stricken nations facing more numerous and more severe threats than children in wealthier nations, but no nation is exempt. Nations around the world have faced barriers in their attempts to implement the CRC. To assess progress of realization of the CRC, Article 44 calls for states to submit a progress report every 5 years. Unlike other human rights treaties, the CRC did not establish a method for individuals or groups to place complaints against a government for violations of the CRC nor a method to sanction governments for failing to make progress on implementation (Gerschutz & Karns, 2005). Nations have varied in how they have implemented the Convention and in their progress in realizing its aims.

Political ideology also has an impact on the implementation. In Argentina, embedded judicial practices in family courts, as well as among political elites regarding children, were a significant barrier in changing legislation to incorporate the provisions of the CRC (Grugel & Peruzzotti, 2007). Part of this may be due to the civil law nature of Latin American governments, where the judiciary has a fair amount of discretion in interpreting laws. This has also been seen in some African nations with a civil law tradition, such as Angola (Méndez, 2007).

In assessing the progress Lithuania has made in implementing the Convention, Kabašinskaitė and Bak (2006) note that under Soviet rule, social work did not exist for ideological reasons. Currently, the majority of services to children are provided through legal channels. For example, they state that while sexual abuse is now recognized as an issue in Lithuania, services to victims are poor because it is considered a legal problem, not a social problem. Not only does the child not receive social work services, but the child's treatment in the legal system is often poor, including multiple interrogations, sometimes in the presence of the offender. In another example, Lithuania has been working to move toward a system of foster care placement for children who have been removed from their families as opposed to institutional placement common under the Soviets. However, this typically consists only of payments to the foster parents, rather than services to the child or family to help reunify the family.

UNICEF's Innocenti Research Centre (2004) lists a number of measures to assess the completeness of the implementation of the CRC within a nation. Reform of the law to be in concert with the rights of the CRC is necessary as is the development of a national independent institution for the rights of children, such as an ombudsman's office. Nations need to develop a comprehensive national agenda to implement the CRC as well as permanent institutions on children's rights. Lastly, they state that allocation of resources to children to the maximum ability possible, systematic monitoring of implementation, raising awareness of the CRC and its rights, and involvement of the population, especially children, are all needed.

The study by UNICEF's Innocenti Research Centre (2004) found that reform of a nation's laws was the most common undertaking for implementing the CRC. Therefore, it is more likely that the negative rights, where children have a right not to experience something such as maltreatment, are more likely to be implemented than the positive rights, such as socioeconomic rights, including food, shelter, and health care. However, the rights are indivisible, meaning nations cannot pick and choose which to grant and thus cannot be divided. Additionally, in nations where there is little democratic participation in government, there is little child participation (Goonesekere, 2007). Rios-Kohn (2007) notes that how international human rights standards are implemented at the national level is affected by several factors, including "the political commitment to human rights, the social and cultural conditions and the existence of a human rights culture within the society, as well as the overall economy of the country" (p. 52).

A number of nations, especially those in Latin America and Central and Eastern Europe, have also revised their constitutions to be in line with the CRC. Many countries have developed codes regarding the rights of children, as well as independent human rights institutions, such as ombudspersons, for children. However, coordinating efforts across government agencies has been a challenge in many nations since so many agencies affect the lives of children. In some cases, the coordinating bodies are housed in a department that is concerned with both women and children, thus weakening the focus, or assigned to a minister of low position in the government (UNICEF Innocenti Research Centre, 2004).

In order to achieve this coordination, Northern Ireland has revised its services for children and youth based on a rights-approach anchored in the CRC. Utilizing the ecological model, they conceptualize the child as an integral part and active participant of varied systems, and they design services for the child accordingly. Services were designed across agencies to meet high-level outcomes, such as "all children are ready for learning and school," and outcomes are measured across agencies as well to encourage inter-agency cooperation. Obtaining the views of children and youth, as required by the CRC, is viewed as an essential part of the scheme (McTernan & Godfrey, 2006). The United Kingdom has not yet incorporated the CRC into its laws, preventing it from enacting its rights directly. However, the Children's Act, passed in 1989, is based on a number of the same principles, including that children do best in a family, children should participate in decisions that concern them, and the welfare of the child should be the primary consideration in making decisions (Rios-Kohn, 2007). In the Netherlands, similar to a number of other European nations, responsibility for youth-related policy has been moved from the national to the local level in order to increase the participation of youth in the formulation and implementation of said policy. However, research has found that while youth voices are sought, they are often used as a political tool as opposed to involving youth in an ongoing interactive, democratic process (Timmerman, 2009).

While South Africa began integrating the CRC right after ratification in 1995 into its laws and programs, including incorporating the rights of children in its constitution, its impact took a while to develop. An analysis of the impact of the CRC on court decisions in South Africa found that from its initiation into the South African constitution in 1996 to 2001, the rights were not fully realized and the majority of those using it were actually adult litigants. However, in examining decisions made between 2002 and 2006, it was found that children's interests were primary in the cases and the rights inherent in the CRC were used to overcome customary law, such as male inheritance (Sloth-Nielson & Mezmur, 2008). Globally, increases in the number of women in national legislatures lead to more effective children's policies. For example, in Rwanda, women hold approximately 50% of the legislative seats and have been able to develop policy to protect children from violence, including gender-based violence (Powley, 2008).

Tang (2003) analyzed the implementation of the CRC in Canada and noted a number of achievements as well as barriers. For example, national bodies were established to help implement the Convention in the areas of juvenile justice and child welfare. Schools worked to identify children with disabilities at an early state and the province of Nova Scotia worked to incorporate education on the rights of children in their school curriculum. Perhaps the most significant achievement was the usage of the CRC by the Canadian Supreme Court in decisions even prior to its ratification by Canada.

However, Tang (2003) states that barriers remain. Funding for health, education, and welfare has been cut since the 1980s as Canada focused more on an economic growth model and on increasing their international competitiveness. The CRC has been adopted by neither federal nor provincial legislation. Due to its federal system of government, child welfare laws and services vary between provinces. So while British Columbia bases their model of child welfare on the best interests of the child, Alberta criticizes the model of the CRC, stating that it undermines the family system. In 1999, an "election" regarding the rights of children was held to help educate children about the rights contained in the CRC and about the democratic process. Ten rights were selected and children were asked to vote for the one they regarded as most important. However, protests ensued with some claiming that the lack of parental involvement in this poll undermined parental authority and some school districts banned the election in their schools. Ironically, the right selected as most important was the right to a family.

The economic resources available to a nation affect its ability to achieve the goals of the CRC. Debt burden and structural adjustment policies have made it difficult for impoverished nations to achieve the promises of the CRC (Goonesekere, 2007). In assessing the progress made by Kenya in implementing the CRC, Onyango and Lynch (2006) state that Kenya has done a laudable job in many areas, including government and legislative reform as well as increasing public awareness. In Kenya, the Children's Act of 2001 was passed in order to consolidate previous legislation and to implement the CRC. As stated previously, the concept of documents focusing solely on rights without their complementary responsibilities and duties has been criticized as a Western ideology. Therefore, the Kenyan Children's Act also includes the responsibilities and duties provided under the African Children's Charter. The African Children's Charter notes that children have the duty to respect their parents, community, and society; to serve their national community; and to preserve African cultural values, social and national solidarity, and the independence of their nation (Njungwe, 2001).

It was ambitious to consolidate all of these goals into one bill while being inclusive of the local culture and customs in Kenya. However, those cultural practices that were deemed to be harmful to the child were outlawed under the Act, including Female Genital Cutting (Odongo, 2004). The Act accomplished several other notable goals, including outlawing of child labor for children under 16 years and free, compulsory primary education. However, Odongo notes that while the Act defines and lists the types of children in need of the protection of the state, it leaves unanswered the questions as to what type of protection these children are entitled. Additionally, Kenya does not have the funds to follow through fully. For example, while there has been an increase in the number of sexual abuse cases reported, there have not been sufficient funds for child welfare services. The spending of funds tends to be dictated by international donors, and countries may not have control over how monies are spent within their country (Onyango & Lynch, 2006).

Additional international pressure can result from the structural adjustment policies mandated by the World Bank and the International Monetary Fund that required borrower nations to restructure their economies to reduce government spending, including social spending on education, health care, and housing, in order to increase the ability to repay the loan (Polakoff, 2007). This policy caused widespread increases in poverty and has been revoked by the World Bank (Polakoff, 2007; World Bank, 2004). In Argentina, the social and economic rights of children deteriorated markedly under structural adjustment, which was compounded by an economic crisis in 2001 (Grugel & Peruzzotti, 2007).

Thus, while all but two nations have ratified the CRC, progress in implementing it and working to achieve the standards set forth within the document have varied widely throughout the world. Poverty, whether it is within a family or within a nation, has proven to be a significant barrier in realizing the goals. This will be further illustrated in the following chapters, which examine specific threats to child well-being.

2

Child Labor

Many of the threats to child well-being fall under the umbrella of child labor, including farm and factory workers, street children, trafficking, and child soldiers. Although the first convention addressing child labor was passed in 1919, the problem continues. According to Article 32 of the Convention on the Rights of the Child (CRC), children have the right to be protected from economic exploitation. The Article states that children should not perform "any work that is likely to be hazardous or to interfere with the child's education, or to be harmful to the child's health or physical, mental, spiritual, moral or social development." It is important to differentiate child labor that is harmful from child labor that is culturally appropriate and designed to assist children in their long-term goals, such as assistance with household chores or apprenticeships (Ajayi & Torimiro, 2004), as not all working children are child laborers. The CRC definition recognizes that some work performed by children can enhance their well-being, for example, by contributing to the family business, learning a trade, or earning some extra money. However, there is also work that is detrimental to a child's well-being, by harming the child physically or mentally or prohibiting the child's access to other guaranteed rights such as education. The CRC focuses on protecting children from this harmful work, not from all work.

The International Labour Organization (ILO) Convention 182 on child labor defines certain forms of labor as the "worst forms of child labor": children who have been trafficked; children in forced and bonded labor; children in armed conflict; children involved in the sex trade; and children involved with illicit activities (children serving in armed conflict and children who have been trafficked are discussed in greater detail in Chapters Three and Four). Additionally, children may be involved in hazardous labor, which is defined as any child working in mining or construction, working with heavy machinery or with exposure to pesticides, or working more than 43 hours per week (International Programme on the Elimination of Child Labour [IPEC], 2006).

The number engaged in child labor has been dropping markedly in recent years. Approximately 218 million children worldwide were engaged in some form of labor in 2004—a rate of 1 in 7 children. Of these, about 126 million are engaged in one of "the worst forms of child labor." These numbers represent an 11% overall decrease since 2000, and a 26% decrease in those involved in the worst forms (ILO, 2006a). These numbers have continued to decrease, and in 2007 UNICEF estimated the global number had dropped to 158 million by 2006. The Caribbean and Latin American countries saw the greatest decrease in child laborers, with numbers falling by two-thirds between 2000 and 2004. The least progress was made in sub-Saharan Africa, which currently has the highest proportion and number of child laborers of any region; approximately one-third of all children ages 5 to 14 years are engaged in labor (ILO, 2006a; UNICEF, 2007). However, it must be remembered that accurate figures are difficult to obtain due to the hidden nature of much of the labor, and thus these numbers may not match estimates for specific types of labor presented later in this chapter. For example, in India, the government census stated there were 12.66 million child laborers, while other sources have estimated 25–30 million children (Global March Against Child Labour [Global March], 2006a).

Children who live in poor countries are much more likely to be engaged in child labor than those in wealthy countries. There are 157 million child laborers in countries still developing their economies as compared to 1 million in countries with developed economies (UNICEF, 2007). Thus, while the vast majority of child laborers are found in countries in the Global South, it should not therefore be assumed that countries in the Global North are immune to this phenomenon. For example, the International Labour Organization (2004) states that there are approximately 300,000 underage children working illegally in the United States (primarily in agriculture). Furthermore, approximately 50% of children aged 13–15 years in Great Britain work—the majority of them illegally—while Portugal has more than 35,000 children aged 6 to 14 years working, 40% of whom work 6 to 7 days a week. However, ILO notes that in developed nations, children are more likely to be able to combine work with school and are less likely to be exposed to the more harmful types of labor.

When the status of children engaged in child labor is examined, it is typically the children who experience structural inequalities who are most likely to work and to be engaged in the more harmful forms of labor. For example, children who are poor or experience discrimination based on their sex or social class are more likely to work. Children who have been orphaned by the HIV-AIDS epidemic can experience a double blow; they are stigmatized due to the disease and are also often thrust into poverty with the death of their parents and thus must work in order to survive (Save the Children, 2003). Even children who are not orphaned may be forced into the role of provider for the family due to this epidemic when their parents become too ill to work.

The main reason that children around the world work is due to poverty. There is a circular relationship between poverty and child labor. While poverty leads to an increase in child labor, child labor leads to an increase in poverty. Children who work during their childhood are not able to receive a solid education, which inhibits their ability to obtain well-paying jobs as adults. Additionally, they will most likely suffer long-term health consequences from their labor, which will impede their ability to work as adults.

In order to earn enough income for survival, some families need all of their members to be economically productive and contribute to the household budget. Historically, children of poor families have typically worked and their labor was vital for the survival of the family (Polakoff, 2007). For example, in Nigeria, the most common reason children gave for working was to provide their parents with money (Omokhodion, Omokhodion, & Odusote, 2006) and in India, 23% of family income is earned by children working in part due to adult unemployment or wage cuts (Cunningham & Stromquist, 2005).

A survey in India found that 70% of parents of working children stated that their children worked in order to gain enough income for familial survival, while one-quarter stated it was to repay a debt (see discussion of bonded labor under the section "Children as Farm Workers") (Global March, 2006a). This was echoed by findings in Bangladesh in which 70% of parents of working children stated that if their children stopped working, their living standard would fall (Global March, 2006b). The expectation of the assistance of the child is often cultural and can fall along gender lines. Girls are more likely to be barred from school and thus be forced to work (for a more in-depth discussion of gender differences, see Chapter Three). On the other hand, gender expectations may require boys to help contribute to the family. In Afghanistan, it is the oldest son who is expected to work if additional income is needed for the family. In addition, boys' chores are more likely to require them to be far from the village, while girls' chores at home are more likely to enable them to combine education and labor (Hunte & Hozyainova, 2008). In Honduras, it is the responsibility of the oldest son to help provide for the family if his father is unable to do so, while the oldest daughter assists her mother with domestic labor. The increasing number of women-headed households due to paternal unemployment, migration for seasonal labor, or inability/unwillingness to provide has thus created a need for child labor (Groves, 2004).

The familial poverty can result from conflict in the child's country. In Khartoum, the capitol of Sudan, almost 30% of children living on the street stated they were there due to displacement caused by conflict in their home area (Plummer, Kudrati, & Yousif, 2007). Families in the displacement camps by Khartoum were exceedingly poor, and this placed economic pressure on the children to work (Abdelmoneium, 2005). In both Iraq and Afghanistan, the number of working children has risen due to increasing poverty, stemming in part from the death of family wage-earners in the political violence as well as adult unemployment. The number of orphans in these countries has increased rapidly and so has the number of street children ("Child labour," 2007; "Children work," 2007). The loss of parents through death or separation is a risk factor for the increase of child labor. In Uganda, children who have been orphaned by the conflict, or those separated from their families, often turn to the street for survival ("Children eke," 2008). Armed conflict in a country also increases the number of children whose births are not registered, children being born to young mothers, unknown fathers, and former child soldiers—all factors decrease the likelihood of accessing an education and having a supportive family system ("More children," 2008). Natural disasters can also cause loss of, or separation from, parents, leading to increases in child labor. Other children who lost their parents were placed with relatives or other caregivers who required them to work in order to help bring needed income to the family ("Cyclone orphans," 2008).

In the West Bank of Palestine, unemployment has soared due to the Separation Wall built by the Israeli government. Adults require a permit to cross through its checkpoints. Due to the difficulty in obtaining these permits, many could no longer access their jobs and became unemployed. As a result, poverty in Palestine tripled between 1999 and 2007. Children, however, do not require a permit to cross into Israel. Therefore, it is estimated that 1000 Palestinian children cross into Israel every day to work on the streets to earn money for their family's survival; the majority of these children are unable to attend school due to their labor ("Poverty driving," 2008). Lebanon is facing an increasing number of street children, the majority of whom are children fleeing from violence in neighboring countries, including Iraq and Palestine ("Government could," 2007).

Thus, children may migrate to escape conflict, but they also migrate in the hopes of better opportunities. South Africa is a popular destination for children from Zimbabwe and Mozambique as well as countries farther away due to the perception of greater opportunities, including jobs and education. Children feel they cannot have their needs met in their home country due to the death of a parent or the level of poverty in their native state and migrate for the hope of greater opportunities ("South Africa draws," 2007). One report found that while Thailand had experienced a decline in the number of Thai ethnic children who were in the labor force, it was suspected that their place may have been taken by children brought in from neighboring countries (Ashayagachat, 2006).

Children may also work because they do not have access to an education. If school fees are charged, children may not be able to afford them and thus cannot attend school. Even when there are no school fees, there are often fees for such items as books, uniforms, or supplies, which may create a barrier to school attendance. Nigerian children's second most common reason for working (after familial poverty) was to obtain money for education, and most children stated they would rather be in school than working (Omokhodion et al., 2006). The education offered could also be of poor quality or irrelevant to their ability to survive (Dybicz, 2005; Save the Children, 2003). In Honduras, rapid population growth and limited funding for education resulted in the school being cut to only half a day, leaving the other half as time when children work. Additionally, final exams are conducted during the peak cultivation time, when many children are needed at home and thus cannot attend. If they do not pass the final exam, they must repeat the entire grade. These factors have led to frustration and an increase in dropouts (Groves, 2004).

Types of Child Labor

Child labor encompasses a wide range of types of labor, but the vast majority of these children work in agriculture. It is estimated that two-thirds of working children are in the agricultural sector, while 22% work in the service sector and 9% in industry (IPEC, 2006). This chapter will address children working on the street, on farms or in factories, and in prostitution. While there are a number of children who have been trafficked working in these same areas, they are addressed in Chapter Three.

Street Children

Children working on the streets are among the most visible of child laborers. While their exact numbers are difficult to quantify, UNICEF (2006a) estimates it to be in the tens of millions, possibly ranging as high as 100 million. Article 27 of the CRC states that children have the right to a standard of living adequate for their development. However, for some children, their family either cannot, or does not, provide this. While the term "street children" is used as a generic label, there are subcategories. Children "of the street" work in the streets for income, but they maintain familial ties and often live at home. Children "on the street" live solely on the street and typically have no family ties (UNICEF, as cited in Lalor, 1999). These are general definitions because, of course, there are always children who do not fit these categories. It varies by region as to whether a child is more likely to be of or on the streets. Children in countries such as El Salvador and Turkey are more likely to live with their families than children in such countries as Nepal and China (ILO, n.d.a; Lam & Cheng, 2008).

Worldwide, most children come to the streets due to poverty, being orphaned, or familial conflict. The reasons why a child is in the streets will vary by whether the child is "on the streets" or "of the streets."

Children of the street are more likely to be there because of poverty. These children typically need to work in order to support their families, and they return home in the evenings (Kombarakaran, 2004). On the other hand, children on the street are more likely to have experienced familial problems such as parental death, abuse, or other conflict. They live on the street because they have nowhere else to go (Lalor, 1999). Family dysfunction, including child maltreatment, is a common reason in countries of the Global North why children wind up on the streets, in addition to poverty (Karabanow, 2003).

Other reasons may be more regional, such as armed conflict in their country, as previously discussed. How poverty affects the rise in street children can also vary by culture. For example, in several countries in southern Africa, including the Democratic Republic of the Congo and Angola, there is currently a rise in the number of street children because there has been an increase in accusations of sorcery against these children, which has led to their maltreatment or being forced to leave their homes. The accusation may be tied to a death in the family or a job loss, but it is often the result of a family member not having the financial resources to care for a child and needing a culturally acceptable reason to push the child onto the street. These children are rarely being cared for by both biological parents, but more often by step-parents or extended family members (Human Rights Watch, 2006; LaFraniere, 2007).

The majority of street children worldwide are boys for a number of reasons, part of which is definition. For example, girls on the street are often viewed as prostitutes, not street children. Furthermore, female child laborers who are not working in the sex trade are often working in jobs located off the streets (such as in the case of maids), while male child laborers are more visible on the streets working as shoeshine boys or peddlers (Lalor, 1999). Finally, girls still living with their families are less likely than boys to work on the street because they are more vulnerable to violence on the streets and are more often needed at home for chores (International Labour Organization, n.d.a).

These children perform a number of different types of jobs, including peddling items, begging, or polishing shoes. The types of labor performed will vary by region and by gender. In Ghana, the children considered it to be culturally unacceptable for them to beg and would work several jobs in order to make ends meet and avoid begging (Orme & Seipel, 2007). Depending on whether children are on the street or of the street, some children will give most or all of their earnings to their parents, while others keep it for their own use. A study in Sudan found that children who are living with their parents were more likely to work the whole day or shift, while children living on the street worked only long enough to earn sufficient money for that day's needs (Plummer et al., 2007).

There is a subset of children, mainly street children, who work as garbage pickers. They scavenge the dumps searching for things that can be sold, such as waste paper, scrap metal, glass, and bottles. They rescue food from the garbage to help feed themselves (Parker, 2002). This work is highly risky because some children have been buried under loads of new garbage being dumped. They also risk contracting diseases because they scavenge among areas of animal fecal matter and can also cut themselves on materials in the trash (Parker, 2002).

There are a number of health risks to street children. They typically do not get sufficient food, do not have access to clean water or toilet facilities, and lack access to medical care (Kombarakaran, 2004). In malaria-prone areas, they are more likely to contract the disease because they are not sleeping under mosquito nets (Orme & Seipel, 2007). They are also likely to have psychological and emotional problems; one study in Kyiv, Ukraine, found that 70% of children in their study had some form of behavioral and emotional difficulty, while three-quarters were depressed (Kerfoot et al., 2007). Harmful habits are common among street children, including use of drugs and alcohol as well as risky sexual practices. One study in Guatemala found more than half of the 170 street children included did not know the name of the first person with whom they had had sexual intercourse, and 100% had at least one sexually transmitted disease. This was not unsurprising because they averaged four to five sexual encounters a day, all unprotected (Harris, 2000). In Sudan, it was found that a number of street boys thought AIDS was only transmitted through intercourse with a girl and that anal intercourse with another boy was safe (Kudrati, Plummer, & Yousif, 2008).

Drug use and abuse are quite common among street children, partly as attempts to forget their desperation and partly to help stave off hunger pangs. In 1999, it was found that 100% of street children seeking attention at a medical clinic in St. Petersburg, Russia, had some type of addictive drug use, including smoking, glue sniffing, alcohol, and other drugs, which was a marked increase from the previous year

(Akimov, 2000). In Nepal, approximately 95% of street children sniff glue, often as a substitute for meals. The chemical inside, toluene, can cause neurological damage, paralysis, or death ("Street children sniff," 2007). In Sudan, the use of glue has taken a unique form as street children in Khartoum ingest the glue (chew or suck) as well as sniff it, possibly leading to more severe damage (Plummer et al., 2007). For children who use injecting drugs, usage of a shared syringe is common, increasing the risk of spreading disease (Karabanow, 2003).

Although street children typically receive attention for being perpetrators of crime, including theft, assault, and drug use, they are even more likely to be victims of crime (Lalor, 1999). For example, Lalor (2000) found that 73% of juvenile prostitutes in his study in Ethiopia had been raped, 93% had been physically assaulted, and 83% had experienced theft of their belongings. While boys do not frequently experience sexual assault, they are frequent victims of physical assault and theft (Lalor, 1999). While the perpetrators of these crimes are commonly other children, children are also at risk from those assigned to protect society: the police. These findings were echoed by research in Sudan, where both boys and girls were found to have experienced multiple sexual assaults while living on the streets, again commonly at the hands of police and other authorities (Kudrati et al., 2008). In Guatemala, one study with street children found that 100% of the participants had been mistreated while on the streets, often by the police, and it was considered to be expected. Most of the children did not file a claim of rights violation due to fear of reprisal as well as the belief that it would do no good. Indeed, those children who had filed a claim found that nothing happened (Godoy, 1999).

In the Congo, police have been found to physically and sexually assault street children, as well as rob them. They also have pressured the children into participating in police operations, despite their youth. Leaders of political parties will pay street children to participate in demonstrations prior to elections in order to create disorder. This is perilous for the children because security forces typically respond violently, which has led to the injury, and even death, of some of the children (Human Rights Watch, 2006). Police brutality against street children has also been documented in Brazil, India, Guatemala, and Colombia (Human Rights Watch, 1994, 1996, 1997a, 1997b). This includes such torture as removal of eyes, ears, or tongues as well as severe beatings (Harris, 2000). Street children are also vulnerable to forcible recruitment into armed forces, both governmental and rebel forces (Singer, 2005; UNICEF, 2001).

Children as Farm Workers

Despite the millions of street children, the majority of child laborers do not work on the streets, but on farms. Approximately 70% of child laborers are in agriculture, which equates to 132 million children under age 15 working in agriculture worldwide (ILO, n.d.b). Human Rights Watch (2003) estimates that in India alone, 60 to 115 million children are employed in some form of labor—the majority of them in agriculture. Working on farms can be a very positive experience for children, however. Ajayi and Torimiro (2004) note that parents in Nigeria stated that child participation in agricultural labor was cultural because their parents tend to be farmers and it is only right for children to help their parents in their livelihood. The parents felt that it provided training and socialization essential to a productive future. This sentiment is an illustration of the discussion at the beginning of the chapter in which it was noted that not all work performed by children is harmful. These children who work for and with their parents were not assigned dangerous or technical jobs nor did they work to the exclusion of schooling.

In contrast, the children under discussion are those who meet the definition set forth in the CRC who are harmed by their participation in agricultural labor. Many of these children are bonded laborers, one of the worst forms of child labor. Bonded labor is where the child owes a debt to the employer and is unable to stop working for the employer until this debt has been paid. There are three main pathways through which a child may enter debt bondage: working as part of a family that is bonded; inheriting debt from a parent or other family member; or being pledged to work as an individual in such types of labor as domestic work or in factories, for example (Child Workers in Asia, 2007). Despite its illegality, bonded labor is most common in South Asia: India, Nepal, Pakistan, and Bangladesh (Save the Children UK, 2007).

Agriculture can be hazardous for children due to the chemicals and heavy machinery often involved. The most common source of accidents for children involved in this form of labor is from operating motor vehicles, including farm machinery. These vehicles were not designed for use by children and require specialized training that children typically do not receive. Cutting tools are another source of frequent injury for the same reasons. Other threats can include the chemicals used for fertilizer because they are often more harmful for children's developing bodies than adult systems (ILO, n.d.b).

Children working on banana plantations in Ecuador are exposed to pesticides distributed by airplane while they are working in the fields. Some of the effects children reported from this exposure were headaches, fever, dizziness, vomiting, trembling and shaking, burning nostrils, and aching bones (Human Rights Watch, 2002). In Ghana, research on the cocoa farms found that almost all were unaware of the hazards associated with pesticides, and 95% of children applied pesticides without any protective equipment with the pesticide containers typically carried on top of their heads (Mull & Kirkhorn, 2005). In Egypt, approximately 1 million children younger than 12 years of age are hired for seasonal agricultural labor, even though this violates the Egyptian law stating these workers must be at least 12 years old. They work in the cotton fields manually removing pests from the cotton. While the work is typically performed during school summer vacation, work days are typically 11 hours a day, with a 1- to 2-hour break, 7 days a week (Human Rights Watch, 2001).

In the United States, while children working in agriculture are only 8% of the child workforce, they represent 40% of the work-related deaths. Approximately 100,000 children suffer an agriculture-related injury each year in the United States (Human Rights Watch, 2000). They are often exposed to pesticides, one-third earn less than minimum wage, and only 55% will graduate from high school. Despite these risks, child laborers in agriculture have fewer protections than children in other forms of labor. Children may begin work at 12 years of age as opposed to 14 years for other fields, while the age at which they may begin hazardous labor is 16 compared to 18 for other forms of labor. Additionally, there is no limit on the number of hours they work, and overtime pay is not required (Human Rights Watch, 2000).

While not the most common form of child labor in agriculture, the one that has received the most worldwide attention is the involvement of children in cocoa production in West Africa. As of 2002, it was estimated that 284,000 children were working on cocoa farms in this region, primarily in Cote D'Ivoire. The majority of these children were related to the head of the farm household, with two-thirds being their children. During the harvest, relatives in neighboring countries such as

Burkina Faso and Mali sent their children to work on the farm (Murphy, 2007). Only a small percentage of these children, approximately 12,000 (4%), are believed to have been trafficked across borders ("Efforts too small," 2008).

In an effort to reduce the number of children working on these farms, the United States passed the Harkin-Engel Protocol in 2001, also known as the Cocoa Protocol, in which the cocoa manufacturers stated they would eliminate forced child labor on the farms. Harkin and Engel pressed originally for a mandated labeling system but had to compromise on a voluntary protocol (Parenti, 2008). The initial deadline was 2005, which was extended to 2008 due to lack of progress; this was due in part to civil war between 2002 and 2004 in Cote D'Ivoire.

Tulane University, hired to assess progress, notes that progress is being made, with national task forces set up and public awareness increasing (Payson Center, 2007). Additionally, the number of children working with dangerous chemicals has been reduced ("Efforts too small," 2008). However, due to the fragmented nature of the many small farms and the previously discussed familial nature of the work, true elimination is difficult to monitor or achieve (Payson Center, 2007). However, Tulane also notes that progress would be difficult to measure because the cocoa industry has failed to establish standards and measurable objectives. While the chocolate industry states it has spent tens of millions of dollars, progress on the ground has been scarce and difficult to find. The cocoa manufacturers have established a foundation, the International Cocoa Initiative, which has but one staff member in Cote D'Ivoire (Goodman, 2008; Parenti, 2008). The government of Cote D'Ivoire is widely regarded as one of the most corrupt in the world and thus has been of little aid. Currently, only chocolate labeled as "Fair Trade" can be guaranteed to have been produced without child labor or bonded labor. Fair Trade manufacturers pay the farmers a higher than average cost for their chocolate, thus freeing the children to be able to go to school (Parenti, 2008). This supports the idea that the underlying poverty that drives the need for the labor of children has not been adequately addressed ("Efforts too small," 2008).

Children as Factory Workers

Bonded labor can also lead to child labor in factories and has been documented in nations such as Afghanistan and India. Over 2000 children in eastern Afghanistan work in brick factories alongside their parents to help their parents pay off debt to the factory owners. These children work 8 to 12 hours a day, and 90% of them do not attend school ("Children work," 2008). Children also work for brick manufacturers in India, again typically alongside their parents (Bales, 2004). Among child factory workers in India in such industries as garments or carpets, it has been found that they are forced to work in small spaces and maintain the same repetitive work for hours on end, resulting in chronic pain and growth deformities. Children working with looms often develop lung or skin diseases resulting from prolonged exposure to the wool (Child Workers in Asia, 2007). Others are employed in factories making silk and weaving it in to saris. Following is the story of Yeramma, one of the children working in the silk industry:

At 4:00 a.m. I got up and did silk winding.... I only went home once a week. I slept in the factory with two or three other children. We prepared the food there and slept in the space between the machines. The owner provided the rice and cut it from our wages. He would deduct the price. We cooked the rice ourselves. We worked twelve hours a day with one hour for rest. If I made a mistake-if I cut the thread-he would beat me. Sometimes [the owner] used vulgar language. Then he would give me more work.

–Yeramma S., eleven years old,
bonded at around age seven for Rs. 1700 [U.S.$35],
Karnataka, March 27, 2002
[Human Rights Watch, 2003, ¶1]

Other children in countries in Central America, such as Honduras, are employed in the *maquilas*, or textile factories. They often produce clothes for major American companies, such as Disney, Gap, and Nike. There have been cases in these factories of girls forced to take birth control pills or undergo abortions in order to keep the workers productive (Zelaya & Larson, 2004). Ironically, Disney in particular has a long history of utilizing sweatshop and child labor for production of its items (Co-op America, 2006).

Children who work by making fireworks in India often work in a dark and dingy shed where they roll and pack the fireworks. The gunpowder mix that is used is corrosive, and over time it eats away at the children's fingers. They breathe in the chemicals constantly, such as zinc oxides and powdered potassium chlorate, leading to long-term breathing problems and blood poisoning (Bales, 2004).

Child Prostitution

One of the worst forms of child labor is the use of children in sexually related activities, which is discussed in greater detail in Chapter Three. Article 34 of the CRC explicitly forbids the use of children in prostitution. Due to the increase in child trafficking, an Optional Protocol to the CRC was ratified by the United Nations in 2000 that addresses the sale of children, child prostitution, and child pornography. As of this writing, 135 countries were parties to this protocol, including the United States. The number of children experiencing commercial sexual exploitation is difficult to estimate, but it is estimated to be around 1 million children, the majority of whom are girls (UNICEF, 2006b; U.S. Department of State, 2005). The effects of sexually related labor on children can be traumatic. Willis and Levy (2002) estimate that 67% of prostituted children suffer from Post-Traumatic Stress Disorder and 16% have attempted suicide. In addition, 50% have suffered physical and/or sexual assault. In Ethiopia, one study found that three-quarters of juvenile prostitutes had been raped, 93% had been beaten and 83% had been robbed while on the street (Lalor, 2000).

Despite this, not all children who enter the sex trade do so under duress; some children opt to engage in sex work in order to earn the money it can bring. In Thailand, government officials found that girls as young as 12 years old were working in the sex trade during school holidays in order to earn pocket money for such items as cell phones and clothes (Ngamkham, 2006). Some Thai girls opt to work in prostitution in order to earn money to repay their parents for their sacrifices, and some state that in a society where there are still fewer opportunities for women than for men, prostitution remains an option (Bower, 2005). In Ghana, child sex workers were recruited from the estimated 20,000 children on the street in the capitol, Accra, to service the adolescent males who were coming to the brothel. While the girls were not forced to participate, their decision to do so cannot be considered a free choice because it was the only way for them to make enough money to live as well as send home money to their families ("Profile," 2008;

"Response," 2008). In Ethiopia, extreme poverty has also been found to be the main factor for working in the sex trade. Girls typically tried other occupations before being recruited into prostitution (Lalor, 2000). In Indonesia, high unemployment and lack of access to education combine with poverty to fuel child prostitution. Those children who are rescued from prostitution will typically return to it quickly—-either from their own need to earn money or from being sent back by their parents ("Poverty at root," 2008).

Mining

Approximately 1 million children work in mines in Africa, Asia, and South America (Save the Children UK, 2007). This may be gold mining, salt mining, or rock quarry mining. It is difficult to adequately assess or protect children involved in mining because many of the mines where they work are small, illegal, and extremely rural (ILO, 2006b). Children are working in such diverse locations as the Philippines, Peru, India, and the Sahel region of West Africa (where about one-third of the workforce is children) (Save the Children UK, 2007). Some of the children come to work in mines with their families, while others are trafficked there or forced to work by soldiers (ILO, 2006b). In the Democratic Republic of the Congo, around 40,000 children work in mining, sometimes at gunpoint of government or rebel troops ("Gem slaves," 2007).

Children who work in mining face a number of hazards. Confined underground, they breathe toxic fumes from such elements as mercury to crushed ore. They do not have protective equipment while using these toxins and use tools designed for adults, which can lead to the same types of hazards facing children in agricultural labor. Children involved in salt mining experience adverse effects from the corrosive nature of salt, including cracking of the skin on their hands and discoloration of their irises (ILO, 2006c). Children working in stone quarries in regions as diverse as Guatemala, Nepal, and Madagascar carry loads far too heavy for their abilities, develop respiratory problems from the constant exposure to the fine dust, and experience injuries from flying rock shards as they smash the rock (ILO, 2006d).

In Tanzania, 4000 children between the ages of 8 and 14 years work in tanzanite mines. The mine shafts are poorly constructed, and the children face being struck by falling rocks or being trapped in a mine collapse ("Gem slaves," 2007). A study of those involved in gold mining in Burkina Faso found a very high proportion of child workers; one-third of all workers were children, with the majority between 10 and 15 years old. Their workday typically started at 7 a.m. and lasted until dark. The pay was extremely low, and most of the children had never attended school. Children were involved in all phases of the work, including dynamite blasting, use of mercury, pounding rock, and digging (Groves, 2005).

Reduction of Child Labor

While in the short term, child labor appears to add to the economy, its long-term impact subtracts more than it adds. It is estimated that the cost to eliminate all child labor over a 20-year period would be U.S.$760 billion; the long-term economic benefit of doing so would be over U.S.$4 trillion due to the improved education and health that these workers would gain by not engaging in labor as children (International Labour Organization, 2003). Due to the fact that these economic gains are long term, it is important to maintain a systems perspective when battling child labor. Many children are working because their families are dependent upon their income in order to meet basic needs (Save the Children, 2003). If child labor is banned, but no attention is given to wages earned by adults or social supports, the situation may worsen through increases in malnutrition and other calamities. As stated by a Bangladeshi official, a long-term approach is necessary because, "If we take them away from their jobs, we would directly contribute to the hunger and desperation of their families ("Skills," 2008, ¶11). For example, bonded labor was outlawed in Nepal, which is a positive social good, but little attention was given to how to integrate these workers into the economy. As a result, approximately 25,000 of their children are working in order to try to help support the family ("Children of former," 2008).

In cases such as these, alternative means of familial income are needed. The International Labour Organization (2003) proposes income transfers to families to offset the income lost in the short term when children attend school rather than work. In addition, they state that societal structures that promote child labor such as social exclusion of certain groups as well as cultural acceptance of all forms of child labor must be addressed in order to successfully reduce child labor.

Community development to help improve the economy and the availability of jobs, as well as develop infrastructure, is vital (Dybicz, 2005). The Bolsa Familia program in Brazil gives very poor families a stipend if their children attend school and get regular health check-ups. This program is seen as the one in Brazil that has the greatest impact because aid is directed at those who are most in need and who have not traditionally benefited form other social programs; 94% of the funds reach the poorest 40% of the population (World Bank, 2007).

Therefore, those working to reduce and eliminate child labor have sought a number of different paths in order to achieve their goal, including improving the quality of and access to education, improving laws regarding child labor, and changing traditional attitudes. Education has been stated to be one of the most important factors in eliminating child labor. However, the education must be available and of good quality as well as relevant to the situation of the child. For children who are overage for their grade, it can be important to have other schooling options so that they can catch up to those of their own age without experiencing the shame of being placed with younger children. For older children, vocational training can be important to help them gain the skills to obtain a job at a living wage (IPEC, n.d.b).

International pressure can help achieve these ends as well. In Bangladesh, the number of female child laborers has been reduced substantially due to the pressure from international garment makers (Global March, 2006b). A number of manufacturers have created codes of conduct that outline the expectations for the production of goods for their company and their refusal to purchase products that do not meet those standards, including child labor. However, due to the multinational locations of production and subcontracts, production is not always monitored and violations can flourish (ILO, 2004).

Save the Children states that in developing programs to combat child labor, a true partnership is vital to success (Groves, 2004). This requires involvement of all stakeholders, including those not traditionally included such as labor unions, as well as the children themselves. The direct involvement of the children has a number of benefits, including empowerment, better information gained in research, and better dissemination of information as the children spread the information to their friends. Groves also stated that is was important to let go "of the leash that so many donor organizations feel they need to retain over those to whom they give funds" (p. 175). By doing so, it increases domestic ownership of the project and increases capacity within the nation.

Programs must be perceived as inviting to the children, and the programs must help children meet their needs as they see them. In Sudan, if street children are caught and arrested, they are whipped and sentenced to government camps, where they experience frequent beatings and sexual assault (Kudrati et al., 2008). Lam and Cheng (2008) note that the shelter for street children in Shanghai is desperately avoided by children because they are not free to leave once they enter, and even within the compound their movements are controlled. They must wear a uniform and are required to be picked up by their parents, whose abuse many of them have fled. Also, they are not offered classes or services to meet their needs. In short, the design of the shelter does not regard children as active agents in deciding their future.

In contrast, Karabanow (2003) notes that programs that incorporate street education, where the cause of children on the street is viewed as a societal structural deficit, and concurrent prevention strategies have higher levels of success than programs that view street children as delinquents or in need of rehabilitation. He notes that organizations should meet basic needs and avoid cumbersome regulations. Providing a place where the children feel comfortable and welcomed is key to helping to rebuild linkages between them and mainstream society. Respecting the children is vital to recognizing their strengths and independence, as well as acknowledging implicitly the disrespect they typically receive from society (Dybicz, 2005).

In the Philippines, one program uses "street educators" in an attempt to perform outreach with street children. These street educators are young people, some of whom are former street children themselves. They provide the street children with education about sexually transmitted diseases (STDs), sexual abuse, drug abuse, HIV, as well as intangible things such as attention and concern. The street educators will also escort the children to temporary shelters, if they desire, where social workers help them to reconcile with their families and work toward getting off the street (Silva, 2002). Schwinger (2007) notes that reconciliation is an underutilized option in Brazil, where foster care tends to dominate and many children desire to return home but need assistance in doing so.

Some countries have passed laws to try to reduce the number of child laborers. Adding to the existing ban on hiring children in occupations considered hazardous, India passed a new child labor law in 2006 that forbade the hiring of children under 14 years of age to perform domestic labor or work in hotels and restaurants (Gentleman, 2007). Additionally, Jordan passed a "code of conduct" in 2007 to try to effect a change in the lives of their child laborers. The thousands of child laborers in Jordan work 60–65 hours per week on average to try to earn enough money for survival. Approximately 13% are held in forced labor, and many are sexually abused. It is important to educate everyone, including children and their parents, about the laws on child labor, as well as the hazards that the labor creates and why it is outlawed. Furthermore, it is important to ensure the laws are enforced. Activists noted that labor inspectors would often ignore child laborers during inspections ("Code of conduct," 2007). Many countries do not have sufficient numbers of labor inspectors, and corruption can occur if salaries are low or if the inspectors themselves do not understand the reason for the laws.

Malawi has been working to improve its enforcement of laws regarding child labor; UNICEF estimated in 2006 that 30% of its children under age 14 years were engaged in child labor due primarily to the high poverty rate in the country. More than three-quarters of the population live on less than U.S.$2 a day. Child labor was especially bad on the tobacco plantations, where the children performed the same work as adults, including applying pesticides with their bare hands, but received only a fraction of the pay—U.S.$2 as compared to U.S.$11 for women and U.S.$14 for men. Therefore, Malawi more than doubled the number of child protection officers to enforce the child labor laws. However, they must still develop adequate laws to address situations of trafficking and must address the widespread poverty ("Attitudes," 2007; "Government intensifies," 2007). Reducing familial poverty is essential because many families depend on the earnings of their children for survival.

Attempts to reduce child labor must be truly multisystemic and take multiple variables and stakeholders into account. Attention to those children who are at risk should be focused not only on the country in question but on neighboring countries as well. If the number of children in the labor force from within the nation is reduced, but no attention is paid to the child labor system itself or to neighboring countries, those children will only be replaced by children from other countries. The reduction and elimination of child labor is a goal that requires remarkable coordination but, as illustrated by the recent drops, is achievable.

3

Child Trafficking

Not recognized as a form of child exploitation until relatively recently, child trafficking was first officially defined in international law in the 2000 United Nations Convention against Transnational Organized Crime, also known as the Palermo Protocol. The definition established in Article 3 states the following:

> *"Trafficking in persons" shall mean the recruitment, transportation, transfer, harbouring or receipt of persons, by means of the threat or use of force or other forms of coercion, of abduction, of fraud, of deception, of the abuse of power or of a position of vulnerability or of the giving or receiving of payments or benefits to achieve the consent of a person having control over another person, for the purpose of exploitation. Exploitation shall include, at a minimum, the exploitation of the prostitution of others or other forms of sexual exploitation, forced labour or services, slavery or practices similar to slavery, servitude or the removal of organs.*
>
> *The recruitment, transportation, transfer, harbouring or receipt of a child for the purpose of exploitation shall be considered "trafficking in persons" even if this does not involve any of the means set forth in subparagraph (a) of this article.*

The three core elements of trafficking are typically regarded as movement, recruitment, and intention to exploit (Kelly, 2005). While trafficking is often defined as involving movement of the person being trafficked, it is not required per the official definition. Child trafficking is difficult to discuss apart from child labor because the two share many commonalities. However, there are differences between the two, namely the use of deception and the use of forced labor in which the child is not free to leave.

Movement of the child is often encompassed in order to separate trafficking from other forms of forced labor because it separates the children from their social support systems and places them further at risk. The movement can be across borders or within their own nation. UNICEF (2002) notes that with this migration and separation associated with trafficking, the violation of the child's rights begins long before the child's labor ever starts. First, they are separated from their home and support systems; then they typically experience abuses during the transit to their workplace. Additionally, while trafficking of adults must involve some form of deception or threat to force compliance, the document notes the inherently vulnerable position of a child by removing that requirement. If a child is experiencing the exploitation defined in the protocol, he or she is a victim of trafficking regardless of whether coercion was used.

A number of international documents address the issue of child trafficking. As noted, the Palermo Protocol was the first international document to define trafficking; as of January 2010, 135 countries were party to this Protocol (United Nations, 2009). Article 35 of the Convention on the Rights of the Child (CRC) requires nations to take all appropriate measures to prevent child trafficking, while Article 39 states they must provide rehabilitation services to the victims of child trafficking. Article 32 of the CRC states that the child has the right to be protected from economic exploitation. Additionally, children who have been trafficked are not able to exercise numerous other rights guaranteed in the CRC, including access to education, health care, and freedom from abuse.

In 2002, an Optional Protocol to the CRC on the sale of children, child prostitution, and child pornography entered into force. As of this writing, 135 nations are parties to the Optional Protocol. The United Kingdom was a late ratifier, only becoming a party to the treaty in 2009 (United Nations, 2010). The International Labour Organization's Convention 182 on the Worst Forms of Child Labour includes child trafficking in Article 3(a) as one of the worst forms of child labor; this Convention has been ratified by 171 countries (International Labor Organization, 2010). The Council of Europe developed its own Convention on the Protection of Children against Sexual Exploitation and Sexual Abuse, which was opened for signature in late 2007. As of 2008, 27 members had signed it, but none had yet ratified it (Council of Europe, 2008a). The Council of Europe Convention on Action against Trafficking in Human Beings entered into force in Spring 2008. This Convention was deigned to help protect those who have been trafficked as well as to prosecute traffickers (Council of Europe, 2008b).

UNICEF (2006) estimates that 1.2 million children are trafficked worldwide each year; however, due to the clandestine nature of this problem, it is extremely problematic to gain accurate statistics on how many children are affected. Even within one region or country, approximate numbers are difficult to gather. This is further complicated by the fact that most assessments focus on children trafficked from one country to another and do not assess children trafficked within their own nation. In Australia, while cases have surfaced, it is very difficult to assess the scope of the problem because few statistics have been kept or cases prosecuted due to the relative newness of the laws (Murray, 2008). One literature review published in 2005 found no studies at all on trafficking for Australia, New Zealand, or the Pacific Islands (Piper, 2005). Countries in Latin America, Africa, and those of the former Soviet Union are common countries of origin, while Central and Eastern European nations serve as transit points to countries in the Global North, including Western Europe, certain Asian countries, and the United States (Monzini, 2004). However, as will be discussed, these are only generalities and exceptions are numerous.

Trafficking is a very profitable enterprise and earns U.S.$32 billion each year for its profiteers—third in earnings after the trafficking of drugs and small arms (International Labour Organization, 2008). However, the majority of human trafficking networks are not run by large international cartels as are gun and drug trafficking schemes. The majority of human trafficking networks are small scale and decentralized (Terre des Hommes, 2003).

It is also difficult to track the types of trafficking into which children fall prey. Most official attention is paid to trafficking for the purposes of sexual exploitation, such as prostitution and child sex tourism. Since this garners the most attention, those who are trapped in this form of exploitation are more likely to be included in official statistics than those in other forms of trafficking such as trafficking for the purposes of labor. This also shapes the gender analysis: girls are much more likely to be trafficked for the purposes of sexual exploitation, while boys are more likely to be trafficked for the purposes of labor. Males are also more likely to be seen as "migrants," while females are more likely to be seen as "trafficking victims" (Ali, 2005; Piper, 2005). Another difficulty in determining the number of children who are trafficked is that women and children tend to be combined into one category and are often not treated as separate entities despite the fact that they are often very different. As stated by Terre des Hommes (2003, p. 13), "Women are not children. Women need to be empowered and children need to be protected."

Boys and girls tend to be trafficked for different purposes, although they are certainly not immune to any type of exploitation. Boys are often trafficked for use in agriculture, mining, and armed conflict. Girls are trafficked primarily for the purposes of sexual exploitation and domestic labor. For example, in Pakistan, more and more children are being sent by their parents to help earn money to help their families; however, boys are typically trafficked to Europe for labor, while girls are forced into prostitution within Pakistan ("Trafficking of children," 2008). Both boys and girls are vulnerable to trafficking to force them to become beggars, and for the purposes of international adoption. The purposes of trafficking also vary by region, with the majority of trafficking in Southeast Asia occurring for sexual exploitation, and in Western Africa for domestic labor and agricultural labor.

Root Causes of Child Trafficking

There are a wide variety of causes that can act as push and pull factors resulting in the trafficking of children. These factors may vary by region; in some regions, children may be fleeing abuse at home, while in others familial poverty may be the primary reason (Willis & Levy, 2002). Natural disasters can also place children at risk because they may be orphaned and/or separated from their social support systems. After Cyclone Nargis in Myanmar in 2008, trafficking recruiters were arrested in refugee camps as they tried to recruit children (Mydans, 2008).

While children of all social groups may experience trafficking, those who are living in impoverished families or without both birth parents are more vulnerable primarily due to increased risks of deprivation and abuse. The International Labour Organization (2007) has identified a system of factors that can place children at risk for trafficking (see Table 3.1). It is important to view these risk factors as a system and not individually, as children's risk and resiliency to trafficking have been found to be related to the interconnections and cumulative effect of factors (De Sas Kropiwnicki, 2007).

Migration to find work has long been common in many parts of the world, and it has only been increased by recent global trends such as globalization and internal wars. Political and social violence has been identified as a factor that increases child trafficking in a number of areas around the world, including Africa and Latin America (Adepoju, 2005; Langberg, 2005). For example, in Nepal, the migration to India for work to support a family is a very old tradition, which has been exacerbated by the conflict between the Nepalese government and the Maoist rebels (Terre des Hommes, 2003). In some cases in northern Uganda, girls have been abducted from conflict zones to be sold to men in Sudan and in the Gulf States (Adepoju, 2005). Also, during the turmoil in Kenya following a disputed election in 2008, there were instances of children being taken from the displacement camps ("Healing the children," 2008). In Colombia, the displacement of more than 3 million people due to the internal conflict, 55% of whom are children, has helped lead to the commercial sexual exploitation of children (ECPAT, 2006). The flow of refugees out of Iraq following the war to oust Saddam Hussein has increased trafficking in such nations as Syria, where the dire poverty of the refugees has increased the already existing problem of trafficking into that nation, particularly for prostitution and domestic work ("New draft law," 2008). The flood of people fleeing Zimbabwe for South Africa has helped to disguise those seeking to traffic children, but as South Africa has no law against human trafficking as yet, perpetrators can only be charged with a lesser offense such as kidnapping ("Zimbabwean migration," 2009).

Poverty has been identified as a primary cause for trafficking in regions all around the world (Dottridge, 2002). Families seek money to enable them and their children to survive. The concept of children working to help support their families is a long tradition in most of the world. As discussed in the previous chapter, it is only comparatively recently that those in the Global North have moved away from this as a norm. Families in some parts of the world are still dependent on all

TABLE 3.1 Risk Factors for Vulnerability to Trafficking

Individual Risk Factors	
General • Age & Sex (i.e. young girls); • Marginalized ethnic minority – little access to services; • No birth registration / Lack of citizenship; • Orphans and runaways; • Lack of education & skills; • Low self-esteem; • Innocence / naivety / lack of awareness; • Consumerism, negative peer pressure In source/sending areas • Difficulties in school – drop -out of school; • Experience of family abuse or violence; • Feeling bored with village/rural life; • City attraction / perception of a better life	In transit • Traveling alone rather than in a group; • Traveling without money; • Traveling unprepared & uninformed; • Traveling without destination address or job; • Emotionally upset, drugged, threatened, constrained; • Traveling without ID & registration; • Traveling illegally; • Go through non-registered agency or smuggler; • Traveling at night. At destination • Isolation; • No social network; • Inability to speak the language; • Inability to understand system in which they live/work; • Illegal status; • Dependency on drugs, alcohol; • No contact with family; • Work in bad conditions – may result in WFCL*; • Inability to recognize exploitation/bondage

Family Risk Factors

- Marginalized ethnic group or subservient caste;
- Poor single parent families;
- Large family in poverty;
- Serious illness (HIV-AIDS) & death in poor family;
- Power relations within HH – often patriarchal – fathers decide (e.g. LA, Africa, South Asia);
- Son/male preference;
- Domestic violence & sexual abuse;
- Alcohol & drugs in family;
- Past debt / bondage relations of the family;
- Traditional attitudes & practices (e.g. send daughter to extended family);
- History of irregular migration & migration network

Community Risk Factors

- Youth unemployment;
- Location – i.e. close to border with more prosperous country;
- Distance to secondary school & training centres;
- Road connection, exposure to city;
- Quality of village leadership & community network;
- Lack of policing, trained railway staff, border guards;
- Lack of community entertainment;
- History of migration

External and Institutional Risk Factors

- War/armed conflict;
- Large youth population vs. low labour market absorption capacity;
- Natural disaster (e.g. draught, flooding, earthquakes);
- Globalization & improved communication systems;
- Absence of cheap, fast & transparent migration/job placement services for youth (i.e. youth may go illegally);
- Strict migration controls contribute to pushing movement underground, with large profits for traffickers;
- Weak legal framework & enforcement;
- Corruption;
- Weak education not relevant to labour market;
- (Gender) discrimination in education & labour market
- Shifting social mores, ambiguity in teens' roles

Workplace Risk Factors

- Unsupervised hiring of workers (e.g. in border areas);
- Limited reach of labour law;
- Poor labour protection & enforcement;
- Unregulated informal economy and 3D jobs (dangerous, dirty, demanding) with poor working conditions;
- Lack of law enforcement, labour inspection & protection;
- Inability to change employer;
- Male demand for sex with girls & sex tourism;
- Undercover entertainment (hairdresser, KTV, massage);
- Public tolerance of prostitution, begging, sweatshops;
- Lack of organization and representation of workers

---

* Worst Forms of Child Labor

Source: Reproduced with permission from International Labor Organization (2007)

family members to be economically productive. As one example, 87% of child domestic workers in Latin America are girls from large, poor families from either rural areas or living on the edges of a city (International Labour Office [ILO], 2004). Children in Togo were commonly found to enter the trafficking stream after being forced to drop out of school due to a lack of money. While education in Togo is free, there are additional school fees that can create a barrier to education (Human Rights Watch, 2003). In Albania, familial poverty was viewed by families to be the most important factor that led to the trafficking of children (Gjermeni et al., 2008).

Children often want to work in order to help their families. This desire to contribute to the family can make assistance to children who have been trafficked a delicate matter, especially when they are older teens. When they are trafficked to countries in the Global North, with very different ideas about the appropriateness of children working, these differing ideas about the nature of childhood can clash. The children do not understand why they are prohibited from helping their families and often do not wish to stop working. They are highly motivated to earn money to send home and only wish to be treated better. If they have been trafficked to countries where schooling is mandatory at their age, they may chafe at this requirement (Loiselle, MacDonnell, Duncan, & Dougherty, 2006).

Another common tradition in many parts of the world is child fostering in which parents will send their child to live with a member of the extended family who is financially better off to work for them. This traditionally worked well for all concerned; the parents were relieved of the financial burden of caring for that child and often received payment for the work of the child, the receiving family had additional help, and the child was cared for (Goździak, 2008). Certain types of work also have traditional roots that were not harmful, including girls helping with domestic labor and boys working in agriculture. However, in recent times, this tradition has led to trafficking in some cases because extended families take advantage of the child sent to their care. Additionally, it has created a norm for parents to send their children away to work, which removes them from parental protection (Dottridge, 2002). UNICEF (2002) states that in West Africa, many families were unaware of the new risks that can result from this traditional practice.

The loss of one or both parents is a risk factor for becoming trafficked for a number of reasons. The loss of a parent may increase poverty in the family, causing a need for the child's labor and wages, or remarriage may create discord with the step-parent. It may also create a push factor for the child to become fostered with extended family, as discussed earlier. While that foster family may not traffic the child, research has found that extended family are more likely to abuse a child, which can push the child to run away and then become vulnerable to traffickers. Children may also flee their home due to abuse and dysfunction and end up being trafficked (Dottridge, 2008; Gjermeni et al., 2008).

Gender roles also play a part in child trafficking. Girls have traditionally engaged in domestic work, while boys have traditionally engaged in agricultural labor. Girls are seen as more obedient and are trained to do domestic chores, while boys are viewed as having greater physical strength and better suited for manual labor (Dottridge, 2002). Additionally, girls are viewed as likely to leave the household due to marriage, so parents have accustomed themselves to the idea of sending their daughters away (Dottridge, 2002). These traditional roles can lead to exploitation and thus trafficked labor. Restrictions on girls have also been cited as a push factor. If girls do not have access to an education or employment, escape from the village will be a tempting offer. This can be especially true if they are being sexually abused or face an early forced marriage (Terre des Hommes, 2003). In some cultures, such as Thailand, children, especially girls, are expected to help support their families and owe them a debt for the gift of life (Bales, 2004).

Trafficking is rarely begun through abduction; its essential nature is deception. Children often, but not always, enter the trafficking stream through a person known to them such as their parents, a relative, a teacher, or a fellow villager. In Albania, for example, traffickers are part of the same ethnic group as those being trafficked and are typically someone known and trusted by the family (Gjermeni et al., 2008). Some are professional recruiters and will work in villages to recruit children who they then pass on to others for trafficking purposes. Most children begin their entry in trafficking with the knowledge of their parents, though parents typically do not know that the child will be exploited. Recruiters typically offer parents money or the promise that the children will receive an education or learn a trade, things parents are unable to give their children due to poverty. In the majority of cases, parents are not "selling" their children; they are sending them away in the hope that they will be able to succeed elsewhere as they cannot at home (Dottridge, 2002). In other cases, recruiters will approach children directly, especially boys, and offer them goods such as a radio or a bicycle or vocational training (Human Rights Watch, 2003).

In some cases, there is also a lack of knowledge about the actuality of the work to be performed. When village girls in Thailand were asked what a prostitute is, the most common answer was "wearing Western clothes and eating in restaurants" (Caye, 1996 as cited in Bales, 2004). In some nations, "employment agencies" are set up as fronts for recruitment into sex trafficking. Girls are told they will be working in Western nations as models, nannies, or waitresses (Hodge & Lietz, 2007). Girls have idealized notions of these countries and eagerly sign up with the "employment agencies" because they believe they will become wealthy there. These have been found in such diverse countries as Malawi, Mozambique, the Philippines, Thailand, and Colombia (International Organization for Migration [IOM], 2003; Lee, 2005) as well as countries in Southeast Europe (Dottridge, 2006).

The idealization of the nation to which the child is trafficked can also create vulnerability. While globalization has increased the awareness of opportunities in other nations, legal migration channels have not kept pace, increasing desire for irregular migration (Piper, 2005). A study of child trafficking in Zimbabwe found that South Africa was viewed "as a place flowing with hard currency where all problems would be solved" (Khan, 2005, p. 30). Families' lack of knowledge about the realities of life in the country to which their child is traveling is a major risk factor in trafficking (UNICEF, 2002). Globalization has also increased knowledge of, and desire for, commercial goods, which creates a push for increased income by the parents, children, or both (Bales, 2004).

Thus, there are a variety of factors that can lead to child trafficking. Both the twisting of traditional practices as well as new knowledge of goods and places brought by globalization have resulted in an increase in child trafficking. There are a variety of forms of labor in which children may be forced to participate, which may vary by geographic region as well as gender.

Forms of Child Trafficking

Trafficking for Commercial Sexual Exploitation

Trafficking for the purposes of sexual exploitation is the most well-known form of trafficking and occurs in nations all over the world.

A large portion of the world's nations are sending, transit, or receiving nations (Monzini, 2004). Of the estimated 1.4 million people involved in forced labor involving commercial sexual exploitation, approximately 98% are women and girls. However, as stated previously, women and children are often combined into a single category, and thus it is unknown how many of these are children (International Labour Office, 2005). Trafficking for commercial sexual exploitation is not the same as prostitution, although the two are often conflated (UNICEF, 2005). Girls who have been trafficked typically have little control over their lives, including freedom of movement, the number of clients they must service, the hours they work, or the acts they must perform (Hodge & Lietz, 2007). Children working in the sex trade have been found to be at risk for a variety of adverse effects, including sexually transmitted infections, Post-Traumatic Stress Disorder, suicide attempts, physical assault, and rape (Willis & Levy, 2002).

Trafficking for commercial sexual exploitation does occur within a nation's borders, and it has been documented in such nations as the United Kingdom and the United States (Boxill & Richardson, 2007; Department for Children, Schools, and Families, 2007). Children living on the street are at high risk for commercial sexual exploitation. Within the United States, approximately 10%–15% of those living on the street have been trafficked for sexual exploitation (Estes & Weiner, 2002). In Lesotho, children have migrated to urban areas to escape domestic violence or as a result of the impact of HIV/AIDS, which impoverishes the family. These children, who typically wind up on the street, have been kidnapped and held in a house where they are sexually assaulted by groups of men before being dumped back out. They have also been trafficked by long-distance truck drivers along their routes (IOM, 2003). Despite this internal trafficking, foreign girls are often preferred because they will be isolated from their support networks, will fear immigration authorities, and do not speak the local language. This encourages dependence on the trafficker, especially with the use of threats against family members in the home country (Hodge & Lietz, 2007).

As stated, the majority of those children experiencing this type of exploitation are females; however, boys experience it as well. For instance, boys are trafficked into child sex tourism (PLUS, 2007). In one example, boys from Romania were trafficked into Rome for commercial sexual exploitation (Dottridge, 2006). Another example is the Launda dancers in India. These boys are often gender variant and are more effeminate. They are hired to dance at weddings by those who cannot afford female dancers. After the dancing, the boys are often forced into intercourse by groups of men (PLUS, 2007).

The most common trafficking patterns involve girls (almost exclusively) being trafficked from less developed nations in the Global South to more developed nations. The line between children and adults is often very fine in the case of sexual trafficking as most are within a few years of 18 years of age in either direction. Common destination countries are Japan, the United Kingdom, the United States, and India. Research has found that the most common form of trafficking in the United Kingdom is for the purposes of sexual exploitation, although other types certainly do occur (Hughes, 2008).

A subcategory of commercial sexual exploitation is child sex tourism, which reverses this migration patterns. With child sex tourism, residents of one country, typically in the Global North, travel to another country, typically in the Global South, for the purpose of having sex with a child. While this is a relatively small category, it has received a great deal of attention due in large part to the universal revulsion against such acts. It is increasingly being found in diverse countries such as The Gambia and Colombia ("Sex tourism," 2008; "Sex tourists," 2008). A number of countries in the Global North, including the United States and Canada, have enacted laws criminalizing such acts and have sent their citizens to prison for violating them ("First sentencing," 2005; Madigan, 2004).

Trafficking for Domestic Labor

It is primarily girls who experience trafficking into domestic labor, due in large part to perceptions of female roles. Girls are expected to perform household chores, while at the same time, their education is not viewed as important as that of boys (Human Rights Watch, 2007). While there are boys who work in domestic labor, research has found that in most nations over 90% of child domestic workers are girls (ILO, 2004). While not every child engaged in domestic labor is a victim of trafficking, the isolation of the position can easily lead to abuses that create exploitation. While there have been substantiated cases of trafficking for domestic labor into countries in the Global North, a large portion of this type of child trafficking occurs from countries that are extremely poor to nearby nations that are comparatively wealthy, such as from Togo to Gabon (Human Rights Watch, 2003).

In this form of trafficking, girls are sent to live with a family and perform domestic labor in their household. While sometimes the families with whom they live are strangers, in other cases they are extended family, such as aunts and uncles, reflecting the tradition of child fostering discussed earlier. However, in cases of trafficking, they are often either paid inadequate wages or are not paid at all. Maltreatment is common, including sleeping in the kitchen, working extremely long hours, as well as physical and sexual abuse. They are rarely allowed to attend school. In Nepal, these girls are known as *kamlaris* and are sent to work in a household in exchange for a monetary payment to their parent or guardian, despite the fact that this practice has been outlawed (Haviland, 2007).

A Human Rights Watch (2003) report investigating child trafficking in Togo found that girls from Togo were trafficked into other countries, including Gabon, Benin, Nigeria, and Niger. Girls were typically responsible for all household labor, including cooking, baking, and child tending, as well as gardening and selling goods in the marketplace. While children as young as 3 years old were found to have been trafficked for domestic labor, more commonly the girls ranged between 7 and 11 years old. Physical abuse was reported by a majority of the girls. The following quotes are taken from a study conducted by Human Rights Watch (2007) in Guinea of child domestic workers:

I have to get up at 4 a.m. and work up to 10 p.m. I wash the laundry, clean the house, do the dishes, buy things at the market, and look after the children. I am told I get 15,000GNF [US$2.50] per month, but I have never seen that money.

(Thérèse I., age 14)

Sometimes my employers beat me or insult me. When I say I am tired or sick, they beat me with a whip. When I do something wrong, they beat me too.... When I take a rest, I get beaten or am given less food. I am beaten on my buttocks and on my back.

(Rosalie Y., age 9)

[The] husband wakes me up and rapes me. He has threatened me with a knife and said I must not tell anyone. He does it each time his wife travels. I am scared. If I told his wife, I would not know where to live.

(Brigitte M., age 15)

Fighting back can be difficult. In 2008, Nigerian officials stated that the prevalence of this form of trafficking continued to grow due to income and gender inequality. While the Child Rights Act in Nigeria provides for jail terms and fines for perpetrators of child labor, it has not been universally accepted in that nation, as some clauses are seen as controversial by religious and cultural leaders ("Trafficking of girls," 2008). Congolese officials note the impact of that country's civil wars on trafficking, with the numbers of orphans and those living in poverty rising as a result ("Tackling child trafficking," 2008).

Trafficking for Agricultural Purposes

Much of the media attention given to children involved in agricultural labor involves children who have not been trafficked, although they may be involved in dangerous or forced labor. The use of children on cocoa farms has received a fair amount of attention in the Global North. While the vast majority of the estimated 284,000 child workers are child laborers who work with their parents, approximately 12,000 of them have been trafficked into agricultural labor. The majority of child laborers in India work at agricultural labor under debt bondage. Debt bondage occurs when a worker (or their parent) is lent a sum of money by an employer and is unable to leave this employment until the debt is paid. Most of these children do not meet the definition of having been trafficked.

More typical of trafficking for agricultural labor is the experiences documented by Human Rights Watch (2003) examining the experience of children in Togo who have been trafficked. They found that boys were almost exclusively trafficked into agricultural labor. These boys were taken to Benin or Nigeria and forced to work cultivating crops such as cotton, peanuts, and beans. Boys report averaging 15-hour workdays, with few if any breaks, and 7-day workweeks. Children suffered physical injuries, either from beatings by the employer or from the work they did, which included the use of dangerous equipment. At the end of the agricultural season, the boys were released and had to find their own way back to Togo. They usually were given the bicycle or radio they had been promised, but the boys often had these items stolen or had to trade them for passage during the journey home because they had no money or transportation.

Children have also been found to be trafficked from Guinea-Bissau into Senegal, and from Burkina Faso to the border region of Benin, to work in the cotton fields (de Lange, 2007; "On the child trafficking route," 2007). In Burkina Faso, only boys were involved and the practice has been increasing markedly in recent years. The children made the choice to go, often directly contradicting their parents' wishes, usually due to a promised item such as a bicycle. While this migration was voluntary, and they were not physically forced to remain, they were not paid until the end of the year, which entrapped them since they could not afford to leave. Afterwards, almost all the boys interviewed stated it was a mistake to go because the work was too hard and the pay too little. They worked every day from dawn to dark and had too little to eat (de Lange, 2007).

Other Forms of Trafficking

Children are trafficked for a number of other purposes, including begging, factory work, mining, adoption, and armed conflict. (For a discussion on children involved in armed conflict, see Chapter Four; for a discussion of trafficking for the purposes of adoption, see Chapter Six.) While there have been anecdotal reports of children trafficked for body organs, there have been no substantiated reports of this actually occurring.

Begging

Children are trafficked from their home countries to nearby countries with higher tourist populations, such as from Albania to Greece or from Cambodia to Thailand or Vietnam, for the purpose of begging. They may be forced to beg directly or to perform a small service for money such as play an instrument, wash car windshields, or sell small items such as flowers or handkerchiefs. Some children are disabled, while others may have to pretend they are disabled in order to garner more sympathy and thus more money. If children do not comply, they typically face physical punishment or even torture (Derks, Henke, & Ly, 2006; Dottridge, 2006).

Some children are trafficked into urban areas and then forced to beg on the street. Any money they earn goes to their trafficker. Children trafficked from Guinea-Bissau into Senegal often end up as *talibés*—children who are forced to work as beggars in exchange for a religious education. If the children do not gather sufficient money, they are beaten. UNICEF estimated that in 2004, *talibés* constituted the majority of the 100,000 child beggars in Senegal ("On the child trafficking route," 2007). By 2008, it was estimated that about 200 children were trafficked every month in this form (UNICEF, 2008). Children are also trafficked from Nepal to India to beg on the streets of large cities such as Delhi and Mumbai (Terre des Hommes, 2003).

Factory Work

Children have also been found to be trafficked into labor in factories in such countries as India and China. In India, children from rural areas are trafficked to factories in urban areas, including sari, carpet, and *zari* factories. *Zari* is a type of embroidery often involving gold and silver threads. It is popular in exports, and subcontracting of production increases the need for low labor costs in order to make a profit. Children who have been rescued from forced labor in this industry were found to work a minimum of 12 hours a day, ranging up to 20 hours a day. They were confined in a small room with dim light and were beaten if their work production was not deemed satisfactory (Centre for Child Rights, 2006).

A notorious form of factory work in India has been the carpet factories. Children were preferred for these jobs, not only because they were more easily able to tie the small knots that weave the carpets, but because they are more easily manipulated than adults (Terre des Hommes, 2003). In 2007, children were found in a sweatshop making clothes for a subcontractor for The Gap fashion store. The children were working up to 16 hours a day hand-sewing clothes and were not permitted to leave the factory, where they lived in filthy conditions.

They were not being paid for their work because they were classified as trainees. The Gap immediately stated this violated their policies and they would not sell any of the clothes produced in the factory ("Children found," 2007). The Gap penalized the contractor and made a grant to help improve working conditions for all in its factories in India (Liedtke, 2007).

The rapid economic growth in China has created a need for large amounts of cheap labor, therefore spurring a rise in child labor and child trafficking. While Chinese law prohibits these occurrences, activists claim the government ignores abuses for the sake of profit (French, 2007, June 21). A common scheme is that of a work-study program, which has no limits on age, hours worked, or type of labor performed. Students go away to school and are told they will work in an internship to help them gain experience. However, the children commonly experience 14-hour workdays, mandatory overtime, and are often forbidden or limited in contact with their parents (French, 2007, June 21). In other instances, children have been kidnapped outright and forced to work in sweatshop conditions. In 2007, children were found who had been kidnapped and forced to work at a brick kiln in horrific conditions (French, 2007, June 16). In 2008, more than 100 children were rescued from factories manufacturing electronic goods. Not only were these children too young to work under China's laws, but their wages and working conditions also violated the laws of that nation. A number of these children had been kidnapped while others were tricked. Most of these children were from an extremely impoverished rural region of China where residents have little access to employment or education and many do not speak Mandarin. (Barboza, 2008, May 1; 2008, May 10).

Services for Trafficked Children

Specific services for children who have been trafficked are needed for a variety of reasons. Children who have been trafficked will often experience numerous potentially long-term consequences, including physical health problems such as untreated injuries and sexually transmitted diseases, as well as psychological difficulties such as low self-esteem, PTSD and depression (Department for Children, Schools and Families, 2007). For those for whom poverty or abuse were factors, they are at risk of being re-trafficked if these are not addressed. Reintegration to their home communities can be problematic for children who have been trafficked. In Nepal, one study found that 94% of returned girls reported that the community looked upon them with hate. For those who were trafficked into the sex industry, shame and community rejection for violating moral standards can make reintegration difficult, if not impossible. Children may also lack the necessary social skills to interact with their peers (Save the Children, 2004). This can make removing girls from brothels extremely difficult; the girls believe that they will have nowhere to go because their community will not accept them back (Terre des Hommes, 2003).

In other nations, children have developed relationships with their traffickers due to their dependence and isolation. Even once the children have been removed, they may try to contact the trafficker (Loiselle et al., 2006). In the United Kingdom, approximately half of the trafficked children who had been placed in care went missing; some may have returned to their trafficker, while others may have fled for fear the trafficker would find them (ECPAT UK, 2007; Silen & Beddoe, 2007). This also relates to the earlier discussed factor that many do not see themselves as children and want to earn money to help their families.

Many children who escape trafficking do not receive services. Children from Yemen who are trafficked into Saudi Arabia to work as beggars or car washers are typically dumped back over the border when they are caught (Lyon, 2008). Adolescents from Albania who had been trafficked to Greece were often jailed until there were enough children to fill a truck; they were then transported back to the Albanian border and left there, making them vulnerable to re-trafficking. This practice is now banned under a 2006 agreement between the two countries (Gjermeni et al., 2008). Some countries have small-scale organizations working to assist children who have been trafficked, but these services are typically overwhelmed by the number of children. Psychological support is particularly in short supply (Thomson, 2007).

In one example of an agency that provides comprehensive services, the Kiota Women Health and Development Organization (KIWOHEDE) of Tanzania has 22 locations throughout the country that provide health care, counseling, and vocational training to survivors of trafficking. They help reunify children with their parents, in some cases providing grant money to help parents develop a business to support their family.

Some girls are sent back to school, while others learn a trade ("Group battles," 2008; "KIWOHEDO," 2007).

Unfortunately, the response to child trafficking in many nations of the Global North has been developed from a legal perspective that tends to focus on the trafficked child as the perpetrator of a crime such as illegal immigration or prostitution as opposed to the victim of a crime. In the United States, assistance to adult trafficking victims is given only if they cooperate with law enforcement officials *and* would face extreme hardship if they were returned to their home country. Those who are not acting as witnesses are typically forbidden from receiving assistance. While this requirement of legal cooperation was not intended under the law for children, children are forced to talk with law enforcement in order to obtain the letter of eligibility that qualifies them for services. If the child is unwilling or unable to tell his or her story to a law enforcement agent due to traumatization or fear of retaliation, the child will be deported (Women's Commission for Refugee Women and Children [Commission], 2007). Additionally, services have focused on children who were brought into the United States, and they do not address the needs of native children (Boxill & Richardson, 2007). In Canada, children who have been trafficked are typically viewed as ineligible for refugee status despite their vulnerability to retaliation and re-trafficking if they are returned to their home country (Grover, 2006).

In the United Kingdom in the early part of this century, there was little training for social workers on the issue, and there was poor communication between agencies (Bokhari, 2008). The United Kingdom established the UK Human Trafficking Centre in 2006 in order to coordinate the law enforcement response within that nation. The Centre will also help create and implement prevention programs. The United Kingdom has also formed The Refugee Council Children's Panel with approximately 35 members who travel around the country to assist unaccompanied asylum-seeking children (Department, 2007). However, some still note that many victims of trafficking are removed from the United Kingdom as illegal immigrants and returned to their home countries without consideration of risks they may face. Since their traffickers are often not prosecuted, especially if they have been trafficked for labor as opposed to sexual exploitation, these risks can be quite serious. Additionally, it is felt that there is no comprehensive strategy to address the specific needs of children; services are developed on an ad hoc basis by nonprofit agencies (Craig, Gaus, Wilkinson, Skrivankova, & McQuade, 2007).

Responses to Child Trafficking

Efforts to eliminate child trafficking have taken a multiprong approach, including prevention strategies, policy initiatives, and legal consequences for traffickers. Prevention efforts have focused primarily on educating those in areas deemed at risk about the actuality of trafficking by providing them with information about the truth behind the promises. Less common are developmental efforts to reduce poverty, such as microfinance operations, and increasing enrollment in schools. Addressing poverty in a developmental fashion is essential to preventing trafficking. A study conducted in India of children who had been rescued from *zari* factory work found that approximately one-third were re-trafficked within a year due to the continuing poverty in their families. However, families who had received the governmental payment to which they were entitled under the Bonded Labour Act, or knew about the availability of it, had not re-trafficked their children (Centre for Child Rights, 2006).

UNICEF (2002) also noted that other poverty reduction interventions, such as microfinance, are not widespread. Togo holds one example of an effective program in which small business loans are made available to the mothers of children who have been trafficked or are deemed at risk of trafficking. While occurring in only a few areas, the success has surpassed expectations with the children now receiving an education or learning a trade and the amount of money available for loans increasing markedly. In India, the Society to Help Rural Empowerment and Education (STHREE) started in 1998. This organization works to strengthen the community to take appropriate legal and rehabilitative interventions; it also addresses causes of trafficking in order to prevent it in the first place. They have helped form self-help groups to work on issues of education, inequality, and employment. Loans are provided through the self-help groups to help with housing issues, as well as to establish income-generating businesses (UNICEF, 2005).

The International Labour Organization (2007) states that effective interventions must address not only poverty but other root causes as well. Keeping children in school is an important prevention strategy. For example, in Thailand, the number of years of mandatory education was raised in 1999 in order to keep children in school longer and to help reduce vulnerability to their trafficking (World Outreach UK, n.d.). Employment opportunities should also be created for older teens who are no longer in school in order to decrease the need to migrate for work (Dottridge, 2006).

Prevention efforts are often concentrated in urban areas and typically do not reach rural or marginalized areas, which is where the majority of children at risk reside (UNICEF, 2002). In order to overcome this, Benin has created a system of village committees to address risk factors as well as identify potential cases of trafficking. Committees inform fellow villagers about the importance of birth registration, education, and the risks of trafficking. They also report cases of potential trafficking and assist with the reintegration of children who have been trafficked (UNICEF, 2002).

Involvement of children in projects has been found to give projects more legitimacy as well as increase knowledge and monitoring of potential abuses (Save the Children UK, 2007). Save the Children has done extensive work in the Mekong subregion in Southeast Asia utilizing a participatory action research approach. In each project area, volunteer groups of local young people were formed to assist in conducting assessments, developing actions to raise awareness of trafficking issues, helping families gain access to services, and monitoring those at risk. These groups appear to be quite successful in their goals of raising awareness, reducing trafficking, and increasing access to services (Save the Children UK, 2006).

In Southeast Europe, a region where there is extensive trafficking, there are programs in school warning about trafficking, and many parents are aware of the dangers and warn their children against it. However, many of the warnings focus on "stranger danger," even though research in this region has found that the majority of children are recruited by people known to them, including family members, neighbors, and boyfriends (Dottridge, 2006; Save the Children, 2004). The education also does not address specific risk factors or what children can do to reduce their risk, utilizing a fear approach, rather than building resiliency (De Sas Kropiwnicki, 2007). School attendance even fell in Albania because parents kept their children home for fear they would be abducted (Dottridge, 2006). The other problem is this school-based strategy does not reach the most vulnerable children: those not in school. One study of trafficking of children in Albania found that one-third had never enrolled in school at all (Gjermeni et al., 2008).

Increasing awareness in the general public of the various forms of trafficking is important. Perceptions of trafficking differ depending on whether a nation is a sending, transit, or receiving country. Sending countries tend to be the most aware and concerned, while transit countries tend not to see the issue as relating to them. Receiving countries have traditionally been indifferent or view the problem as residing in the countries of origin, but increasingly, they are deemed to have the most accountability in the international media (UNICEF, 2002).

Nations in West Africa were hampered in early efforts due to the lack of data regarding trafficking in their nations and the low level of awareness surrounding the issues. The efforts that did occur were not coordinated and were not sustained. This created a lack of media coverage—regarded as essential to informing the public about the issue (UNICEF, 2002). Awareness of the problem tends to raise concern; in West Africa, where more research has been conducted and awareness is higher, 70% of countries identified trafficking as a concern as compared to 33% in East and Southern Africa (UNICEF, 2003). In a campaign against commercial sexual exploitation in Honduras, there were over 100 media reports in 6 months on the issue as a result of a targeted effort by the interdisciplinary local team (Save the Children UK, 2007). In Greece, one nongovernmental organization (NGO) worked to increase public awareness of the abuse that child beggars face and warned the public that to give money to the beggars would only worsen the circumstances (Dottridge, 2006).

Raising Awareness in Receiving Countries and Reducing Demand

Addressing demand in the receiving country or locale has therefore been one prong to try to reduce trafficking. If the demand is lessened, the supply will automatically reduce. A primary area where efforts around this have occurred has been in the area of child sex tourism. While it is one of the least common areas of trafficking, it has garnered a lion's share of media attention. As stated earlier, a number of Global North countries have passed laws illegalizing child sex tourism and have successfully prosecuted their citizens who have traveled abroad

FIGURE 3.1 This poster in Vietnam encourages tourists to report suspicious behavior to a hotline.

for this purpose. However, it is not just those who perpetrate the crime who must be targets for intervention but also those in the general public who are aware it is occurring and do nothing to intervene. In Madagascar, there are signs starting at the airport in the capitol alerting visitors about sex tourism, with saying such as "NO to sex tourism" and "Malagasy women are not tourist souvenirs" ("No welcome," 2008). Figure 3.1 is from a poster in Vietnam encouraging other tourists to report suspicious behavior to a hotline.

The majority of media messages prepared in the United States have been aimed at members of the general public to educate them about the occurrence of trafficking and how to intervene. For example, in Atlanta, a coalition of women developed a strategy to inform the public by holding a meeting and inviting a representative from over 200 women's groups in the area, in the belief that if people know about the sexual exploitation that is occurring, they will work to stop it (Boxill & Richarson, 2007). However, these media messages have primarily been directed at the general public, rather than at those who have been trafficked. Materials in languages other than English, as well as hotline numbers on inconspicuous items such as matchbooks or prayer cards, are still needed to spread the message to those who need assistance (Commission, 2007).

Training has also been a focus of many anti-trafficking efforts. Those receiving training have included judges, social workers, border personnel, law enforcement officials, and NGO staff. Research in the United States has found that law enforcement personnel who received training on trafficking were significantly more likely to perceive it as a problem in their jurisdiction and have a more accurate picture of perpetrators than those who did not receive training (Wilson, Walsh, & Kleuber, 2008). Another focus for training has been border officials to help them identify children at the border who are in transit for the purposes of exploitation (Department, 2007). Training of male officials and personnel has been especially important in some countries due to lower awareness and sensitivity, especially as related to sexual exploitation (Save the Children UK, 2007). Journalists have also been an important focus because they are able to utilize their media to educate a broader population. Those in the travel industry have adopted a code of conduct to help stop sex tourism, including training staff, providing information to travelers, and annual reporting (UNICEF, 2004).

One of the examples of how global attention can help reduce the use of child labor is in the use of children as camel jockeys. Thousands of children as young as 2 years old were trafficked from countries such as Bangladesh, Pakistan, and Sudan to countries in the Persian Gulf region for use as camel jockeys. These children faced numerous risks in this task: they were often physically and sexually abused; they were at risk of serious injury from the camels; and the children were forced to live in camps enclosed in barbed wire by the racetrack (U.S. Department of State, 2005). However, after the U.S. State Department cited the United Arab Emirates as a destination for trafficked children, that country began enforcing a ban on child jockeys and sent over 1000 children home to their countries ("United Arab Emirates," 2006). The child jockeys were replaced with lightweight robots operated by remote control ("Robot jockeys," 2005).

Policy Against Trafficking

The development of effective policy has been an ongoing effort. As stated at the beginning of the chapter, human trafficking did not even have a formal definition until 2000. When nations were encountering these crimes within their borders, many did not have appropriate laws with which to prosecute the traffickers, as the old laws against slavery did not quite fit. Representatives of the International Programme on the Elimination of Child Labour have stated that "clear, specific and unambiguous" laws are needed; however, many nations either lack laws addressing trafficking, or they only address trafficking for the purposes of sexual exploitation (van de Glind & Kooijmans, 2008). In Mozambique, it was noted in 2008 that since there was no law specifically against human trafficking, traffickers felt free to operate knowing they would be charged only with a lesser crime such as sexual harassment or kidnapping ("Scratching the surface," 2008). In another example, South Africa has no law against human trafficking as yet, so perpetrators can only be charged with a lesser offense such as kidnapping ("Zimbabwean migration," 2009). In Syria, because there was no separate law against trafficking, the existing laws frequently resulted in the victims being punished more severely than the trafficker ("New draft law," 2008). Jordan (2002) noted that many laws either did not provide any protection to victims or only to some victims, such as those who had been trafficked for sexual exploitation.

In the United States, the Victims of Trafficking and Violence Protection Act (TVPA) of 2000 was created to fill this void. It is based on three core "P's": prevention, protection, and prosecution. Under the TVPA, those who cooperated with federal law enforcement and would face extreme hardship if deported would become eligible for the "T" visa, which would enable them to remain in the United States. They would also become eligible for federal benefits. The TVPA developed the office to Monitor and Combat Trafficking in Persons that now produces the yearly report assessing the progress of nations around the world against human trafficking. However, due to the focus of the United States, most of the cases prosecuted within its borders have been cases of sex trafficking, which does not provide an accurate picture of the range of trafficking occurrences within the United States (DeStefano, 2007). In addition, the laws do not target the demand for sexual services by focusing on the purchasers. According to Schauer and Wheaton (2006), 25 of the 50 U.S. states have no laws to punish the purchasers of sexual services, as opposed to 47 states that make selling sexual services a crime.

Sweden has taken a different approach regarding the sex trade in order to reduce the focus on the seller. Since 1999, the sale of sex is not illegal in Sweden; however, buying it is. It is based on the concept that people are not commodities to be bought and sold as goods (Ekberg, 2004). This law does not criminalize the seller, instead viewing them as exploited, but targets the buyer in order to reduce demand. Those found guilty of buying sex can receive fines or face up to 6 months in jail, as well as the shame of public exposure. Pimps and brothel owners also face penalties under the law. Prostitutes are offered a variety of services and supports to help them leave the trade. The law applies to Swedish citizens all over the world and thus can be used to prosecute sex tourists as well as peacekeeping troops stationed in other nations

(Ekberg, 2004). While the law does have its critics, the number of prostitutes is estimated to have dropped 40% between 1998 and 2003, and officials from all over the world are coming to Sweden to assess implementing a similar law in their nations (Ritter, 2008). New York was the first state in the United States of America to pass a similar law that viewed the prostitutes as victims and provided services to them while increasing penalties to those who bought sex. Ironically, the most prominent person to be arrested under this law was Eliot Spitzer, the governor who signed the bill into law (Bernstein, 2008).

Countries have varied on how well they have integrated the Optional Protocol to the CRC on trafficking. Norway has received positive feedback on how well it has integrated the Protocol into its national laws, while other nations such as Iceland, Denmark, Ukraine, and Kyrgyzstan have been noted as having legal inconsistencies or criminal justice problems in their national laws and the Protocol. Morocco has been identified as a leader in the Arab-African region for its campaign to fight sexual exploitation and for developing specialized police units to deal with these crimes (Buck, 2008).

Thus, in order to work to eliminate child trafficking, the multiprong approach is necessary. Raising awareness among both those who are at risk for trafficking as well as the general public is essential. Effective policies that penalize the trafficker, not the person who has been trafficked, must be developed in order to assist those who have been victimized and punish those who committed the crime. By working to reduce the need for child labor, educating about exploitation, and developing severe consequences, progress toward eliminating child trafficking will be made. At the same time, effective and appropriate services for those who have been trafficked must be developed to help them recover from the trauma and be able to establish productive lives.

4

Child Soldiers

The involvement of children in armed conflict is considered to be one of the worst forms of child labor. Recent attention in the popular media has helped to draw attention to the issue of child soldiers. For example, the conflict in Sierra Leone and the widespread use of child soldiers was illustrated in the movie *Blood Diamond,* a fictional account, as well as *A Long Way Gone,* the memoir of former child soldier Ishmael Beah (2007). Currently there are approximately 250,000 active child soldiers in the world, both boys and girls, who are involved in more than 30 conflicts worldwide (UNICEF, 2006a). However, this is only an estimate because not only do armed forces using children not report this fact—never mind the numbers—but the specific children involved are constantly changing as some children leave and new ones are recruited.

While the use of children in combat is not new to our time, there has been a dramatic increase in the numbers for several reasons. One reason is the proliferation of light, inexpensive assault weapons that are easier for children to carry and use (Fonseka, 2001). The changing nature of war has also contributed to the increase in the use of child soldiers. The past century has seen a shift from most wars being between nations to being within a nation between its ruling government and an insurgent force, causing a change in the location of battles. War no longer occurs on isolated battlefields but in everyday locations such as towns and villages. This change has caused a dramatic increase in the impact of war on civilians. Civilians accounted for 10% of deaths in World War I,

50% of deaths in World War II, and 90% of deaths in some recent conflicts such as in the Balkans (Schaller, 1995 as cited in Singer, 2005).

These changes have also led to an increase in the use of child soldiers because they are more likely to be used by rebel forces fighting against a government within a country, although they are used by government forces as well. Rebel groups have less access to men of fighting age and therefore need younger participants to increase their ranks. Children may choose to join due to the glamour of the cause (as described later). Also the presence of conflict disrupts normal society so that it is easier to forcibly recruit children. Armed forces find children to be effective fighters because they have been trained to follow the instructions of adults and are less likely to question orders. Children are not likely to demand payment as would older soldiers and are trained to become fearless in battle. This fearlessness is achieved in part through their less fully developed sense of mortality, as well as forced usage of drugs. In Liberia and Sierra Leone, groups would forcibly apply what was called "brown-brown," which is cocaine or heroin mixed with gunpowder. The gunpowder increased the strength of the drug, and the children were told that the gunpowder would render them invincible to bullets. An incision would be made on the child's arm and the drug would be packed in and covered with a bandage (Singer, 2005).

Article 38 of the Convention on the Rights of the Child (CRC) requires that those taking a direct part in combat must be at least 15 years old; children younger than 15 years may not be recruited into armed forces. In 1998, the recruitment of child soldiers under the age of 15 years was declared to be a war crime (Fox, 2005). However, the weakness of this article is that the Convention is only applicable to nations, not non-state armed forces such as rebel forces (where the majority of child soldier usage currently occurs), and it only requires states to take "all feasible measures," rather than all *necessary* measures to prevent it. However, it does require states to limit recruitment into all armed forces, not just their own (Fox, 2005). In contrast, the African Charter on the Rights and Welfare of the Children (Article 22) compels states to take "all necessary measures" to ensure that children under 18 years of age do not participate in combat.

The Cape Town Principles, adopted in 1997, addressed these shortcomings by establishing that a child soldier is considered to be any child under the age of 18 years who is recruited (compulsorily, forcibly, or voluntarily) or otherwise used in hostilities by armed forces, paramilitaries, civil defense units, or other armed groups. This definition is not limited to children who serve as combatants; they may also be porters, cooks, messengers, and forced sexual partners (UNICEF, 1997).

Based on these principles, an Optional Protocol to the CRC on the involvement of children in armed conflict was ratified by the United Nations in 2000 to increase the protections afforded to children. This Optional Protocol raised the age of mandatory recruitment and involvement in combat to 18 years. It states that there will be no compulsory recruitment of children under 18 years of age, and voluntary recruitment must be truthful, genuinely voluntary, and only with the consent of parents or guardians. The Optional Protocol is also written to apply to all armed groups, regardless of whether they are the official armed group of the nation. As of this writing, 131 countries have ratified this Optional Protocol (Office of the High Commissioner for Human Rights, 2010). In 2007, the Paris Principles were developed by representatives from 58 nations. The Paris Principles "are a detailed set of guidelines for protecting children from recruitment and for proving effective assistance to those already involved with armed groups or forces" ("Paris conference," 2007, ¶6) as active recruitment of child soldiers continues in at least 13 countries.

Children are used by both governmental forces as well as forces fighting against them. Between 2004 and 2007, nine governments used child soldiers: Chad, Democratic Republic of the Congo, Israel, Myanmar, Somalia, Sudan, Uganda, United Kingdom, and Yemen. The United Kingdom, despite ratifying the Optional Protocol, sent 17 year olds to Iraq (although most were not involved in direct combat), while Israel was cited for its use of Palestinian children as human shields (Coalition to Stop the Use of Child Soldiers [Coalition], 2008a). In 2008, the United States (another ratifier) reported it was holding about 500 children in Iraq for working with armed forces fighting their troops, including such activities as serving as lookouts, as well as active fighting. In addition, the United States reported it had held eight children in its facility in Guantánamo Bay, Cuba. Six were released, and the remaining two were charged with crimes relating to their activities as child soldiers ("U.S. says," 2008). Human Rights Watch states that the United States held approximately 2400 children in custody in Iraq between 2003 and 2008. These children were not provided with lawyers, nor did they attend the 1-week or 1-month detention reviews. The average length of detention for a child was more than 130 days, but some have been held for more than a year with neither charges filed against them nor a trial—a violation of procedure (Human Rights Watch, 2008).

The country with the largest use of underage fighters is Myanmar. Myanmar is estimated to have 75,000 child soldiers fighting within its borders—both in the official army and in the rebel armies (Singer, 2005). The situation in Myanmar has deteriorated to the point that children are bought and sold by military recruiters. There is a shortage of soldiers in the national army due to high desertion rates and lack of volunteers, and the government is trying to make up this lack through the forced recruitment of children as young as 10 years of age (Human Rights Watch, 2007a).

Why Children Join

The reasons why children are involved in armed conflict vary from the macro to the mezzo to the micro level. On the macro level, children are more likely to be involved in conflict in countries where there is a general lack of respect for human rights, where the government has been unstable, and where the armed conflict is of a long duration (Høiskar, 2001). This prolonged instability can lead to a lack of educational or vocational opportunities, making children more vulnerable to recruitment. Additionally, the conflict can cause children to become separated from their parents, again rendering them more vulnerable to recruitment.

On the mezzo level, familial wealth plays an important role. Children from wealthy families are typically not at risk for involvement in armed conflict because their families are able to protect them through legal measures, bribes, or relocation. It is the children from poorer families who are most at risk for recruitment (Machel, 2001). This is even true in industrialized nations, such as the United Kingdom and the United States, where volunteers who join the armed forces come disproportionately from families of lower socioeconomic families, especially as enlisted soldiers rather than officers (Wessells, 2006a).

On the micro, or individual, level, a common idea is that children are always involved through forcible recruitment, but in actuality, this is not always the case. In some cases, children voluntarily join the forces, believing in the cause for which they are fighting or searching for stability in the upheaval generated by armed conflict. It may be the only manner in which to get daily food and some semblance of protection from harm. Some child soldiers have said that they joined in the fighting in order to escape the poverty in their families (UNICEF, 2001). War and conflict, due to the instability they cause, often lead to increased poverty and hunger. War zones typically have very high unemployment rates, up to 80% (Wessells, 2006a). This has been seen in the recent war in Iraq. Many adults have lost their jobs due to the conflict and therefore children have had to leave school in order to help their parents earn money to support their families. One of the best-paying jobs for these children is to make bombs for the insurgents. The children are in contact with dangerous materials, and a number have died in this work ("Poverty drives," 2007).

Other incentives to join may include the perceived power and excitement (Wessells, 2006b). Parents may also offer their child for military service in order to earn the salary for the child's work (Machel, 2001). For some girls, it may offer more opportunities than traditional life seems to offer, and it can offer an escape from a forced early marriage or sexual abuse (Denov, 2007; Wessells, 2006b). In other societies where honor and shame are important concepts, this may become a motivating factor for children to join; they may wish to avenge the death of a family member (Singer, 2005).

A qualitative study of 19 former child soldiers in Sri Lanka found that 18 of them stated they had volunteered. While the most common reason given was the "virtue of being a freedom fighter" and the glorified role of martyr, this was followed closely by a stated fear of abduction by the "enemy" (de Silva, Hobbs, & Hanks, 2001). When exploring the cultural impacts on the decision to volunteer, de Silva et al. (2001) stated that public address systems continuously broadcast the glory of serving in the rebel forces and becoming a martyr for the cause with posters of martyrs broadly displayed. Even the children's playgrounds have play guns. The children in the study were also all from lower socioeconomic families with no opportunities for success available to them through education. Thus, this study exemplifies the concept that even for those children who state they volunteer for the conflict, there is not a true choice of options. In conflict-filled societies, employment options are often slim, especially for those with low levels of education (Wessells, 2006a).

However, in most situations, the children are forcibly recruited in some manner, especially girls (Save the Children, 2005a; Singer, 2005).

In comparison to the previously described situation in Iraq, many other children are forced to participate; their parents are threatened into allowing their children to do so. In Nepal, children are kidnapped—individually or in groups—into the Maoist rebel forces. It is estimated that between 2002 and 2006, approximately 22,000 children were abducted (Special Representative of the Secretary-General for Children and Armed Conflict, 2007). Even though the peace process is ongoing in Nepal, these forces refuse to release the children they have and continue to "recruit" more. In some areas, the Maoists had a "one family, one child" policy in which each family was expected to provide a recruit or face severe punishment (Human Rights Watch, 2007b).

Some forces will abduct children from places where they gather, such as schools, churches, or orphanages. Street children can be particularly vulnerable to recruitment, due in part to their poverty and isolation. In addition, soldiers sometimes conduct mass "recruitments" in the street, where they round up children and force them into service (Wessells, 2006b). Children are also made more vulnerable to recruitment as a result of the upheaval and death during wartime, which can result in their separation from their caretakers during displacement or in becoming orphans (Wessells, 2006b).

In order to better understand the manner through which children become involved in armed conflict, the roles they play in it, and the impact on them, conflicts in three different countries, each on a different continent and experiencing very different kinds of conflict, will be examined.

Uganda

One of the most infamous users of child soldiers has been the Lord's Resistance Army (LRA) in Uganda, a rebel group that has fought against the government since 1986 (Briggs, 2005). The conflict appears to stem from the historic inequity created under colonialism in which those in the South of Uganda were given favored positions over those in the North (Cheney, 2005). In 2007, a peace agreement was signed, the Agreement on Accountability and Reconciliation; however, fighting continues and the LRA continued to hold approximately 2000 women and children it had abducted (Coalition, 2008b).

The LRA has kidnapped as many as 25,000 children since the start of the conflict; 7500 of them girls (Amnesty International, 2005).

The boys were trained to be soldiers, and the girls were given to officers as "wives" and forced to become sex slaves. Children also serve as porters and cooks. Children are abducted from their schools, from their homes, and from the roads. In order to avoid being captured by the LRA, approximately 30,000 children slept en masse at their schools, churches, hospitals, and other central locations every night, watched over by the adults in their communities (Amnesty International, 2005). These children became known as the "night commuters" for their nightly journey and were the subject of a movie entitled *Invisible Children* (http://www.invisiblechildren.com).

These child soldiers experienced violence in multiple forms and methods. One study found that 77% of the sample of former Ugandan child soldiers had seen someone being killed, and 39% were forced to kill someone themselves (Derluyn, Broekaert, Schuyten, & De Temmerman, 2004). Violence occurred not only in combat but was also used as a disciplinary technique. In order to force the children to remain with the army, harsh violence was used against those who revolted in any manner. When abducted, children were sometimes forced to kill those they knew, such as family and friends. This led to such strong feelings of guilt that the children thought they could not return to society after such shame. Children who tried to escape or who disobeyed were tortured or killed, often by the other children. The following quote from a child kidnapped by the LRA illustrates this method:

One boy tried to escape [from the rebels], but he was caught... His hands were tied, and then they made us, the other new captives, kill him with a stick. I felt sick. I knew this boy from before. We were from the same village. I refused to kill him and they told me they would shoot me. They pointed a gun at me, so I had to do it. The boy was asking me, "Why are you doing this?" I said I had no choice. After we killed him, they made us smear his blood on our arms... They said we had to do this so we would not fear death and so we would not try to escape.... I still dream about the boy from my village who I killed. I see him in my dreams, and he is talking to me and saying I killed him for nothing, and I am crying. (Human Rights Watch, 1997)

Colombia

While countries in Africa often receive the bulk of attention for the use of child soldiers, countries in other regions are among the worst violators. More than 11,000 children fight in Colombia, 80% of them fighting for the guerrilla groups— the Revolutionary Armed Forces of Colombia (FARC) and the National Liberation Army (ELN)—and 20% fighting for paramilitary groups aligned with the government (see Mapp, 2008 for a description of the conflict). The formal military also uses child soldiers, but not nearly as frequently as the irregular forces (Human Rights Watch, 2005). The military names the children "little bells" due to their use as sentries, while FARC refers to them as "little bees" as they can "sting" the enemy before they realize what is occurring (Singer, 2005).

Human Rights Watch estimates that approximately 25% of guerilla forces are child soldiers, with several thousand under the age of 15 years. Children as young as 8 years old are recruited by FARC, typically by force, and face severe punishment if they attempt to return home. Younger children are used to spy and run messages, and then as they age, they learn to place bombs as well as participate in direct combat (Briggs, 2005; Human Rights Watch, 2003). If children try to escape or if they disobey orders, they can be killed (Coalition to Stop the Use of Child Soldiers [Coalition], 2007). The guerrilla groups have a relatively high use of females, with one-quarter to one-half of their soldiers being females, including girls as young as 8 years (Human Rights Watch, 2003). The paramilitary groups had promised in 2002 to release all of their child soldiers but failed to do so. FARC has refused to even engage in talks on their use of child soldiers.

Some children are coerced into joining the fighting, but most join voluntarily due to the need for food, affection, safety, or the perceived glamour of fighting (Human Rights Watch, 2003; 2005). Many of the children choose to join the armed forces because they feel it is safer than living without its protection (Human Rights Watch, 2003). The violence in Colombia has been continuing so long that this generation has never lived without its impact; violence is the second leading cause of death for children aged 5–14 years. Children may also join armed groups in order to gain vengeance for violence against their families (Briggs, 2005). Additionally, children often have behavioral issues, such as being highly aggressive or withdrawn, and have difficulty concentrating in school (Médecins Sans Frontières, 2006). This impediment to educational success may cause some children to join the fighting. Gender roles are also perceived to have an influence on children choosing to join. It is an opportunity for boys to fulfill the machismo role, while it offers girls a chance to break out of the passive role allotted to females (Care International, 2008).

Many families have been displaced from their rural lands by the conflict and forced to flee to urban areas, where they live in desperate poverty. The poverty rate in Colombia increased from 23% in 2000 to 31% in 2003; almost 25% of those living in poverty are under 10 years old (Coalition, 2007). Additionally, a lack of jobs and educational opportunities helps to feed the children's movement into the rebel groups. Schools are regularly attacked and/or occupied by armed factions, and schoolteachers are threatened or killed (Coalition, 2007).

Sri Lanka

The conflict between the government of Sri Lanka and the rebel group known as the Liberation Tigers of Tamil Eelam, more commonly referred to as the Tamil Tigers or LTTE, began in 1983 when the LTTE began fighting for an independent Tamil state. It lasted until 2009, when the Tigers were defeated during a brutal military campaign. It is estimated that between 80,000 and 100,000 people were killed and about 1 million displaced (Charbonneau, 2009). More than 6000 children were recruited by the Tamil Tigers, but this number does not include those recruited in the final months of the war when these numbers are thought to have jumped markedly ("Retraining Tiger cubs," 2009). The Tamil Tigers received international condemnation for the regular use of child soldiers, with one of their brigades known as the "Baby Brigade" due to the youth of its members. Approximately 40% to 60% of their forces were under the age of 18 years, most of them recruited when they were between 10 and 16 years old. The Leopard Brigade was one of the most elite units with its members consisting of children who were raised in LTTE orphanages and indoctrinated from birth with its politics (Singer, 2005). The Tamil Tigers were particularly known for their use of girls in direct fighting; about half of the soldiers are female (Singer, 2005).

Children were often forcibly recruited. The Tigers visited the homes of families in the area of the conflict and informed them that they must provide a child to the group. Those families who resisted were threatened and harassed (Human Rights Watch, 2004). Other children were simply abducted off the street while walking home or participating in festivals (United Nations Security Council, 2006). The children who joined were treated harshly; they were allowed no contact with their families and were beaten if they tried to escape or made a mistake (Human Rights Watch, 2004).

As noted previously in this chapter, not all children in the Tamil Tigers were forcibly recruited; some children chose to volunteer for different reasons. One reason was that they were continually exposed to propaganda extolling the benefits and glory of serving in the rebel forces; martyrs for the cause were glorified (de Silva et al., 2001). Second, safety could also be a driving factor. One survey found that 40% of Sri Lankan children stated that either their home had been attacked or shelled or that they personally had been shot at, beaten, or arrested, while 50% said that a family member had been killed, abducted, or detained (Senanayake, 2001 as cited in Singer, 2005). The Sri Lankan government forces committed abuses against the civilian population, especially the Tamil ethnic group, such as unlawful detention, torture, and rape. Tamil women have been raped by government forces while in their custody (Amnesty International, 2002; Briggs, 2005). Between January 2006 and August 2007, over 1000 "disappearances" were reported, the vast majority of them being Tamil men between 18 and 50 years old, with witnesses alleging government involvement (Hogg, 2007). Knowledge of, or witnessing, these abuses drove some children to join the rebels either through a need for protection or a desire for revenge (Human Rights Watch, 2004). Lastly, poverty and a lack of access to education were driving factors. There are few economic opportunities in the area of the conflict, and there has been a destruction of infrastructure, including schools (Briggs, 2005; Human Rights Watch, 2004).

A paramilitary group known as the Karuna Group splintered off from the Tamil Tigers in 2004 and fought against them in support of government forces. The Karuna group has also actively recruited child soldiers, including children as young as 9 years of age (UNICEF, 2007; United Nations Security Council, 2006; United Nations Security Council, 2007). They generally targeted poor families, especially families who have already had a family member taken by the Tamil Tigers (Human Rights Watch, 2007c). The government of Sri Lanka was accused by a United Nations official of assisting the Karuna Group in abducting children to serve as soldiers (Senanayake, 2006). The Karuna Group was also accused of infiltrating camps for those displaced by the fighting and abducting residents (Amnesty International, 2007).

Experience of Girls Involved with Armed Groups

It is estimated that approximately 40% of child soldiers worldwide are girls (Save the Children, 2005a). The different needs of girls involved with armed forces are becoming more recognized. The Paris Commitments, a plan for child soldiers developed in 2007 by representatives of nations worldwide, noted the particular needs of girls in programming were all too often not being met (Paris Commitments, 2007).

The productive work of girls is often central to an armed force because females fulfill such traditional duties as cooking and cleaning (McKay, 2006). In fact, Denov (2007) calls the work that girls perform as "fundamental" to the success of their efforts and states that this is exemplified by the fact that girls are typically the last to be released at the end of the conflict. Girls complete additional duties, including carrying goods or gathering information. However, this does not mean that girls do not fight; many girls also fight in armed combat. In 2002, over half of the girls associated with armed groups in the Democratic Republic of the Congo stated their primary function was "fighter" (Save the Children, 2005a). Between 1990 and 2003, girls were a part of armed forces in 55 countries, and in 38 of them (70%), they were involved in armed conflict (McKay & Mazurana, 2004).

While girls share many of the same experiences as boys involved with armed groups, one thing will differentiate their experience: sexual assault. In most, though not all, groups, sexual assault of the girls is common. In most groups, girls are routinely gang-raped until a high-ranking officer claims them as his property (Denov, 2007). In some groups such as the LRA, a girl may be given to a commanding officer as a "wife," and she is then bound in sexual slavery. However, in some aspects, this can make her life easier than that of other girls because she is forced to service only one man and she may receive extra food or other goods due to his status. Due to such compensations, girls in FARC in Colombia will choose to align themselves with a commander. Although forced sexual intercourse in FARC is rare, this is not to say there is not coercion involved. Girls are required to use contraception, and if they do become pregnant, they must have an abortion (Human Rights Watch, 2003). These strictures can be additionally traumatizing because Colombia is a predominantly Catholic country. Once the children leave the armed forces, they typically stop using contraception (Care International, 2008).

It is also more difficult for girls to escape from the groups that kidnapped them. As they are less likely to be involved in conflict, they have fewer chances to escape or for protection workers to find them, since they are typically limited to staying at the base camp. In many groups, they are likely to bear children, and the presence of a young child inhibits their ability to escape. Additionally, they are less likely to feel they can return to their home village due to the stigmatization they would face for bearing a child out of wedlock. Even after the fighting has formally ended, girls can face difficulties returning to their former lives. This is due not only to the stigmatization they face from their communities, but that the rebel forces who captured them are reluctant to allow them to leave due to the sexual services they are forced to provide (Singer, 2005).

Impact of Child Soldiering

Unfortunately, the impact of being involved in armed conflict lasts beyond the immediate combat situation and can include not only physical but also social and psychological damage. Using a biopsychosocial approach can be a useful tool for examining the barriers to reintegration for former child soldiers. Biologically, they may have suffered wounds from combat in addition to having been under- or malnourished. Thus, physically, they may encounter difficulties. Socially, the former child soldiers may encounter resistance in the community to which they are returning due to anger at their actions while in combat. In addition, they will encounter difficulties in education because they are typically substantially older than other school children at their level due to their lack of educational opportunities while engaged in combat. They often experience shame at being behind younger children and become easily frustrated (Care International, 2008). As discussed, they may have been forced to kill family or community members by the group that captured them. This, as well as the other deaths they caused or witnessed, can create psychological difficulties. There may also be posttraumatic stress disorder (PTSD) from the conflict and the children will have difficulties in dealing with stress in a nonviolent manner (UNICEF, 2001).

Derluyn et al. (2004) found that almost 100% of their Ugandan sample reported PTSD symptoms at the clinical level. The length of time since their escape and the length of time of their abduction did not affect the level of symptoms. This was supported by Kanagaratnam, Raundalen, and Asbjørnsen (2005), whose sample of former Sri Lankan child soldiers also found no difference in impact by length of time to exposure to traumatic events, length of time since the events, or age of exposure. However, Kanagaratnam et al. did find a difference by ideological commitment to the cause with those with strong ideology reporting fewer posttraumatic symptoms than those with weak ideological commitment. This is important to remember because much of the knowledge of PTSD as a result of combat is based on U.S. soldiers who served in the Vietnam War and other clinical samples who typically have weak ideological commitment. Additionally, the U.S. soldiers were able to leave the combat zone and return to a safe environment, an option often not available to those living in war-torn areas. It is difficult to overcome PTSD when there is no "post" and the trauma is ongoing.

When assessing the psychological impact of combat, it is important to remember that other cultures often have different concepts of mental health than those in the Global North. Westerners tend to locate psychological difficulties as being solely in the mind without consideration of biological or spiritual factors. The solution for these mental difficulties is to "talk them out." However, this is in contrast to the cultural beliefs of others around the world and may not be the most effective method for helping former child soldiers overcome reintegration difficulties (Honwana, 2006). The beliefs of the society are an important factor in shaping the impact on the child. When programs for former child soldiers were implemented in Mozambique and Angola, the communities asked not for assistance with psychosocial issues, but rather for help with family reunification, reestablishing schools, and creating job opportunities for youth (Green & Honwana, 1999).

In Mozambique and Angola, those who have engaged in conflict are considered to be "polluted" by the war and must be cleansed before they are accepted back into society. They are carriers of the spirits of the dead; if the former soldiers are not cleansed, they will carry the anger of the spirits back into the community. Any psychosocial issues experienced by the combatant are caused by the anger of those who have died (Green & Honwana, 1999; Honwana, 2006). Traditional healers may also be sought out to help individuals who are having a difficult time returning to community life. The healer will conduct a biopsychosocial assessment, looking not just at the individual, but their relationships with their family as well as the community. Rituals and healings will be conducted to help the individual, the nature of which will depend on the primary religious identification of the individual and how rural his or her village is (Honwana, 2006).

Reintegration

Blattman (2006) suggests that the largest cost of child soldiering is not in its impact on mental health, but on human capital. His longitudinal study found that the impact of lost education due to involvement in the conflict, together with the risk of injury, had a long-term result of lower income by nearly a third. This has strong implications for reintegration programs.

Once child soldiers have been released from the armed force with which they were fighting, it can be difficult for them to reintegrate into society. As Briggs (2005) states, while not every child will suffer from PTSD, most will need assistance in reentering society and moving past their experiences to resume their life. Longitudinal studies have found that most former child soldiers grow up to lead productive lives, but they continue to struggle with psychological distress caused by their experiences (Boothby, 2006). If reintegration is not carried out well, the children will be vulnerable to re-recruitment. A flare-up in fighting in the Democratic Republic of the Congo caused leaders of armed forces to seek out youth who had previously fought but had failed to reintegrate back into their families and communities due to lack of resources for education and programs ("Youth again forced to fight," 2007).

Research with former child soldiers in El Salvador approximately 10 years after the end of the conflict found a similar lack of programming for former child soldiers. The respondents said that in order to even receive a demobilization kit, they had to lie and say they were older than they were. Even among the almost 30% who had received an injury resulting in a physical disability, only 5% of them received any physical therapy. Illustrating the long-term psychological impact, even a decade later, almost 60% currently always or frequently think of situations from the war, while approximately 35% each were depressed quite often, felt nervous, or were easily annoyed. Only half of the respondents were currently working for pay (Santacruz & Arana, 2002). These findings underscore the necessity of effective programs for reintegration of former child soldiers.

Traditional programs to assist with reintegration are typically offered at the end of the conflict, which ignores the reality of child soldiers who will escape from the fighting when they can and thus often return home in the middle of a conflict, not at its end. As an illustration of this, only 15% of former child soldiers in Colombia receive reintegration assistance (Care International, 2008). Additionally, what programs there are for child soldiers often focus on fighters who are currently children and do not address the needs of those who may have begun as children, but due to the length of their involvement, are now adults. As discussed later in this chapter, because of gender stereotyping the needs of girls have traditionally been excluded from such programs and thus few girls have used the programs.

Another barrier has been that in order to access the programs, the former soldier must typically turn in an automatic weapon. Child soldiers, especially girls, usually do not escape with an automatic weapon, thus rendering them ineligible for these services (Wessells, 2006b). The success of these programs is typically assessed by the number of weapons collected, not by the success of the reintegration (Save the Children, 2005a). As is true in most evaluations, what gets measured gets the most attention and what is not measured receives less attention and less funding. This is particularly true for the children involved in armed conflict for whom the reintegration progress is most commonly handled by nongovernmental organizations (NGOs) or UNICEF (Save the Children, 2005a). Due to these difficulties, the Paris Principles called for more effective disarmament, demobilization, and reintegration (DDR) for child soldiers (Special Representative, 2007).

One of the primary services that programs can offer is to identify the location of the child's family. During conflict, families are often forced to flee their villages and family members may have been killed. Thus, locating family to whom the former soldier can return can be more difficult than it may initially seem. After the child is placed in the home, follow-up services to ensure that reunification is proceeding smoothly can be essential. Family, and the support they can provide, has been found to be an important factor in helping to reduce the impact of war on children (Summerfield, 2000).

As an example of an organization that has gathered all of these pieces together, the World Vision Gulu Children of War Rehabilitation Center in Uganda provides care to those who have escaped from the LRA. They are provided with medical assistance, HIV/AIDS education, psychological counseling, community reintegration skills, and help in tracing their family. World Vision has helped more than 15,000 individuals at this center (Cheney, 2005; World Vision, 2007). These types of centers are valued by the children who receive assistance there in order to provide them support in healing before returning to the community. Children in Uganda interviewed by the Coalition to Stop the Use of Child Soldiers (2008b) stated they especially valued the counseling to help them understand and cope with the trauma they experience and to develop self-control abilities before returning home.

UNICEF (2006b) states that reintegration is particularly difficult for girls. One reason is that they typically are not viewed as soldiers since they often do not participate in combat. For example, following the decade-long conflict in Sierra Leone, girls did not qualify for programs as they were registered as "camp followers" (Machel, 2001). As a result, they often do not receive the reintegration services that boys do, leaving their psychological trauma unresolved. In Mozambique, the girls received packages of goods that included men's clothing (Machel, 2001). Additionally, due to the nature of the services they were forced to perform, some will return with children born of the rape, who may be rejected by their family and community. It was not until 2004, after the civil war in Sierra Leone, that these "forced marriages" were able to be prosecuted as a crime against humanity in court (Park, 2006). Communities often need assistance in understanding that these relationships were forced and learning to provide support to the returning girls. In addition, the girls could benefit from services to help with the sexual abuse they have suffered—a topic rarely discussed in a number of countries experiencing these conflicts. The combination of sexual trauma and the trauma associated with violent conflict has been found to have deadly consequences for girls. One study found that former girl soldiers were 52% more likely to commit suicide than their male counterparts (Stavou & Stewart, 2002 as cited in Singer, 2005). Health services for such problems as sexually transmitted diseases, fistulas, and genital injuries are often needed, but rarely provided (Denov, 2007).

Cheney (2005) notes that it can be difficult to reintegrate child soldiers not only because of their actions while with the rebels, but because of the cultural taboos that have been violated. Traditional generational roles in Uganda provided that it was the elders in a clan who decided when to go to war; however, that was upset by Kony's abduction of children and their forced participation in conflict (Singer, 2005). These children become socialized into committing horrific acts in order to survive. It is then difficult for the children to revert to obeying their elders when they return to the community. Adding to the difficulty is the fact that while they may have left the community when they were children, due to the length of the conflict, they may return as young adults. They will be lacking the education and socialization they need to integrate into the community as appropriate to this new role. Girls who return with children are visible reminders of the violations of cultural norms, including maintaining virginity until marriage, the importance of a child's paternity, and community-sanctioned marriage (Denov, 2007).

All too often, reintegration programs ignore the vital role of community. A representative of an NGO working to reintegrate children formerly involved with the Maoist rebel group in Nepal stated, "We still have to work a lot at the community level to ensure that the... children...are treated like children, encouraged to rejoin school and not looked upon as a burden to society" ("Challenges of reintegrating", 2007, ¶2). Boothby (2006) found that when community sensitization programs are conducted, the reintegration of child soldiers is eased. If communities do not understand the nature of the experience of the returning child, they may not accept him or her. The Coalition to Stop the Use of Child Soldiers (2008b) reported that former child soldiers often faced extensive stigmatization by their community and were constantly bullied at school. Save the Children (2005a) found that one of the most commonly stated needs of returning girls was to help the community to understand that their involvement in the armed group was coerced. This is especially true if they are returning with a child. Working with the community and the local healers can help reduce the spiritual contamination of the children and make the community more willing to interact with them and them with the community. A UNICEF representative working with Empowering Hands, a program to help former child soldiers in Uganda, noted that "Placing the centre of support squarely on community members is essential to giving the formerly abducted their lives back" ("Empowering hands," 2007, ¶7).

Additionally if economic opportunities are provided, it will not only help ease the reintegration but also reduce the likelihood that the children will become reinvolved with the conflict because of the reduction of poverty. In Colombia, it has been noted that demobilization programs need to help youth become self-sufficient. "They come from military institutions in which you have to do and not think. Then they come to an institution that gives them benefits but not tools to enable them to be self-sufficient" (Coalition, 2007, p. 11). Children who had been demobilized but lacked job skills were vulnerable to re-recruitment by the army (Coalition, 2007). Vocational opportunities that were offered were typically gender stereotyped. Girls were offered training to be hairdressers, beauticians, or dressmakers (Care International, 2008). It has also been found that if proper supports and reintegration methods are not in place, children are prone to engage in activities that place them at risk for contracting HIV. These activities include injecting drugs and engaging in sex work, due to the difficulties they faced in psychosocial healing, addictions acquired while serving in the conflict, and economic struggles due to lack of job skills and community support ("Former child soldiers," 2008).

Wessells (2006b) found that a program to create economic opportunities for former child soldiers also helped in creating peace. He states that "Having access to immediate income and livelihoods, most former child soldiers came out of the bush, surrendered their weapons, and stayed in their communities" (p. 190). It helped in reducing the stigma associated with these children because they became productive citizens working alongside other community members. In addition, providing a mechanism to earn a living wage helps ease the stress on former child soldiers, helping to reduce the ongoing trauma from their experiences. How well children reintegrate after the conflict, including their ability to earn an income, has been found to help predict if they suffer from ongoing psychological disturbance from the conflict (Summerfield, 2000).

When providing assistance, it can be difficult to strike a balance between meeting the needs of the children and not providing assistance of such a high a level that it will create further adjustment difficulties when they return to their home. Cheney (2005) notes that some children in Uganda pretended to have been abducted child soldiers in order to receive the assistance allotted to the returning child soldiers. This can include material goods such as food and clothing, and other benefits, including vocational training and other education. Additionally, providing assistance to only former child soldiers can stigmatize or, alternatively, be seen as rewarding them for their participation (Special Representative, 2007). Children interviewed by the Coalition to Stop the Use of Child Soldiers (2008b) stated that receiving services to which other children did not have access was stigmatizing and created jealousy in the other children. They stated a preference to participate in services available to the entire community. As Honwana (2006) states, services to aid in reintegration of former child soldiers must be conducted together with social development and services to eliminate poverty in order to remove the structural causes that can lead children into becoming child soldiers. The United Nations Special Representative of the Secretary-General for Children and Armed Conflict (2007) states that providing service to all affected children in a region, such as school materials, can be a more productive method of providing services.

Preventing the Use of Child Soldiers

Prevention of a problem is always better than healing the trauma afterwards. Save the Children (2005b) has developed seven recommendations to prevent the use of child soldiers based on known risk factors. The first is to identify children at risk of recruitment, especially forced recruitment, and physically move them away from the area of the fighting. This place can be a local place, such as a church, or parents may keep their children close to them or hide out in the bush. Since one of the biggest risk factors to recruitment is separation from parents, avoiding the separation of children from their parents or other caretakers is the second recommendation. Some of the ways to accomplish this include educating families about how to avoid separation, ensuring children are well-treated in their families so they do not run away (especially if they are being cared for by an extended relative), and reuniting separated children as quickly as possible.

The third recommendation focuses on voluntary recruitment and advises changing the attitudes that prompt children to want to join the fighters. Save the Children states that the most potent deliverers of that message are the parents, followed by the child's peers. Save the Children Sweden has also been working with the soldiers of 13 African governments to train them about not recruiting children. Some of the soldiers had believed that having children do small chores such as guarding checkpoints or cooking meals was beneficial to the children because it earned the children money. But they said they learned at the training that children should be in school and to hire the children inhibited their education ("Train the soldiers," 2008).

The next two recommendations also focus on factors that can prompt voluntary recruitment: poverty and lack of opportunity. Save the Children states that "reducing poverty through improving household livelihoods" and providing alternatives to fighting for the children, including education and vocational training, are important preventative measures. At the meeting establishing the Paris Principles, the deputy executive director of UNICEF stated that, "you will never end recruitment if you do not address the social issues that lead to their recruitment in the first place ("Paris conference," 2007, ¶7).

The sixth recommendation is to help former child soldiers successfully reintegrate into the community in order to reduce the risk of re-recruitment. Lastly, and perhaps most important, Save the Children recommends creating peace and reducing the demand for child soldiers. As demonstrated in this chapter, not all forces will refrain from using child soldiers, and preventative measures cannot protect all children. By working for peace, all children can be protected as well as adults, and the broader society will be stabilized.

In summary, recent decades have seen an increase in the use of child soldiers, as well as international treaties prohibiting their use. Children become part of armed groups, governmental and rebel, through both voluntary and forced recruitment. However, when examined more closely, both types of recruitment have similar causes, including poverty and lack of stability, and the voluntary recruitment is often not truly voluntary, but the best of a series of bad options. Girls, although not seen as typical soldiers, are often more at risk than boys because they not only serve in all the same ways that boys do but also must meet sexual demands. When helping former child soldiers, it is important to include cultural factors around reintegration and utilize an approach that not only addresses psychosocial impacts but helps with education and vocational skills as well. Girls again will have special needs due to their sexual trauma and violations of cultural norms. Broad-based social development is often an effective method of reducing recruitment of child soldiers, including reducing poverty and increasing education and vocational training. Lastly, by working for peace, all of society will benefit.

5

Children Affected by War and Conflict

War violates every right of a child—the right to life, the right to be with family and community, the right to health, the right to the development of the personality and the right to be nurtured and protected. Many of today's conflicts last the length of a "childhood," meaning that from birth to early adulthood, children will experience multiple and accumulative assaults. Disrupting the social networks and primary relationships that support children's physical, emotional, moral, cognitive and social development in this way, and for this duration, can have profound physical and psychological implications.

—*Graça Machel,* The impact of armed conflict on children *(1996, ¶30)*

The Special Representative for Children and Armed Conflict of the Secretary-General of the United Nations (2007) states that although the involvement of children with armed groups, as discussed in the previous chapter, has garnered the majority of attention in the past decade, it is necessary to address all impacts of armed conflict on children to ensure their well-being. However, as fewer wars are fought between nations and conflicts are more likely to be intranational, they draw less international attention and less humanitarian aid (UNICEF, 2007). Reflecting the changing nature of conflict discussed in the last chapter, today more than 90% of those dying as a result of conflict are noncombatants—half of whom are children. It is estimated that between 1993 and 2003, more than 2 million children died and at least 6 million were permanently disabled or seriously injured as a direct result of armed conflict; another 1 million children were orphaned or separated from their families (UNICEF, n.d.).

These deaths and injuries typically occur far from the battlefield. Children under 5 years of age have the highest mortality rates in areas affected by conflict because the majority of deaths that occur as a result of armed conflict are not from violence, but rather result primarily from malnutrition and poor medical care, to which children are particularly vulnerable (Zwi et al., 2006). This is exacerbated by the forced displacement of children from their homes. An estimated 20 million children have been forced to flee their homes and are living as refugees or internally displaced persons (IDPs) within their own borders (UNICEF, n.d.). In camps for those who have fled the violence, communicable disease is common and is the most common cause of death for children in the camps. Malnourishment is a frequent reason why they are unable to fight these illnesses (Machel, 2001). Access to safe drinking water is also an issue for those who have been displaced by violence (Risser, 2007). Even for children who survive, malnutrition in the first 2 years of life has been found to lead to poor outcomes in adulthood, including shorter height, lower educational attainment, and lower income (Victora et al., 2008).

As an illustration of this impact on children, the conflict in the Democractic Republic of the Congo (DRC) has caused an estimated 5.4 million deaths. Although the conflict officially occurred between 1998 and 2002, an estimated 45,000 people continue to die every month with the majority of these deaths caused by malnutrition and preventable illnesses rather than by violence (International Rescue Committee, 2008). These deaths occur as an indirect result of the conflict due to its impact on the availability of good food and water, as well as medical care. Children under 5 years old are at special risk and constitute almost 50% of deaths, despite being only 19% of the population. It has been estimated that for every violent death in the DRC's war zone, there were 62 nonviolent deaths as an indirect result of the conflict (Lacey, 2005).

Children are also affected by the deaths of those around them, even if they themselves survive. After the genocide in Rwanda, for example, 96% of the interviewed children had witnessed violence, nearly 80% of children had lost immediate family members (half of these lost a parent), and more than one-third of those children had witnessed the murder (Machel, 1996; Machel, 2001). In Afghanistan between 1992 and 1996, 72% of surveyed children had lost a family member, and 40% had lost a parent (Wali, Gould, & Fitzgerald, 2005). These types of statistics make it clear how directly conflict can impact children, even if the children themselves were unharmed. The witnessing of violence, as well as the fear of the occurrence of violence, can cause long-term problems. Living in a state of fear can create permanent trauma for children if it is not addressed. Children can overcome this trauma, but it requires culturally sensitive care, including supportive caregivers and a secure community (Machel, 2001; Punamäki, 2001).

Mental Health Impact of Conflict

It has only been within the past 100 years that clinicians have begun to understand the impact of war on soldiers. The understanding of the impact on civilians, especially children, is still in its exploratory stages, with the preliminary work with children really only beginning in 1996 with the Machel report (Machel, 1996). Much of the previous research focused on assessing the occurrence and severity of posttraumatic and acute stress disorders with limited implications for treatment methodology. The difference between resolving trauma from a conflict that has ended and coping with one that is ongoing is also unknown. While not all children who are exposed to violence and trauma develop severe reactions, the majority of children will show some behavioral impacts. This can range from heightened anxiety, particularly in situations that resemble the original, to severe aggression or dissociation.

Article 39 of the Convention on the Rights of the Child (CRC) states that children should receive assistance necessary to promote "physical and psychological recovery and social reintegration" following armed conflict. Children who receive assistance earlier and for a longer duration have better adult mental health outcomes (Punamäki, 2001). Healing the trauma caused by war is essential for building a peaceful society after the end of the conflict. Children with higher posttraumatic stress disorder (PTSD) scores have been found to be less willing to reconcile and have a higher desire for revenge than children with lower scores (Bayer, Klasen, & Adam, 2007). While some studies have found symptoms of PTSD to reduce after the end of the conflict (Barenbaum, Ruchkin, & Schwab-Stone, 2004), this is not always the case. One study of German children exposed to violence during World War II found for the majority who reported PTSD symptoms immediately following the war, they continued 60 years later (Kuwert, Spitzer, Träder, Freyberger, & Ermann, 2006).

Children living in conflict areas have been found to score high on assessments of psychological difficulty, including depression, suicidal ideation, and PTSD, in varying areas including Yemen ("Children in clash-prone," 2008), Iraq (Dyregrov, Gjestad & Raundalen, 2002), El Salvador (Walton, Nuttall, & Nuttall, 1997), Sierra Leone (Morgan & Behrendt, 2008), Sri Lanka (Elbert et al., 2009), and Croatia (Živčić, 1993). While the cultural relevance of the diagnosis of PTSD remains controversial, it appears that the symptoms associated with it—such as intrusive thoughts, fear of reminders of the events, and sleep disturbances—are common across cultures.

Baker and Shalhoub-Kevorkian (1999) note that due to the collective nature of Arab society, trauma is also experienced collectively. Therefore, an event does not have to personally affect a child's family, nor be directly experienced, for secondary traumatization to occur. Kuwaiti children exposed to the Iraqi occupation and first Gulf War through media, including a large sample out of the country for all or some of this conflict, still experienced psychological difficulties, with approximately 62% experiencing some level of PTSD. The level of exposure to violence was a significant predictor of both PTSD and depression (Hadi & Llabre, 1998). This effect of viewing graphic scenes on television has been found in other studies as well, leading some to call for an investigation on limiting scenes of graphic war violence (Nader, Pynoos, Fairbanks, Al-Ajell, & Al-Asfou, 1993).

Both the type of trauma and the number of traumatic events have been found to have an impact on the development of psychological difficulties such as PTSD (Thabet, Abed, & Vostanis, 2004; Thabet & Vostanis, 1999). Children in Palestine experiencing bombardment or home demolition were found to have higher levels of PTSD and fear than children living in the same area who experienced other forms of political violence (Thabet, Abed, & Vostanis, 2002). The psychological distress was widespread; Thabet and Vostanis (1999) found that almost three-quarters of their participants had symptoms of PTSD of at least mild severity, with 39% of them experiencing moderate to severe difficulties.

These difficulties have been found not only in countries with a full-scale war but also in countries with more isolated conflicts, such as Northern Ireland. "The Troubles," as they were called, also impacted the youth. While research has found that the intensity and severity of the violence which children experienced was less severe than in other conflicts, it has been one of the most studied conflicts due to its location (Muldoon, 2004). In Northern Ireland, one of the common coping mechanisms was to maintain "a conspiracy of silence" in which the Troubles were not to be discussed. This helped to reduce potential conflict with others of possibly differing views, but it also inhibited dealing with the impact of the trauma that was occurring (Murphy, 2004). Additionally, by not discussing the conflict with those of different views, it prevented the people from learning about different views and understanding how the Troubles affected people in other communities, leading to a sense of victimization (Gallegher, 2004).

While depression was not a common outcome among children exposed to violence from the Troubles, there is evidence that their externalizing behavior increased. As with most conflicts, children from more economically distressed backgrounds and members of ethnic minorities were disproportionately more likely to experience political violence than children from more economically affluent backgrounds (Muldoon, 2004). These groups are not only more vulnerable to experiencing violence but can also be more vulnerable to its effects due to other stressors.

Maintaining a systems perspective—viewing the child in the context of the community—is essential to understanding the potential relationship of multiple stressors on the child. Farwell (2004) notes that focusing solely on intrapsychic difficulties resulting from war trauma ignores the importance of the fact that war and conflict are inherently community based. She argues that examining the community's socioeconomic and political contexts is essential. Her research found that in addition to exposure to trauma, a significant amount of psychosocial distress was predicted by poor economic circumstances. Additionally, the difficulties resulting from war and conflict can affect the child not only on an individual level but also on the family level. A correlation between exposure to war and the occurrence of violence within the family has been found among children living in Afghanistan and Sri Lanka (Catani, Schauer, & Neuner, 2008).

It is important to maintain a strengths perspective when examining the psychosocial reaction to trauma. This can be accomplished in part by regarding the situation as dysfunctional instead of the individual, and viewing the individual's difficulties as attempts to manage a dangerous environment in the manner he or she is best able to do so. Symptoms of reactions such as PTSD do not necessarily mean dysfunction. This view maintains the focus on their active ability to cope rather than viewing them as passive victims (Boothby, Strang, & Wessells, 2006; Kostelny, 2006).

Education

War and armed conflict also disrupt children's education; an estimated 43 million children are out of school due to conflict (UNICEF, 2007). This is the number one reason why children are out of primary school, affecting one in three out-of-school primary-school-aged children (Save the Children, 2006). As attacks on schoolchildren, teachers, and school buildings have been increasing, this number may only continue to grow (United Nations Security Council, 2007). Children who are displaced from their homes by the violence are especially likely to be out of school due to lack of access to schools. For example, in the Darfur region of Sudan, the refugee camps have no secondary schools and primary schools are typically understaffed and overcrowded (Women's Commission for Refugee Women and Children, 2006). Save the Children (2008a) estimates that over half of the children in the region are not receiving an education. In Sudan, 90% of children between 6 and 14 years old in two displacement camps by the capitol, Khartoum, do not attend school (Abdelmoneium, 2005). In Colombia, 85% of displaced children do not have access to primary education (Machel, 2001). In both Sri Lanka and Nepal, it has been found that children who are internally displaced typically do not have access to education facilities because there are no such facilities, education is not offered in their language/dialect, or they do not have the proper paperwork to attend them ("Escalating war," 2008; "Plight," 2007; Risser, 2007).

The impact of conflict on education is starkly clear when looking at the example of Somalia. Lacking a functioning national government since 1991 and beset by warring regional factions, Somalia's educational attendance is the lowest in the world: 12% for boys and 10% for girls (UNICEF, 2006). In 2006, 70% of schools in Mogadishu, the capitol, were closed when students and their families fled the city due to surges in violence ("One-third," 2007). These correlations between armed conflict and school attendance are echoed throughout the world.

Approximately half of all Afghan children are currently out of school, the majority of whom are girls. Girls are targeted by the Taliban insurgents because they do not believe in the education of females. Boys also struggle to attend school because they may have expected duties to help provide for the family, especially if their father has been killed and they are the eldest son, regardless of their age ("Civilians complain," 2007). In Iraq, while attendance has risen every year since the American invasion, there are still large gaps in attendance and success (Tavernise, 2006). In the summer of 2007, only 28% of 17 year olds in the conflict-ridden south and central part of the nation sat for final exams and of those only 40% received a passing grade. Approximately 20% of elementary school–aged children and 30% of all children were out of school in 2007 ("Children have been," 2006; UNICEF, 2007).

Even children who are not combatants or displaced due to the conflict often have their educations affected. During times of violence, parents are more apt to keep children home in order to protect them. Children can be at risk of becoming targets of violence during their journey to school. They also fear being accused of giving aid to the "other" side during their travels or being forced to help one side or the other (IBON Foundation, 2006). While schools should be a safe place for children, isolated from the conflict, this is too often not the case. Teachers in Northern Ireland during the Troubles noted a number of ways in which schools were affected by the conflict; they described the school as operating in the shadow of the conflict (Kilpatrick & Leitch, 2004). Teachers can also be a target for armed forces, due to their high status in the community or their strong political views. Teachers in Sri Lanka who have tried to protect the children from forced recruitment by armed forces have been targeted by guerrillas, while in Colombia, schools are regularly attacked and/or occupied by armed factions and schoolteachers are threatened or killed (Coalition to Stop the Use of Child Soldiers [Coalition], 2007; Machel, 2001).

School buildings themselves can also be targets for attack, either for physical destruction or recruitment of child soldiers (Kilpatrick & Leitch, 2004; Machel, 1996; Risser, 2007). Immediately following the fall of the Taliban in Afghanistan, there was a surge in school attendance that has since lessened due to violence. Hundreds of schools have had to close due to violence and even for those that are open, students may be too afraid to attend (Bearak, 2007; "Civilians complain," 2007). In one province, there were 224 schools in 2003, but in 2008 only 54 were functioning ("Attacks deprive," 2008). Schools for girls are especially at risk (United Nations Security Council, 2007).

Schools are often attacked both by rebel groups as well as official state forces. In the occupied Palestinian Territories, schools have been attacked and occupied by both the Israel Defense Forces and Palestinian armed groups. The Israel Defense Forces have stormed schools using tear gas and stun grenades as well as guns, while Palestinian militants have used hand grenades in schools. In Sri Lanka, assaults by both the Sri Lankan Army as well as the Tamil Tigers have resulted in the destruction of schools and the death/injury of teachers and pupils (United Nations Security Council, 2007). Schools in the Aceh province of Indonesia were deliberately targeted during hostilities there, with only fragments of the buildings remaining (Risser, 2007).

Even for those schools that are functioning, they do so at less than optimal levels. In Afghanistan, only 20% of teachers are even minimally qualified, and more than half of the schools have no buildings; classes are held in tents or outdoors (Bearak, 2007). Teachers in the Gaza Strip have difficulty teaching lessons due to a shortage of materials, including paper and chalk. Girls must share the toilet with boys because there are no building materials to build a second toilet (O'Loughlin, 2007). When energy sources in Gaza were cut off by Israel in response to attacks, children's schools did not have power or heat. Classes that required a high level of energy, such as science or computer classes, were skipped for months ("Students return," 2008).

The psychological impacts can also affect education. The teachers and students of one school in Northern Ireland felt permanently psychologically affected when its principal was seriously injured in a targeted attack and was unable to return to work. Children who lived in Bosnia during the conflict in that region were sometimes afraid to use the playground, even in a new country, as the schoolyards there were often mined (Lamberg, 2007). The trauma the children have witnessed and their state of fear can inhibit them from concentrating and learning, and malnutrition can impact their cognitive development and thus their ability to learn (Kohli & Mather, 2003; Machel, 2001). Teachers in the Gaza Strip of the occupied Palestinian territory note that students often cannot learn due to hunger and fear (O'Loughlin, 2007).

Even after conflict ends, restoring education can be a difficult task. In Sierra Leone, the government built and restored hundreds of schools, but there are too few teachers to staff them. Nationally, 40% of the teachers are considered unqualified. It has been difficult to attract new teachers due to the low salaries being offered and the irregularity of the payment of the salaries. Although school attendance is mandatory, only about 70% of elementary school children and 20% of secondary school children attend and the system could not handle full enrollment if it did occur. Many schools operate in shifts with students attending either in the morning or in the afternoon, and there still may be 70 students per class. Education is supposed to be free, but school administrators charge fees equal to about one-third of the average national income and teachers will often mandate private classes in order to supplement their meager salaries ("Schools without teachers," 2007; UNICEF, 2008). Additionally, since many students have missed out on education due to the conflict, a large proportion are overage, creating additional difficulties in the classroom (Save the Children, 2006).

Twenty-two Global North countries pledged monetary assistance for education aid in 2005, but only the Netherlands and Norway are contributing their fair share, calculated based on gross national income. The United States ranks 20th of the 22, but ranks highest in contributing education aid to countries in conflict (primarily Afghanistan and Iraq). Only 3% of the U.S. development aid goes toward education, but 40% of that goes to nations in conflict (again primarily Iraq and Afghanistan). Overall, only 18% of aid for education goes to countries experiencing conflict, despite the fact that these nations often have the greatest need. They experience a much higher proportion of children being out of school than other nations (Save the Children, 2007). As demonstrated throughout this book, not receiving education places children at risk of a host of other problems, and this is especially true for children living in a war zone.

Landmines and Other Unexploded Ordinance

Landmines have been identified as a special threat to children. Between 8000 and 10,000 children are killed or maimed by landmines every year, and they are the sixth-most preventable cause of death of children (Pearn, 2003; UNICEF, n.d.). Landmines often remain as a threat long after the end of a conflict. As one example, in 2008 a city in northwest Egypt stated it is unable to expand due to over 22 million landmines and other unexploded ordinance left from World War II ("Unexploded mines," 2008). It takes approximately 100 times longer to clear a mine than to place it; and while the initial cost of landmines is about U.S.$3 each, they can cost up to U.S.$1000 to clear.

Children are at special risk for being landmine victims because they are less able to read and less likely to be aware of the dangers of landmines. Children in poor families are at particular risk because these children are more likely to be in mined areas when scavenging for firewood, fetching water, cultivating their crops, or herding animals (Machel, 2001). Additionally, some of the landmines are brightly colored and can appear as toys to a child. The "butterfly" mine, once common in Afghanistan, came in several colors and had a "wing," creating an attraction to young children (Machel, 2001).

Afghanistan has one of the highest casualty rates from these dangers in the world due to extended periods of conflict in that nation. In 2007, 143 people were killed and 438 injured by landmines in Afghanistan alone, a 13% increase in deaths from the previous year. The majority of those affected were males aged 1–26 years ("Landmines," 2008). In order to cope with the dangers already present, programs to educate children about the risk of landmines have been developed. The government of Afghanistan, together with the United Nations, has designed a train-the-trainer program to develop educational programs for children. Trainers conduct program for teachers across the countries who then train other teachers and then schoolchildren about the dangers of landmines and unexploded ordinance. They plan for all children to receive at least basic information on the topic by the end of 2008 ("Six million schoolchildren," 2007).

Due to the risks of death and injury from landmines long after the end of a conflict, the International Campaign to Ban Landmines (ICBL) was formed. It is made up of over 1000 nongovernmental organizations (NGOs), 60 governments, the International Committee of the Red Cross, and UN agencies. The ICBL developed the 1997 Convention on the Prohibition of the Use, Stockpiling, Production and Transfer of Anti-Personnel Mines, and on their Destruction, which 156 countries have now adopted, leaving 39 countries which have not (ICBL, 2010). The ICBL and its Coordinator, Jody Williams, received the Nobel Peace Prize in 1997 for their efforts. The provisions of the treaty fall in two broad categories: those that prevent future use of landmines, including a ban on production and destruction of stockpiles; and those that solve the existing landmine problems, including clearing currently placed landmines and assistance for survivors (ICBL, n.d.).

Since this Convention, the global production of landmines has greatly decreased; the number of producing countries has dropped from 54 to 15, and there has been no intercountry trade of landmines since the 1990s (Landmine Survivors Network, 2007). Almost 42 million antipersonnel mines have been destroyed, and 83 member nations have destroyed their stockpiles of mines ("Mine ban," 2008). However, the Convention is not an unqualified success. All nations did not clear their minefields by 2009 as required due to such reasons as a large number of mines, a delay in starting, and/or a lack of funding. These nations with uncleared minefields include Bosnia and Herzegovina, Chad, Denmark, Thailand, United Kingdom (Falklands), and Zimbabwe. The nations of Belarus, Greece, and Turkey failed to destroy their stockpiles by their deadlines ("Mine ban," 2008). Two nations were known to have used anti-personnel landmines—Myanmar and Russia (ICBL, 2009). Thus, while a great deal of progress has been made, there remains work to be done in eliminating this threat.

While the United States has not produced any landmines since 1997 because its stockpiles are full, it remains on the list of producing countries together with such countries as China, Cuba, Iran, Iraq, and Pakistan (Landmine Survivors Network, 2007; Machel, 2001). Under the Bush Administration, the U.S. government refused to be a party to the convention because landmines remain a tactical weapon in warfare that they perceived as irreplaceable. Instead, it plans to convert to the usage of "nonpersistent" landmines, which are designed to turn themselves off after the end of the conflict (U.S. State Department, 2004). However, this technology is not always reliable.

In recent years, other forms of ordinance and their risk to children have been gaining more attention, especially cluster munitions. Cluster munitions are defined as "a weapon comprising multiple explosive submunitions which are dispensed from a container" and are considered to pose a larger threat to civilians than other types of munitions because they cover a large area with shrapnel and explosions and have a higher rate of unexploded ordinance than other munitions (Cluster Munition Coalition, n.d.). The countries most affected by cluster munitions are Afghanistan, Cambodia, Iraq, Laos, Kosovo, and Vietnam

(Cluster Munition Coalition, n.d.). The cluster bombs used in Kosovo by NATO, brightly colored and shuttlecock shaped, contributed to over 100 deaths between June 1999 and April 2000, after the return of most refugees to their home (Machel, 2001). Children in Lebanon are also at high risk because approximately 1 million unexploded cluster munitions remained of the 4 million dropped in the barrage by Israel on Lebanon in 2006 (Special Representative of the Secretary-General for Children and Armed Conflict, 2007). During the conflict, cluster munitions caused only two deaths, but after the conflict, when civilians returned home, deaths rose to a rate of three a day in the first month, then continued at two a day for a number of months thereafter ("Is this the end," 2008). Clearing them is estimated to take almost a decade, with the majority of the funding coming from the European Union ("Funding shortfall, 2009).

Motivated in part by the Israel-Lebanon conflict, work has begun on an international treaty to ban these weapons. There were debates over whether those with a "self-destruct" mechanism should be exempt because their predicted failure rate is 1%–2%, but in the field appears closer to 10% ("Cluster bomb ban treaty," 2007). However, this exception was not included in the final draft. By January 2010, 104 nations had signed it including Britain, which had inititally opposed the treaty (Burns, 2008; ICBL, 2010),. Unfortunately, a number of the largest users, including Israel, the United States, China, and Russia, did not join. A spokesperson for the U.S. government stated that cluster munitions continue to have military utility and that to ban them would place the lives of U.S. soldiers at risk ("Experts see," 2008). However, in March 2009, the new Obama administration in the United States signed a law tightly limiting exports of cluster munitions (Beaumont, 2009).

Child Refugees

As stated earlier, an estimated 20 million children have been forced to flee their homes due to conflict—45% of all internally displaced persons (IDPs) and refugees (United Nations High Commissioner for Refugees, 2007; UNICEF, n.d.). If children are displaced within the borders of their own country, they are known as IDPs; if they cross the border into another country, they are refugees. Children of impoverished families are more likely to be caught in the conflict to become child soldiers,

IDPs, or refugees in bordering nations, while wealthier families are more likely to be able to send their children abroad to nations in the Global North to escape the conflict. The United Nations has noted a linkage between recruitment of child soldiers and the displacement of families. Some families will become displaced in an effort to avoid armed groups recruiting their children, while other families will have their children forcibly recruited from camps for IDPs (United Nations Security Council, 2007).

Children who have been displaced by the conflict are likely to have more severe mental health issues than children who have been affected by the war but not displaced (Elbedour, Onwuegbuzie, Ghannam, Whitcome, & Hein, 2007; Živčić, 1993). A cross-sectional survey of adolescents living in refugee camps in the Gaza Strip found extremely high levels of psychological problems. Almost 70% of the sample was classified with PTSD, 40% had moderate or severe depression, while 95% suffered from severe anxiety. This may be due to the additional burden of living in a refugee camp, where both the ability to meet basic needs and the availability of community support are typically lower (Elbedour et al., 2007).

Some children may be sent without their parents or other caregivers to third countries for a number of reasons: in a bid to keep them safe; because they were separated from their family during the conflict; or because their caregivers may have died in the conflict (Mitchell, 2003). However, the arrival of children as unaccompanied minors in a third country creates additional issues, including the lack of adult support to seek asylum in these countries, an issue that has concerned human rights activists for some time. These children are known as "unaccompanied children" or "separated children" to indicate their vulnerable position; the vast majority (over two-thirds) of unaccompanied or separated children are male and tend to be older teenagers (UNHCR, 2004).

While Article 22 of the Convention on the Rights of the Child requires nations to provide protection and assistance to child refugees, a number of issues have arisen. A common problem is that of documentation of minor status (being under the age of 18 years in most countries). Minors must supply documents to prove their age if their appearance does not substantiate their claimed age. Due to the nature of their flight and the conflict that they are fleeing, many lack documentation and may be erroneously referred to adult services, where they will not receive services appropriate to their age (Cemlyn & Briskman, 2003; Mitchell, 2003). Some countries use X-rays to examine bone structure to help determine bone structure, but this is a less than certain procedure (UNHCR, 2004). Israel has recently outlawed infiltration into the country, punishable by up to 7 years in prison and will apply the law to refugees and asylum seekers. They also utilize the concept of "hot return," which involves immediately deporting asylum seekers illegally entering the country without allowing them to make an asylum claim ("New law," 2008).

Refugee children face additional stressors caused by the flight, in addition to those caused by exposure to the conflict. This can include the stress of the escape to a third nation and living in a refugee camp or detention facility while one's case is decided (Lustig et al., 2004). Detention for asylum-seeking youth, while against international policy, is often common. In Australia until July 2005, all unaccompanied minors were placed in detention facilities (Crock, 2006). Children in the community have been found to lack access to postsecondary education and counseling services (Cemlyn & Briskman, 2003). Unaccompanied children are less likely than either accompanied children or adults to be granted asylum in Europe or Canada (Halvorsen, 2004 as cited in Lidén & Rusten, 2007; Grover, 2006). However, in Denmark, because most unaccompanied children who seek asylum are granted a residence permit, their asylum claims are generally not examined. This means that although they are granted residence, they do not receive the assistance to which an asylum claim would entitle them (McAdam, 2006).

In Britain, although it is against policy to detain unaccompanied minors longer than 24 hours, in practice it does occur, especially if there is a difficulty in documenting age (Cemlyn & Briskman, 2003). While the United Kingdom has developed positive laws to assist unaccompanied children seeking refuge, research has found that these are often not implemented. There appears to be a cultural gap in understanding the types of persecution that a child can face. U.K. officials tend not to accept that a child may face persecution for political ideals, as well as the fact that the child may face child-specific forms of persecution, including recruitment as a child soldier, trafficking, and female genital cutting. In 2004, only 2% of children were initially granted asylum, and only 12% succeeded on appeal (Bhabha & Finch, 2006).

In the United States, children are held to the same legal standards and requirements as adults under U.S. law; they are not entitled to legal aid and can be held in detention indefinitely (Bhabha & Schmidt, 2006). Minors are detained for up to 2 years in detention facilities for refugees and asylum seekers, and even occasionally in facilities for juvenile delinquents when other facilities are full. For instance, approximately 7000 children were detained by U.S. immigration authorities in fiscal year 2006, more than half of whom did not have legal representation (Women's Commission for Refugee Women and Children, 2007).

Policy regarding unaccompanied minors is difficult even for those who work in the system. Some professionals in the United Kingdom report routinely having to inform other service providers about policy. This was made even more difficult by frequent policy changes. They also reported administrative errors regarding age, sex, and language that made it difficult to prepare to properly meet the needs of the child (Dunkerly, Scourfield, Maegusuku-Hewett, & Smalley, 2005).

The difficulties for these children do not end once they are granted refugee status because they face the stress of acclimating to a new country, a new culture, and often a new language. In some cases, symptoms of PTSD do not start developing until 8–10 months after resettlement as they become comfortable in their new surroundings and begin to process the trauma to which they have been subjected (Schmidt, 2005). In addition, they frequently have the stress of concern for those who have remained behind and are still in danger (Cambridge & Williams, 2004). Even youth who migrate with their families may have a difficult time adjusting. Although they have the support of their families, there may be tensions with their parents as they try to adapt to the new culture. These children may wish to fit in with their peers, yet their parents may desire that they maintain their native culture and values. Furthermore, there will often be financial difficulties in the new country because working parents are typically not able to obtain employment at their previous level from their home country. Parents can also be coping with their own trauma and adjustment issues and may not be available as a support for their children. Xenophobia in the new country may also be a barrier to successful adjustment.

The ability of accompanied children and their parents to gain asylum varies between nations. In Sweden, which has fairly liberal asylum policies, the child's best interests must be considered per the requirements of the CRC, but they may not trump the standards of immigration. The child must still demonstrate that he or she meets the requirements of asylum/refugee status (McAdam, 2006). Norway established "child conversations" as part of the asylum process in order to encompass the child's right to be heard, as required by the CRC. Less formal than the adult interview, child conversations are an attempt to include the voice and opinion of the child (Lidén & Rusten, 2007).

Sexual Violence

Children face many physical risks during times of conflict, but one particularly affects girls: sexual assault. The Special Representative of the Secretary-General for Children and Armed Conflict (Special Representative) notes sexual violence against girls as a particular focus of her office (Special Representative, 2007). Rape has a long history as a tool of war to terrify and degrade the enemy and to propagate one's offspring on them. In the twentieth century, Jewish women were raped by Russian soldiers, the Japanese trafficked thousands of women for sexual purposes during World War II, and approximately 100,000 women were raped during the fall of Berlin at the end of World War II (IRIN, 2007). Rape during the genocide in Rwanda was extremely widespread (Human Rights Watch, 1996). In the Bosnian conflict, the number of rape victims ranged up to 50,000 (IRIN, 2007). During the last rule of the *mujahideen* in Afghanistan, rape was so common in Kabul that women were terrified to go outside and in the beginning, the rise of the Taliban was seen a welcome event (Benard, 2002). Human Rights Watch (2003) found a similar situation in Iraq in which girls reported that they were too frightened to go outside to work, school, or on errands due to a high fear of sexual assault. As noted in the previous chapter, girls are also often kidnapped by armed forces for use as sexual slaves.

Despite this long history, it has only been since the Bosnian conflict in the 1990s that rape has been recognized as a war crime for its tactical use during warfare. While females of all ages are at risk, girls are more vulnerable because they are perceived as less able to defend themselves and less likely to be infected with HIV/AIDS (Machel, 2001). The United Nations notes that 60% of victims of war-related sexual assaults occurring in the Democratic Republic of the Congo were between the ages of 11 and 17 years (United Nations Security Council, 2007).

Examining current conflicts occurring on the continent of Africa highlights the widespread occurrence of sexual violence as a war tactic.

The United Nations' top relief official stated in 2005 that "organized, premeditated sexual attack had become a preferred weapon of war … with rapists going unpunished and victims of rape shunned by their communities" (Hoge, 2005, June 22, ¶1). He stated that the United Nations had documented more than 25,000 rape victims in one region of the Democratic Republic of the Congo in one year. In northern Uganda, 60% of the women in a displaced persons camp were known to be victims of sexual violence (Hoge, 2005, June 22), while a report assessing human rights abuses during the conflict in Sierra Leone found that over 50% of females interviewed had been subjected to sexual violence, including 26% who had been gang raped (UNICEF, 2005).

Even within refugee camps, girls are not safe from sexual assault. UNHCR has developed guidelines to reduce sexual violence, including well-lit latrine areas, female guards, and providing water and firewood within the camps to reduce the need to leave, but they have been inadequately implemented (Machel, 2001). Following the genocide in Rwanda, unaccompanied female refugees in Tanzania were housed in bright orange tents designed to denote a "safe" zone. However, this only highlighted their vulnerability, and sexual assaults increased (Machel, 2001). During the turmoil in Kenya in 2008 following a disputed election, some citizens fled to IDP camps, only to find that the risk of sexual assault was as high inside the camps as it was outside of them ("Camps offer little refuge," 2008). Gang rapes became commonplace as well as male leaders requiring girls to exchange sex for the food to which they were entitled ("Sexual violence continues," 2008).

The genocide occurring in the Darfur region of Sudan has caused a high level of chaos and, therefore, sexual violence. A report compiled by Doctors Without Borders/ Médecins Sans Frontières (MSF) (2005a) stated that as a result of the violence, almost 2 million people in the region have fled their homes. However, even when they reach a camp for displaced persons, the violence continues. Girls must leave the relative safety of the camp to collect firewood and water. It is while they are pursuing these daily activities that they are attacked. In a 6-month time period, MSF treated almost 500 rape victims and felt that number was only a portion of the actual victims. In more than half of the cases, physical assault accompanied the sexual assault, and almost one-third were raped more than once. Eighty-one percent of the women were assaulted by military or militia forces that were armed. There is great pressure from the Sudanese government not to report rape, and females are typically discouraged from reporting by police. The President of Sudan stated that rape does not exist in Sudan and unless the NGOs name the victims, which they will not do, they state there is no evidence rape exists ("Too scared to tell," 2008).

Many cases of sexual assault are not reported because the victims fear retribution and social stigmatization for violation of their society's sexual mores, as well as the fact that during times of conflict there may be no authority to which to report the crime. There is a large stigma to being the victim of rape, and girls can face great shame in their community if the attack is known. They are so reluctant that unless they have severe injuries, they will not report the attack, thus preventing themselves from accessing medical help, including medication that could help prevent transmission of HIV ("Too scared to tell," 2008). Therefore, medical clinics treat the victim, but they do not report the crime. Relief International has been training local midwives to help victims of sexual assault in order to increase access to health services. Cooperative Housing Foundation has been working with women to build and use more fuel-efficient stoves in order to decrease the number of trips needed to gather firewood ("Too scared to tell," 2008).

After the release of the MSF report, a director of MSF was detained by the Sudanese government and charged with spying; however, the charges were dropped after a protest by the United Nations (Hoge, 2005 July 30). MSF includes the following case study in their report to illustrate these repercussions of sexual assault, summarized below (Doctors Without Borders/ Médecins Sans Frontières; 2005a):

In 2004, a 16-year-old girl was collecting firewood for her family when three armed men on camels surrounded her, held her down and raped her, one after the other. When she arrived home, she told her family what had occurred. They threw her out of the house and she had to build her own hut away from them. Her fiancé broke their engagement, stating that she was now disgraced and spoiled. When she was eight months pregnant as a result of the rape, the police came to her home and they asked about the pregnancy; she told them she had been raped. They told her that since she was not married, this was an illegal pregnancy. They beat her with a whip and placed her in jail for 10 days in a cell with 23 other women in the same position. These women were forced to clean, cook and fetch water for the police officers. The only food and water she had was that which she could scrounge in the course of her duties.

Although awareness of sexual violence during times of war and conflict has risen and it is now recognized as a war crime, perpetrators continue to act with impunity for the most part. As discussed above, they are often in league with the government, which is therefore reluctant to call attention to their actions. Even UN peacekeepers have been found to sexually exploit women, such as exchanging food for sexual intercourse (Martin, 2005). There has been a correlation between the arrival of peacekeeping troops and a rapid rise in child prostitution (Machel, 2001).

Only in recent years has the United Nations acknowledged this problem with a special conference held in 2006 to examine the issue (IRIN, 2007). In 2007, an entire battalion of UN peacekeeping soldiers was suspended from duty in Cote d'Ivoire while allegations of widespread sexual impropriety were investigated. Girls as young as 13 years old were trading sex with the peacekeepers for food in order to survive ("UN suspends," 2007). A report by Save the Children (2008b) found that children as young as 6 years of age were being sexually abused by humanitarian troops and workers. Victims typically did not report the abuse due to fear of retaliation, stigmatization, and/or the belief it would do no good. Even if peacekeepers are not involved, girls may be called to trade their sexual services for money to survive or for safety. Parents in camps for the internally displaced in Guatemala were forced to prostitute their children in order to survive, while in Colombia, girls had sex with members of paramilitary forces in order to maintain their family's safety (Machel, 2001).

Violent Neighborhoods

It should not be assumed that the issues discussed in this chapter are relevant only to children living in the Global South or in areas with a declared conflict. There are a large number of children who are affected by these issues who live in countries with no declared conflict in its borders but are impacted by the continual violence that occurs around them. While children in nations in the Global North have experienced acts of terrorism, such as the London subway bombings, the train bombings in Madrid, and the attacks on the World Trade Center, other acts of violence occur much more regularly in these nations, though they draw less attention. Violent neighborhoods can have impacts just as detrimental as conflicts and acts of terrorism, and since they do not receive international recognition, there is no humanitarian aid offered.

In the United States, almost 5300 youth ages 10–24 years were victims of homicide in 2004, an average of 15 a day, and almost three-quarters of a million were treated in the emergency room for injuries sustained from violence in 2005 (Centers for Disease Control [CDC], 2007). As in other conflicts around the world, those of minority races and ethnic groups and of lower socioeconomic status are disproportionately affected. In the 10–24 year age range, homicide is the leading cause of death for African Americans and the second leading cause of death for Hispanics (CDC, 2007). Youth living in the inner city in the United States are more likely to have witnessed or experienced community violence, with studies finding up to 43% having witnessed a murder, 11% having been shot at, and 3% having been shot. Almost 80% had witnessed a beating. This was true even for the youngest children; one study found that in a group of 3–4 year olds attending a Head Start program in Washington, D.C., 78% had been exposed to at least one incident of community violence (Stein, Jaycox, Kataoka, Rhodes, & Vestal, 2003).

Exposure to violence among urban children has been found to be associated with a host of negative effects similar to those found among children living in countries where war is occurring. Again reflective of war zones, exposure to trauma has been found to have a cumulative effect with greater exposure resulting in more severe effects (Lynch, 2003). Research has found that exposure to violence is associated with problems such as PTSD (Lynch, 2003; Scarpa, Haden, & Hurley, 2006), substance abuse, anxiety, depression (Lynch, 2003), conduct disorder and externalizing behaviors (McCabe, Lucchini, Hough, Yeh, & Hazen, 2005; Thompson & Massat, 2005), sexually risky behaviors (Voison, 2003), poor health (Boynton-Jarrett, Ryan, Berkman, & Wright, 2008), poor school achievement (Baker-Henningham, Meeks-Gardner, Chang, & Walker, 2009), and lower scores on intelligence tests and standardized reading assessments (Delaney-Black et al., 2002). Additionally, it has been found that youth with higher levels of exposure to community violence are themselves more likely to commit assault and carry a weapon

(Patchin, Hueber, McCluskey, Varano & Bynum, 2006). Despite these effects, exposure to community violence is not routinely assessed and often is viewed as less important than family violence (Voisin, 2007).

As it has been found that children are able to adapt better to continual violence if there is a high level of community cohesion and shared beliefs (Shaw, 2003), the violence that occurs in distressed neighborhoods may have an even greater impact than some conflicts due to the lack of these supports. Garbarino (2001, p. 363) states that "one of the worst features of living in an urban war zone may be the dismantling of the compensatory, salutogenic infrastructure of the community."

While the vast majority of community violence has been conducted in the United States, a few other studies on this concept have been conducted in other nations. In Guyana, it was found that 85% of children in Georgetown had heard gunshots, and over a third had seen people shooting at each other. While only 3% had seen someone being killed, over one-third had seen the body of a murder victim where they were killed (Cabral & Speek-Warnery, 2005). This is comparable to a study in Jamaica that found that 84% of children in the sample had been exposed to two or more types of community violence and half knew someone who had been shot (Baker-Henningham et al., 2009).

There have been high levels of community violence in South Africa. One study in South Africa found that exposure to community violence was associated with attention difficulties, aggression, and anxiety/depression (Barbarin, Richter, & de Wet, 2001). Research in Cape Town with children between 8 and 13 years old found that over 90% of children had witnessed violence, and almost 50% stated they had witnessed a murder. Over 80% had also heard about acts of violence. Both witnessing and hearing about community violence produced similar levels of psychological distress. Psychological distress was mediated by perceptions of safety and moderated by an unknown locus of control, social support, family organization, and family control (Shields, Nadasen, & Pierce, 2008).

Helping Children to Recover from the Impacts of Conflict

In many conflict situations, the focus is on meeting people's basic survival needs. This is especially true for those who have been displaced by the conflict and do not have access to previous support mechanisms.

Maslow's Hierarchy of Needs states if people's basic survival needs, such as food, water, and shelter, are not met, then people are unable to attend to higher order needs such as psychosocial difficulties. However, there have been criticisms that aid agencies have tended to focus *only* on physical needs to the exclusion of psychosocial healing needs (Okitikpi & Aymer, 2003; Sossou, 2006). The mental health impacts of conflict can last long past the physical impacts if intervention is not provided.

In recognition of this fact, Doctors Without Borders/Médecins Sans Frontières (MSF) now offers psychosocial services as well as medical services. As one staff member stated, "What do you do if there is enough food, but no one wants to eat?" (MSF, 2005b, ¶2). UNICEF has offered a number of programs for children who have been affected by conflict. In Lebanon, a train-the-trainer approach was used to educate teachers about the skills needed to help distressed children function effectively in the classroom (Sharar, 2007). They also offer programs in the occupied Palestinian territories to help children cope with the psychosocial trauma caused by the ongoing conflict (Dolan, 2006). In 2008, Mapp and Behrens conducted an intervention in Bethlehem, Palestine to help children affected by the conflict to develop emotional coping skills (see Box 5.1).

The Inter-Agency Standing Committee of the United Nations has published the *IASC Guidelines on Mental Health and Psychosocial Support in Emergency Situations* (2007) to help promote a minimum set of standards during emergencies that will protect and promote mental health. Based in human rights, the document addresses a number of needs that people will have, including meeting physical needs in a culturally appropriate fashion in order to promote psychosocial well-being. Anchored in the concept of resiliency, the Committee aimed the document toward helping coalitions of agencies to work effectively together to meet these needs.

Increasing family support has been shown to help ameliorate the effects of violence (Ozer, 2005; Punamäki, 2001; Shields et al., 2008; Wallen & Rubin, 1997). It can be difficult for parents to offer support to their children when they themselves may be traumatized. This is especially true for a conflict of long standing where the parents themselves did not have a childhood free of conflict. The mental health of children and the impact of war trauma on parents have been found to be correlated (Thabet, Abu Tawahina, El Sarraj, & Vostanis, 2008). Therefore, it is important for social service providers to educate families about the effects of trauma, while understanding the potential

BOX 5.1 Helping to Ameliorate the Effect of War on Palestinian Children

While the impact of war on children has now been recognized, there is a paucity of information concerning the impact of the ongoing conflict on Palestinian children. Much of the previous research has focused on assessing the occurrence and severity of posttraumatic and acute stress disorders with limited implications for treatment methodology. Despite the high profile of the Israeli–Palestinian conflict in the media, the impact on children is rarely mentioned (Aqtash, Seif, & Seif, 2004). Children in the Occupied Palestinian Territory (OPT) have never lived in a society free of violence. Almost all children in the occupied territories have been exposed to at least one traumatic event, ranging from watching mutilated bodies on television, hearing or witnessing the shooting or killing of a relative or friend, to the destruction of their home by Israeli forces.

The mental health system in Palestine is new; therefore, not many services are provided (Srour & Srour, 2006). In 2008, Mapp and Behrens sought to help address this need. Working together with staff from the International Center of Bethlehem, they sought to fill two gaps: assessing children in the West Bank as opposed to the Gaza Strip, as well as working to develop services to assist the children through the community. Utilizing a mixed-methods approach, both qualitative and quantitative data were gathered on the children's exposure to trauma, their coping skills, and the community's capacity to support them. Additionally, Behrens, a licensed music therapist, conducted music therapy sessions with 20 children in Bethlehem.

Interviews with mothers found that they worked hard to help mitigate the impact of the conflict on their children, but they felt hampered by the restrictions on movement imposed by the Israeli government and the Separation Wall. Additionally, since the mothers themselves had been children affected by conflict and had not been able to resolve the effects of that experience in their own lives, they were limited in their abilities to assist their children. Social service providers echoed the ongoing impact of the conflict on themselves as individuals, which affected their ability to help others. Both parents and providers noted that the traditional coping mechanism of utilization of the extended family as support was no longer as effective due to the high levels of ongoing need and the fact that this support mechanism had been overwhelmed. Thus, outside support is needed. The providers noted that although they did receive money from outside agencies to help provide services, the funders were specific in their requirements of which services were to be provided; this resulted in duplication of some services (such as parenting classes, or services for women and children) and left other needs unmet (such as services for men). The providers were also frustrated by their inability to gain additional knowledge and training due to restrictions on their movement by the Israeli government.

Results showed that the music therapy sessions helped the children to learn and identify feeling words, such as *happy*, *sad*, *angry*, and *scared*, and therefore may be a tool to help meet these unmet needs in this community. This is important because research has found that children who receive assistance in resolving the trauma brought about by war are more interested in peace (Bayer, Klasen, & Adam, 2007).

impact of intergenerational transmission (Burrows & Keenan, 2004). A project in the United States entitled SURVIVE (Supporting Urban Residents to be Violence-Free in a Violent Environment) educates both parents and children about types of violence (e.g., media, community, family), their potential impacts, and ways to mediate them. Sessions are conducted both with parents and children together as well as separately (DeVoe, Dean, Traube, & McKay, 2005).

Helping to End Conflict

The World Health Organization (WHO) (2002) states that one of the primary ways to reduce collective violence is to reduce poverty and to reduce inequality between groups. Those living in high-income countries are more than six times less likely to die from political violence than those living in middle- and low-income nations, while inequitable distribution of resources, including education and health services, contributes to conflict between groups. While the conflict in Northern Ireland is typically portrayed as tension between Catholics and Protestants, a more in-depth analysis reveals that there were long-standing injustices relating to political power, housing, and employment. It was in the 1960s with the wave of civil rights movements across the world that the Catholic minority began to struggle for equal rights, leading to the start of the Troubles (Muldoon, 2004). The conflict in Mindanao, Philippines, also stemmed from structural inequalities between groups (Frederico et al., 2007). In the United States, communities with higher levels of poverty are more likely to experience community violence.

Thus, children all over the world are physically and emotionally harmed by the occurrence of violence in their communities. Children suffer directly as well as indirectly from armed conflict; UNICEF (1996, ¶1) states, "Even if they have never seen a gun, millions of children suffer from wars, as resources that could have been invested in development are diverted into armaments." It is imperative for a peaceful future that the damage to these children be healed and work is done to help prevent future violence.

6

Child Maltreatment and Adoption

Article 19 of the Convention on the Rights of the Child (CRC) provides that the state will ensure all children are protected from maltreatment. Around the world, about 86% of children aged 2–14 years experience a "violent method" of discipline by their parents, which can include minor or severe physical punishment as well as psychological aggression. An estimated 40 million children under the age of 14 years experience child maltreatment (UNICEF, 2007a; "WHO calls," 1999). Additionally, approximately 57,000 children under the age of 15 years in the Global North die every year from child maltreatment (Krug, Dahlberg, Mercy, Zwi, & Lozano, 2002). These methods are typically used in order to cause a child physical or emotional distress to discipline the child and correct the child's behavior. These high numbers of violent discipline exist despite much lower support by caregivers for the use of such methods (UNICEF, 2007a). Thus, child maltreatment occurs around the world in a variety of forms, but only recently has it been recognized as such.

Child abuse was initially considered to be limited to Global North nations because that it is where it was written about in the professional literature, starting in the 1960s. Following the widespread use of X-rays in emergency rooms in the United States, C. Henry Kempe wrote a paper noting the common existence of child abuse. This led to mandatory reporting laws in the United States in the early 1970s and growing awareness of the problem. Subsequent research has discovered that similar behaviors occur across the world; it is the definition of what constitutes child abuse that varies (Williamson, 2002).

Even within a country, there are different definitions of what "maltreatment" is. Within the United States, there is no single clear-cut definition of child physical abuse; some would include corporal punishment, while others would not. These definitional difficulties only expand as we look around the world. It has been a concern of many of those working in the area of culture and child maltreatment that a balance be found between respecting a person's culture and not allowing a child to be harmed.

In an attempt to create a cross-cultural definition of child maltreatment, Finkelhor and Korbin (1988, p. 4) defined it as "the portion of harm to children that results from human action that is proscribed, proximate, and preventable." Thus, acts most clearly considered to be child abuse are intentional; socially censured by that culture; abusive according to international consensus; perpetrated by an individual (although governments, religious institutions, etc. can perpetrate child abuse as well); affect children specifically rather than children and other age groups; and affect a child defined as a person by that society. Pierce and Bozalek (2004) describe four categories of child maltreatment:

Societal abuse: includes child labor, child marriage, and child prostitution
Physical maltreatment: includes physical abuse and neglect
Sexual abuse: includes both sexual contact and exposure to sexual stimuli
Nonphysical maltreatment: includes fostering delinquency, parental alcohol/drug abuse, and emotional maltreatment

These definitions allow for cultural variation in childrearing, but they are inclusive of child maltreatment as well. Some behaviors might meet a cultural norm but be considered maltreatment by other cultures. For example, some cultures are appalled at how Americans have their infants sleep in separate rooms from their parents and consider that to be detrimental to the child's development (Small, 1998). Other cultures may accept a behavior that is considered abusive by most other cultures, such as using small children to clear a minefield in Iran (Finkelhor & Korbin, 1988). It is important to differentiate between cultural differences and maltreatment. Despite some differences in definition about what constitutes maltreatment, there is general agreement that certain acts are definitely maltreatment. Globally, sexual abuse is the type of abuse most commonly considered to be maltreatment, followed by abandonment and physical abuse by a parent (Bross, Miyoshi, Miyoshi, & Krugman, 2000).

Mandated reporting of suspected child maltreatment exists in such countries as Australia, Canada, Finland, France, Israel, Rwanda, and the United States to help identify affected children (Pollack, 2007). Mandated reporting for professionals was introduced in Thailand in 2003, but as of 2005, the new law was not well enforced (Assavanonda, 2005). However, these laws are comparatively rare (Krug et al., 2002); some other countries have voluntary reporting laws, while yet others have none. The efficacy of mandatory reporting laws has been debated. Some have raised concerns that mandated reporting increases the number of unsubstantiated reports that must be investigated, which draws resources away from cases where abuse is truly occurring. Another concern is that it sets up an adversarial relationship between families and the state. In response, supporters state that mandated reporting helps identify children in need of assistance who would not be otherwise identified (Mathews & Bross, 2008; Pollack, 2007). Pollack also notes that Article 19 of the CRC calls for the reporting of child maltreatment as a protective measure for children.

Types of Child Maltreatment

Leaving aside societal abuse, types of which are examined in other chapters, the three other types will be examined in more depth. Specifically, physical abuse, sexual abuse, emotional abuse, and neglect will be discussed in the following section. While consequences for specific types of maltreatment are discussed, it is important to remember that many consequences are common for multiple types of maltreatment and can also be cumulative. For example, adults who experienced child maltreatment have been found to have significantly lower health as adults (Corso, Edwards, Fang, & Mercy, 2008). However, those adults who experienced multiple types of maltreatment, such as both physical and sexual abuse, had an even greater risk of poor physical health than those who experienced only one form of maltreatment (Draper et al., 2008).

Physical Abuse

Physical abuse is typically defined as the infliction or endangerment of physical injury as a result of punching, beating, kicking, biting, burning, shaking, or otherwise harming a child. Harsh physical punishment, as stated previously, is one of the actions most commonly considered to be abusive across cultural contexts but yet remains widespread. Surveys across countries have found rates of moderate physical punishment ranging from 29% to 75% and severe physical punishment ranging from 4% to 36% (Krug et al., 2002). Physical punishment, including harsh methods, remains common in some countries, often due to a belief that this is the proper way to discipline children and teach them right from wrong ("Dramatic rise," 2008). For example, in Yemen, more than half of surveyed parents in rural areas and about one-quarter of those in urban areas used harsh methods of corporal punishment, including hitting children with objects, tying them up, or biting them (Alyahri & Goodman, 2008). In Vietnam, caregivers have stated that these actions are done out of love for the children in order to help them grow up to be good citizens ("Dramatic rise," 2008).

Physical abuse can have numerous short-term and long-term consequences, including an increased likelihood of mental health diagnoses, suicide, increased aggression, peer relation difficulties, and behaviors resulting in physical health problems (e.g., smoking and drinking) (World Health Organization, n.d.). It also has a negative impact on brain development, which can result in some of the above behaviors (Pinheiro, 2006).

Sexual Abuse

Child sexual abuse is defined as sexual contact or noncontact episode prior to the age of 18 years with a perpetrator who is at least 5 years older than the victim unless force was used. This can include a variety of actions ranging from intercourse to exposure to sexual material. Globally, it is estimated that 20% of women and 5%–10% of men have experienced a form of childhood sexual victimization (Krug et al., 2002). However, this can range among countries, with some countries such as Canada reporting rates of 13% for women and 4% for men, while studies in South Africa have found rates of 53% for females and 60% for males (Pereda, Guilera, Forns, & Gómez-Benito, 2009).

The most common perpetrators are known to the victim, including fathers/step-fathers, other family members, and professionals such as teachers (Lalor, 2004a; Speizer, Goodwin, Whittle, Clyde, & Rogers, 2008). However, these rates vary widely by country and their reliability varies depending on whether the statistics are drawn from a formal child welfare system, surveys of a college population, or a community survey. A community survey of childhood sexual abuse in Swaziland found that one-third of females surveyed reported experiencing some sort of sexual violence as a child, typically perpetrated by neighbors, followed by boyfriends or husbands (Reza et al., 2009).

Effectively dealing with sexual abuse has been inhibited by the lingering stigma for its victims. Similar to victims of other forms of sexual violence, there remains a shame to having experienced sexual abuse. In addition, the low status of girls in many cultures and the private nature of sexual matters have created barriers. In a society where females are seen as less valuable, women and girls lack power and are more vulnerable to abuse (LaFraniere, 2006; Lalor, 2004b). Additionally, males may be seen as having "uncontrollable" sexual urges that need to be satisfied (Lalor, 2004a).

Consequences of sexual abuse can include depression, substance abuse, and difficulties with sexual boundaries. Women who have experienced child sexual abuse are more likely to be victims of intimate partner violence in their adulthood (Speizer et al., 2008). In regions where AIDS is widespread, children who experience forced or coerced intercourse may become infected with HIV. In some areas, the virus may even cause the abuse due to the rumor that sex with a virgin can cleanse one of AIDS. While the prevalence of this is unknown, it does appear that older men are seeking younger partners in the belief that they will be less likely to be infected with a sexually transmitted infection (Lalor, 2004a; Lalor, 2004b; McCrann, Lalor, & Katabaro, 2006). In Zambia, it was found that as the level of abuse increased, abused children had less knowledge about HIV/AIDS, had more negative ideas about prevention, and had lower levels of self-efficacy regarding prevention of the disease. They were also more likely to participate in sexually high-risk behaviors (Slonim-Nevo & Mukuka, 2007).

Effective justice systems for these types of crimes may also be missing, affecting reporting, availability of police officers, and ability to prosecute. In impoverished countries such as Madagascar, the cost of the forensic exam is expected to be borne by the victims or their families, a cost that can be beyond the means of a family to pay, thus prohibiting prosecution of the offender (LaFraniere, 2006; "War, poverty and ignorance," 2007). Social pressure on children not to testify in cases of sexual abuse has meant that many offenders have escaped punishment. In Lesotho, a hotline for children was introduced in 2007 in order to hopefully increase reporting rates and alleviate this pressure ("Helpline allows," 2007). Thailand has noted the need for more female police officers in order to work more effectively with children who have been sexually abused (Phanayanggoor, 2005).

Emotional Abuse

Emotional or psychological abuse occurs when a child is regularly threatened, yelled at, humiliated, ignored, blamed, or otherwise emotionally mistreated. Surveys have found yelling or screaming at children to be common in countries around the world, ranging in prevalence from 70% to 85% (Krug et al., 2002). It has received relatively little attention because it can be difficult to quantify and is not as obviously harmful as the other types. However, consequences of emotional abuse can include an increased likelihood of involvement in domestic violence as an adult; substance abuse; depression; low self-esteem; as well as antisocial behavior, including fire setting and cruelty to animals.

Neglect

Neglect is the failure to provide for the child's basic needs and can include many different subtypes. Physical neglect is not providing the child's basic needs, such as food, clothing, and shelter, while emotional neglect is not meeting the basic emotional needs of a child for love and acceptance. Medical neglect is not providing appropriate medical care for a child (when it is available), while educational neglect is not making sure a child is receiving the available education. Obviously, many of these types of neglect are more applicable in wealthier countries, where the remedies are available to almost all residents as opposed to poorer nations, where their availability may be limited.

Consequences of neglect are varied depending on the type of neglect. They include the obvious consequences of not receiving what is needed, such as physical harm, including failure to thrive, malnutrition, illness, and death. They also include educational harm, such as failure to achieve in school. Similar to emotional abuse, neglect has historically not received as much attention in the research as physical and sexual abuse. However, it has now been determined that neglect can have long-term consequences similar to those of abuse, including substance abuse, depression, and suicide.

Risk Factors

The risk factors for experiencing child maltreatment are fairly similar around the world. Society can impact these occurrence rates, however, as illustrated by the fact that some European countries have rates lower than would be expected for child deaths by maltreatment (Greece, Italy, Ireland, Norway, and Spain), while others have much higher rates (Belgium, Czech Republic, France, and Hungary) (UNICEF, 2005). Thus, there are factors that will remain difficult to quantify. The ecological model, which examines how individual, familial, and larger systems factors interact, is most commonly used to explain the occurrence of child maltreatment (Krug et al., 2002).

Individual Level

On the individual level of the child, premature infants, twins, and children with a disability have higher rates of maltreatment than average (Krug et al., 2002). Age is a major factor for physical abuse because those who are least able to protect themselves are at highest risk. Thus, infants and toddlers are at the highest risk; the rate of fatal child abuse for children 0–4 years is more than double that of children aged 5–14 years. In contrast, sexual abuse rates are higher in adolescents. The type of child maltreatment experienced varies by sex. Boys are more likely to experience harsh physical punishment, while girls have higher rates of sexual abuse and nutritional neglect. In her study of child abuse in Hong Kong, So-Kung Tang (1998) hypothesized that boys may experience more severe physical abuse due to higher expectations for their behavior due to their higher societal position. In contrast, girls will marry out to another family, reducing the importance of their achievement and causing them to be seen more as "outsiders." Thus, the higher societal role of boys negatively affects them in this case.

These higher expectations may also explain why only children were more likely to experience physical abuse in her study.

Continuing with the ecological model, the next system level is that of the caregiver. Parents who commit physical abuse are more likely to be parenting alone, be young, be unemployed, have low educational levels, and be living in poverty. They also are more likely to have low self-esteem, poor impulse control, mental health problems, as well as unrealistic expectations for child development. Caregivers of large families are more likely to mistreat their children; this may correlate with household overcrowding. Overall, stress and isolation from social support increase the risk of maltreatment (Krug et al., 2002).

Family Level

In countries around the world, these factors are demonstrated in numerous societies. In Taiwan, it was found that children were more likely to be abused in families with poor family functioning, with frequent conflicts, and with parents who drank habitually (Yen et al., 2008). This was echoed by a study in the Kurdistan province of Iran that found that poor parental relationships and parental use of addictive substances were associated with higher rates of child maltreatment (Stephenson et al., 2006). Familial poverty can also create a risk factor for sexual abuse in that children may be tempted to perform sexual acts for a financial reward (McCrann et al., 2006). In the United States, abuse is more likely to occur in households where a nonrelated parental figure resides (McRee, 2008).

Families where corporal punishment is used are at a much higher risk for committing physical abuse. There is no clear-cut difference between where physical punishment ends and physical abuse begins, making abuse more likely. Research has consistently found that corporal punishment is not only an ineffective method of behavior change, but it often leads to the same negative consequences associated with physical abuse (UNICEF, 2005). Corporal punishment itself has been found to lead to not only higher rates of risky sexual behavior as a young adult, but further abusive behavior, as research across 32 nations found correlations between corporal punishment before age 12 years and having coerced or physically forced sex in the year previous to the study, especially for males (Gámez-Guadix & Straus, n.d.). This combination of the ineffectiveness of the method and the high risk of negative outcomes has led a number of countries to limit the use of corporal punishment by authorities other than parents (such as schools and juvenile justice); 19 other countries have banned it completely. The UN Committee of the Rights of the Child has stated that corporal punishment—the use of physical pain to discipline a child—is incompatible with the CRC (Krug et al., 2002).

Community Level

At the community level, poverty and lack of social capitol increase rates of child maltreatment. For example, in Swaziland, the drought has dramatically increased community poverty levels; the rates of child abuse have risen in correlation. In some cases, children are being locked or chained inside houses in an attempt to keep them safe while their parents search for work or food. In other cases, parental frustration has led to severe physical violence against children ("Hard times," 2007; Krug et al., 2002).

At the societal level, it appears that factors such as support for childrearing, armed conflict in the nation, the support of the social welfare system, and cultural norms around parent–child relationships are important influences (Krug et al., 2002). Rates of physical and emotional child abuse have increased markedly in Iraq since the start of the war in 2003 ("Domestic violence," 2007). In southern Africa, rates of reported child abuse have been rising, which is believed to be due in large part to the large number of children left orphaned by the AIDS crisis. In Zimbabwe, rates of sexual violence against children have increased 40% in the past 3 years and 400% in the past decade, which is believed to be caused by the huge number of orphans, the country's economic crisis, and social stress ("Trying to understand," 2008).

Prevention of Child Maltreatment

Many child maltreatment interventions focus on tertiary or, at best, secondary prevention, rather than primary prevention. Thus, the targets for these programs are families where child maltreatment has already occurred or is considered at high risk for occurring. For example, in the United States, the majority of federal funds are available only for families with a child in foster care and not for either prevention or family preservation (Pew Charitable Trusts, 2007).

Parenting education has been the one approach that tends to occur on a broader level. In these classes, parents and potential parents are taught about normative child development as well as nonviolent skills with which to improve their ability to manage child behavior. While many of these classes are targeted to parents already determined to be abusive, they are also available in the community to nonabusive parents as well as in secondary schools (Krug et al., 2002). Germany has used parent education for both primary and secondary prevention, that is, universally and to at-risk populations (Junger et al., 2007). Afghani parents state that while the use of corporal punishment is widespread, they recognized it was not the best way and were interested in learning nonviolent methods of discipline (Smith, 2008).

A survey of parenting education policies in eight countries in the Global North found a variety of supports for families (Canada, Denmark, Finland, France, Germany, Italy, Netherlands, Sweden, United Kingdom, and United States). The Nordic countries provided the greatest level of support for families, including child allowances, paid leave, and childcare provisions, while the United States was the country in the group with no national paid maternity leave policy. No country had specific policies relating to parenting education; rather, they were integrated with other policies. Most countries targeted families who were viewed as "at risk," with the exceptions of Finland, where they were available to all families, and the Netherlands, where they are based on client request. All nations implemented them through local governments, except for the United States, where they were implemented through local service providers. Most countries focused on young children (birth to 5 years of age) except for the Netherlands, which included all children 0–18 years of age, and the United States, which focused on schoolchildren (including preschool) because programs were often delivered through the schools. Thus, there has been no coherent policy among nations and within nations, and there is no specific focus on parenting education (Shulruf, O'Loughlin, & Tolley, 2009).

Home visitation has been found to be an effective strategy to prevent child maltreatment. In the United States, a program in which nurses visited low-income first-time parents had half the maltreatment rate than similar families who did not receive this service. The mothers voluntarily enrolled in the program during pregnancy and the nurses assisted them with having a healthy pregnancy, understanding child health and development, and planning for the future (Pew Charitable Trusts, 2007). Home visiting programs have also become widespread across Canada, with similar positive results (Santos, 2005).

Educating children about abuse can be an effective primary prevention tool. In Thailand, a child abuse prevention project teaches the children the mantra "Why, no, go, tell" to help children protect themselves from sexual abuse by teaching them they have the right to refuse a person seeking to abuse them and to tell another person about what happened ("Mantra may help," 2005). However, many parents consider it to be inappropriate to discuss topics of a sexual nature with their children. For example, in Afghanistan, many parents consider any discussion of sex with their children to be indecent, even though 40% of child sexual abuse occurs within the home. Rates of child sexual abuse have been rising in that nation in the post-Taliban era, but few children will speak of it due to the associated disgrace and stigma ("War, poverty and ignorance," 2007). A survey of parents in China found that although almost half of respondents were concerned that education about child sexual abuse might cause their children to know too much about sex, 95% thought such programs should be offered in elementary school and were willing to have their children attend (Chen, Dunne, & Han, 2007).

Systems of Child Protection

In many countries there is no governmental system for investigating and responding to child abuse. This can affect not only how child maltreatment is dealt with but how it is defined. A national system would require a formal definition of child maltreatment that would encompass the actual variety of cases. A lack of a formal child welfare system is more common in countries of the Global South, due in part to national poverty as well as a historically strong family and community structure that traditionally assisted in such cases. For example, Vietnam has no national system for responding to child maltreatment; indeed, there is no definition of child abuse and no specific laws against physical punishment. Child abuse is typically defined only as sexual abuse, and even then, it focuses on girls as the only victims ("Dramatic rise," 2008). In another example, the Kenyan Department of Social Services is not well-known among professionals in that nation. Additionally, those who are aware of it are hesitant to report abuse because resources are limited and a child who is removed may be placed in a prison cell due to lack of other options (Mildred & Plummer, 2009).

In nations such as South Africa, there is no licensing procedure for foster parents due to the large number of people and amount of money it would involve. Additionally, many orphans are being cared for by family members outside of the formal welfare system (van Delft, 2006). This increase of kinship care due to the AIDS epidemic has further increased pressure on the child welfare system due to the large increase in applications for governmental assistance (September, 2006). In sub-Saharan Africa, extended families are caring for over 90% of children orphaned by AIDS (UNICEF, 2006). The fact that the level of need has overwhelmed the community's ability to provide care has been seen throughout sub-Saharan Africa to the extent that the number of child-headed households has been rising. This family type, once extremely rare, now constitutes 15% of all household types (Lombe & Ochumbo, 2008).

In Uganda, community-based programs are working to provide support to poor families, many of whom are caring for orphaned children, to help them meet their basic necessities (Roby & Shaw, 2008). More formal support is needed by these kinship systems because the level of need has overwhelmed the families' ability to provide. Additionally, cultural shifts such as increased distance between families due to urbanization and a weakening of familial bonds have caused the extended family to be less available than in the past (Akpalu, 2007). Ghana has a long history of informal foster placements for children with low use of institutions. Formal placements in family foster care were unusual due to wide kin networks that were able to assist with the rearing of a child. However, due to the AIDS epidemic and the concomitant rise in the number of children in need, traditional caregivers have been overwhelmed (Ansah-Koi, 2006). As a result, Ghana has seen an increase in the use of institutions to care for children, in contrast to nations in other parts of the world that are moving away from it (Akpalu, 2007). This is echoed by developments in Botswana, where residential facilities for children were first established in 1987 in response to rising need (Maundeni, 2009).

Institutional Care (Orphanages)

In contrast to these African nations, a number of countries that traditionally used large institutions to care for children in need of care are shifting more toward a family environment because institutional care has been found to be detrimental to the healthy development of children (Browne, Hamilton-Giachritsis, Johnson, & Ostergren, 2006) including resulting in lower intelligence levels (Nelson et al., 2007). Moving children from institutions to a family setting through foster care or adoption has been found to significantly improve these developmental delays (Nelson et al., 2007; Wilson, Weaver, Cradock, & Kuebli, 2007).

Australia, Iceland, Kyrgyzstan, Norway, Slovenia, and the United Kingdom have been shifting from large institutions to an emphasis on placements with families (Browne et al., 2006; Maluccio, Canali, & Vecchiato, 2006; "Move to keep," 2008; Sellick, 2006). In Poland, the use of foster care was reduced during Soviet rule due to an emphasis on the use of large institutions. However, there has now been a shift back toward placement with families (Stelmaszuk, 2006). This has been echoed by other nations of the former Soviet bloc, including Georgia, Moldova, and the Ukraine (EveryChild, 2009). However, there is still a growing number of children in countries of the former Soviet Union in formal state care, many of whom are in institutions. Children with a disability are especially at risk (UNICEF, 2007b).

Conditions in orphanages in some countries have been found to be abusive. Extraordinary neglect and abuse have been documented in orphanages in countries such as Russia, Romania, and China. In many orphanages the children are not truly orphans, but have been abandoned. In Russian culture, it is assumed that an abandoned child must be "defective" in some way; due to this prejudice, Human Rights Watch (1998) found that in some cases babies were never removed from their cribs, and older children were often physically and sexually abused.

In Romania at the end of the Cold War, it was found that hundreds of thousands of children had been abandoned due to their parents' inability to care for them often as a result of the prohibition on birth control and abortion. The conditions in these orphanages were squalid, and the children were typically severely neglected (Hunt, 1990). As a condition of being able to join the European Union, Romania promised to move the children from orphanages without resorting to international adoption for them (Laffan, 2005). However, thousands of children are still living in governmental institutions in horrific conditions; they simply have been moved from orphanages to psychiatric institutions and other state-run facilities (Mental Disability Rights International, 2006). In an effort to reduce poor adoption practices in international adoptions and increase domestic adoption, Romania has stopped all international adoptions ("Romania," 2006; Rosenthal, 2005).

China traditionally used institutions to care for its abandoned children, the number of whom rose sharply with the enforcement of the "one-child policy" (Johnson, Banghan, & Liyao, 1998). This name is misleading because the policy is not strictly "one child." Urban families are restricted to one child, but rural families may have two if the first child is a girl, and ethnic minorities are typically exempt from the policy. Families may also pay large penalties for having additional children past their limit. Children who were abandoned were most often girls or disabled boys, due to the need for a son to care for their parents (Johnson et al., 1998). The vast majority of abandoned girls were not abandoned to die but were typically placed where someone else would find them—someone whom the parent believed would be able to care for the child, such as an orphanage or potential adoptive family (Johnson, 2004).

The orphanages in China became overwhelmed and were unable to adequately care for all of the children. Human Rights Watch (1996) found that the mortality rate in the orphanages was frighteningly high, with over 50% of admissions dying in the first year from the lack of proper care. In some institutions, the mortality rate was closer to 90%. The orphanages were also unable to pay high-quality staff to care for the children and, thus, high rates of abuse were documented as well. In recent years, the quality of care in the orphanages has been much improved ("China paying more attention," 2001; Johnson, 2004; Platt, 2000), but there is still more work to be done. A ranking Chinese government official stated in 2006 that orphans were still not receiving adequate care ("China's orphans," 2006). The growing number of children who have been orphaned by AIDS are having difficulty receiving services as well ("Thousands of AIDS orphans," 2005).

While the communal living provided in orphanages fits the traditional communist model well, in recent years China has begun to develop a foster care system similar to that in the United States, where nonrelatives are paid money to help care for children in need (Shang, 2002). In China, the first family foster care program began in Shanghai in 1998 to help move children from orphanages. Most of the children were living there because they were abandoned by their birth families due to the child's disability or female sex. Foster care is not considered a short-term resource as it is in the United States; it is intended to be permanent. While families are anxious about becoming foster parents, for those who desire more than one child, it is a way to grow their family without violating the limitations on the number of children allowed per family (Glover, 2006). The "ideal" family in China is often one child of each sex (Johnson, 2002). While families believe they need a son to care for them, they believe that a daughter is more loving, loyal, and obedient (Johnson, 2002; Johnson, et al., 1998).

Family Foster Care

While extended families in all nations have always assisted in the care of children, the system of family foster care, in which families unrelated to the maltreated children will care for them, varies from country to country. While it has existed in some fashion in countries such as France for centuries, it has been formalized only in about the last 100–200 years as part of the governmental social welfare system. In France, foster parents are considered to be governmental employees (although they do not have the same civil service rights) (Corbillon, 2006). Other countries such as Argentina and China have only formalized foster care in recent years (Dezeo de Nicora, 2006; Glover, 2006). In Argentina, it began in the 1980s as a resource to care for children whose families were unable to care for them due to poverty, the special needs of the child, or older age of the child, which was believed to render the child unadoptable (Dezeo de Nicora, 2006).

Countries with a longer history of family foster care will often have different types of caregivers, such as kinship providers, general foster parents, and therapeutic foster parents (for children with additional needs). In Japan, this last category was only instituted in 2002 and requires additional experience and training (Iwasaki, 2006). The United States uses therapeutic foster parents for children with higher levels of physical or emotional needs (Wehrmann, Unrau, & Martin, 2006). In Sweden, there has been a return to prioritizing the use of kin as providers of care, both because it is seen as important to the child and because of the declining number of foster parents (Hojer, 2006). Kinship care has also been receiving a surge of attention in the United States for similar reasons (National Conference of State Legislatures, 2006). In Spain, family foster care was only instituted in 1987 and approximately half of all children in care still reside in institutions. However, of those in family foster care, about 85% are in kinship placements (del Valle, López, Montserrat, & Bravo, 2009).

The shift to family foster care is not always easy, though, as illustrated by countries such as India, Thailand, Korea, and Japan. In India, this shift has led to limited success to date and is still in progress (Goriawalla & Telang, 2006). While Thailand has been working to increase its number of foster families, foster care is limited in that nation due to financial resources. Additionally, many foster families leave the program when their foster child leaves because of the attachment to the child ("Foster families," 2005). The majority of children in state care in Japan live in large institutions (Bamba & Haight, 2007). Foster care itself has been struggling in Japan due to the declining numbers of available foster parents. This is for a number of reasons, including the importance of blood ties in that nation, lack of support for foster parents, and a lack of parental confidence in their ability to parent (Iwasaki, 2006). Korea has also experienced these difficulties especially as it attempts to move from a reliance on institutional care to foster families, the importance of blood ties in a family (Lee, 2009).

Most countries have experienced difficulties in recruiting sufficient numbers of foster parents, due to changing norms and rising numbers of children, in addition to other factors. For example, in South Africa, the growing number of children orphaned by the AIDS epidemic is overwhelming the abilities of both the formal welfare system as well as their kinship network to be able to care for them (van Delft, 2006).

Adoption

Although being available for adoption in the United States is often associated with having experienced parental maltreatment, this is typically not the case with children worldwide. Children in other countries are often available for adoption due to disabilities, parental poverty, or governmental policies limiting the number of children per family. However, due to the AIDS crisis, there are some nations in Africa that have turned to international adoption to help find permanent homes for their orphaned children (Roby & Shaw, 2006).

International adoption first began in force after World War II with the adoptions of orphaned children from Germany and Greece by

U.S. families. A second wave began after the Korean War with children from Korea (who were often fathered by U.S. soldiers). From these beginnings as a child-focused phenomenon, international adoption has evolved to one that is more focused on meeting the needs of adoptive parents. As fertility has declined in Western nations, as well as the number of healthy White infants available for adoption, interest in international adoption has risen. International adoption is regulated by the Hague Convention on Intercountry Adoption. Developed in 1993, its goal is to regulate procedure and set minimum standards for international adoptions in order to protect all parties: birth parents, adoptive parents, and the children being adopted. As of early 2010, there were 81 contracting states to this convention, including the United States. The United States ratified it in 2007, and it went into force on April 1, 2008 (Hague Conference, 2009). Box 6.1 summarizes the main tenets of the Hague Convention.

Hollingsworth (2003) questions whether social justice is served by international adoption by families in the United States. On the one hand, children are being brought from conditions that are at the best impoverished and at the worst, harmful. On the other hand, the question remains of whether it is the best method to remove a few select children from these circumstances and leave the circumstances unchanged. Box 6.2 describes a U.S.-based non-governmental organization Brittany's Hope that is both trying to help children find permanent homes through international adoption while also working to address the conditions within the sending nation.

The Hague Convention first requires governments to make it a priority that children are able to remain with their birth parents and adoption is an option only after attempts at familial reunification, as well as domestic placement, have failed. However, in some countries, international adoptions are perceived as favored over domestic adoptions due to the greater revenue they provide. For example, in China, each international adoption results in U.S.$3000 being paid to the orphanage; this is not true for domestic adoptions (Johnson, 2002). Other difficulties can result from domestic adoption laws. Prior to 1999, if a Chinese couple wished to adopt a child, they had to be at least 35 years old and childless. In 1999, the law was changed to allow couples 30 years and older to adopt, and if the child was abandoned and living in an orphanage, the couple is permitted to already have one other child as well (Glover, 2006). India has no secular adoption law; adoption is based on

BOX 6.1 The Hague Convention on Protection of Children and Cooperation in Respect of Intercountry Adoption

The Hague Convention on Protection of Children and Cooperation in Respect of Intercountry Adoption (Hague Convention) was developed as a structure for regulating international adoption, both in receiving countries and countries of origin. It was adopted in 1993 and entered into force in 1995. The Convention seeks to ensure that intercountry adoptions are made in the best interests of the child and with respect for his or her fundamental rights. In order to uphold the rights of the child as delineated in the Convention on the Rights of the Child (CRC), the first preference is for the child to remain with his or her birth family when possible. If that is not possible, family placement (i.e., foster care or adoption) is preferred over institutional placement, and permanent placements (birth family or adoption) are preferred over temporary placements (foster care or institutional placement). Lastly, placements that keep the child in his or her country of birth are preferred over ones that move the child to another country (UNICEF, 1999).

If the child is placed for adoption, there must be confirmation that the child is available for adoption, all information about the child must be preserved, and the child must be placed with a suitable family. The Convention also states that all children must be protected against the risk of abduction, trafficking, or other illegal activities by all contracting countries. This is accomplished through the establishment of a Central Authority in all nations who have ratified the Hague Convention. This Central Authority has differing requirements depending on whether the country is sending or receiving children.

Sending countries must ensure that all legal requirements have been met, establish that the child is adoptable by determining that the child is indeed an orphan with no parental ties, and determine that international adoption is in the best interest of the child. All other possibilities of domestic placement must be taken into consideration before the international adoption process can take place. Proper informed consent must be obtained from the birth parent(s).

Receiving countries must take the responsibility of working with countries that abide by the Convention's regulations. They must determine that the prospective adoptive parents are eligible to adopt, and home studies must be conducted to evaluate the parents' ability to raise the child properly. The prospective parents must be counseled on intercountry adoption and confirm that the adopted child will be given a permanent residence. All agencies who provide intercountry adoption services must be accredited or approved by the Central Authority. The agency must provide the prospective adoptive parents with preadoption training as well as extensive medical information on the child (International Social Services, 2008).

a Hindu tradition to provide a male heir for a man who lacks one. The 1956 law based on this tradition states that parents can only adopt a child if they lack one of that sex, while non-Hindus can assume guardianship of a child, but this does not provide the child with the rights of the adoptee (Desai, 2009).

BOX 6.2 Brittany's Hope: A Developmental Model for Orphan Care

While international adoption remains a viable option for many children, it will never meet the needs of all children, and it remains the last resort under the Hague Convention. According to UNICEF, there are 145 million orphans around the world, including children who have lost either one or both parents (UNICEF, 2009). Thus, it is important to take a developmental approach in order to build capacity in children's home countries to reduce the need for international adoption. Brittany's Hope, a U.S.-based nongovernmental organization, has been making this shift.

Originally developed to facilitate international adoption of special needs children who were otherwise unlikely to find a permanent family, Brittany's Hope has been expanding its mission to promote sustainable development projects for orphans and other at-risk children around the world. Many of their projects have occurred in the nation of Vietnam, including Emily's Canes to provide canes to community members with vision impairment and teach them to use them, and Brittany's Cribs to provide safe cribs in orphanages. They also sponsor the House of Love orphanage, where they have funded a number of building projects, such as shower and kitchen facilities; underwritten sustainable development, including potable water and farm animals; and also facilitated sponsorship of individual children at the orphanage. Many children living there are not eligible for adoption because they have a living parent, but in many cases their parent is not able to adequately care for them due to poverty or illness. The money provided through sponsorship helps assure an adequate diet, schooling, and a safe place to eat and sleep for all children living at this facility.

Brittany's Hope is now expanding to the continent of Africa, where they are facilitating projects in Kenya and Uganda. They are helping to build an orphan care village in Injibara, Ethiopia. Being built in stages, it will provide a safe place for orphans to live and develop, as well as provide medical care and facilities to the surrounding community. Later stages will include vocational training facilities and sports fields for the community. In Uganda, they have begun a program to provide food to street children. Begun as a small outreach program, it now feeds hundreds of children a day as word spreads among the children of its availability.

The work of Brittany's Hope helps demonstrate how a wider focus is being developed to help more children than the few who can be assisted through international adoption. While adoption remains the best plan for some children, community development, such as that promoted through Brittany's Hope, casts a wider net to help orphans and others in need. You can read more about Brittany's Hope at http://www.brittanyshope.org.

The number of children adopted by Americans from other nations peaked at 22,884 in fiscal year 2004 and has been declining since. In fiscal year 2009, 12,753 children were adopted from other nations. The top three nations from which Americans adopted children (sending nations) have been Russia, China, and Guatemala for a number of years. However, the number of children adopted from both Russia and China has been steadily declining, which explains a large part of why international adoption numbers have been declining overall. In fiscal year 2004, about 7000 children were adopted from China, which declined to about 3000 in fiscal year 2009. Similarly, almost 6000 children were adopted from Russia in fiscal year 2004, but only a little more than 1500 in fiscal year 2009. In contrast, in recent years, Ethiopia has seen increasing numbers of children adopted to the United States and became the number two sending nation in fiscal year 2009 (U.S. Department of State, n.d.). Ethiopia is one of the few African nations that has welcomed international adoption. The Ethiopian government requires the foreign adoption agencies to provide social services and document the results. Birth information on the children is typically available and adopting families can often meet the birth family, both of which are attractive to couples seeking to adopt (Gross & Connors, 2007).

The changes occurring in the Chinese child welfare system may also be affecting the number of children available for international adoption. As stated earlier, family foster care as a method of permanent placement is becoming available. Additionally, as stated previously, restrictions on domestic adoption are being eased and thus more Chinese couples are now able to adopt children (Glover, 2006). These changes have helped increase the number of domestic adoptions substantially (Johnson, 2002).

Simultaneously, requirements for people from other nations seeking to adopt Chinese children have been tightened. At the end of 2006, China announced that people who are single, obese, older than 50 years, or without good physical and mental health and solid financial status would not be allowed to adopt. There was a greater number of adoption applications than children available to be adopted, and China used this method to narrow the application pool and retain what it considered to be the most well-qualified people (Belluck & Yardley, 2006).

The trafficking of children for adoption continues to be a concern in a number of countries as well. In Afghanistan, children were sold due to poverty; their parents could not afford to raise them ("Stop sale," 2008). A study by UNICEF and Terre des Hommes (2008) in Nepal found abduction and trafficking of children for adoption to be widespread in that nation. Birth parents were deceived about adoption and many believed that their children would return at the age of 16 or 18 years. They did not realize they were permanently giving up all rights to their child and in some cases did not even know they would be sent out of the country for adoption. In Ghana, it was found that up to 90% of children living in orphanages were not truly orphans, and in a number of cases, their parents had been tricked into signing away their parental rights ("Protecting children," 2009).

In Costa Rica, 14 people (including a judge) were arrested in a trafficking scheme in which mothers were paid to give up their infants ("Costa Rica detains," 2008). Vietnam halted adoptions to the United States in 2008 due to concerns about trafficking and fraud (Brummitt, 2008). In China, young boys are being kidnapped and sold to rural families who want a boy (Jacobs, 2009). However, the two countries with the largest problem appear to have been Cambodia and Guatemala.

In 2001, the United States halted the processing of adoptions from Cambodia due to reports of widespread corruption and trafficking. They were joined by France, the Netherlands, Switzerland, Belgium, and Britain in 2004 and Canada in 2005 (Blair, 2005; Ministry of Children and Family Development, n.d.). In some cases, children in Cambodia were being purchased, or even stolen, from birth mothers for international adoption (Corbett, 2002; Mydans, 2001). In other cases, poor women, especially those who were widowed or divorced, were convinced to place their newborn in a "children's center." They were told that the placement would be temporary and they would be able to visit the child; they were also given a "donation." However, when the mothers would try to visit the child, they were refused, and if they asked for the child back, they were told they would have to pay an amount of money several times the amount of the "donation" they had received. Fraudulent paperwork was then created stating that the child had been abandoned and the parents were unknown. Government officials appear to have been receiving large bribes for their assistance in the process (Cambodian League for the Promotion and Defense of Human Rights, 2002).

UNICEF (2009b) estimates that between 1000 and 1500 infants from Guatemala are trafficked to the United States and Europe each year. Guatemala had been sending such huge numbers of children to the United States that 1 of every 100 children born every year was growing up in the United States ("Adoptions," 2008). In September 2008, Guatemala announced that it was suspending international adoption in order to allow itself time to establish guidelines for accrediting adoption agencies as well as process transition cases. At the same time, the United States announced that although Guatemala had ratified the

Hague Convention, it was not meeting its Convention requirements and therefore no new adoptions from there would be processed (U.S. Department of State, 2008). This was despite a new law in Guatemala passed at the end of 2007 that was designed to tighten the adoption system to reduce the widespread corruption ("New Guatemala adoption law," 2007). In 2007, the U.S. embassy in Guatemala began requiring additional DNA testing. A DNA test was already required at the beginning of the process to ensure that the person relinquishing the child was truly a birth parent. The second DNA test was added at the end of the process to determine that it was still the same child (U.S. Department of State, 2007). Canada has suspended adoptions from Guatemala since 2001 (Adoption Council of Canada, 2006). Additionally, the United Kingdom, Germany, Canada, Spain, and the Netherlands all filed objections regarding Guatemala's adherence to the Hague Convention (Huntenburg, 2008).

Conclusion

Around the world, children are at risk of maltreatment, regardless of the country or culture in which they are raised. Societies have developed a variety of mechanisms to try to deal with this, some formal and others informal. For those children who are unable to be raised by their families, alternative families are sought through adoption in many cases. However, this does not alleviate all problems; in fact, it may cause problems. As maintained by the Hague Convention, the first choice of permanent placement should be with the child's own family, the second choice should be an adoptive family in the child's own country, and the last choice should be with a family from another country.

Due to the lifelong impacts of experiencing maltreatment, it is essential for societies to work to reduce and eliminate this occurrence. If the birth family is unable to provide a safe environment, research to date supports the concept that a substitute family is the next best option for the child. Concordant with the ideas of the Hague Convention, this family should ideally be kin, or as a second option, within the child's own culture. As a last option, international adoption should be available so that all children can grow up in a loving safe family.

7

Educational Issues

Since 2000, the number of children, including girls, enrolling in primary school has increased markedly. Spending on education and education aid has also increased (UNESCO, 2007). Progress has been made around the world in increasing and maintaining school enrollment. Much of that success relates to the institution of universal primary education (UPE) and the related removal of educational fees. Even in societies where children are not traditionally educated in formal schools, interest is growing. Pastoralists across Africa are reporting an increased desire to send their children to school because they are able to see the positive results it brings ("Education tops," 2007; "I'm beginning," 2007). However, vast problems in education continue, including access and quality. UNICEF (2008) estimates that globally, 93 million primary-school-aged children are not enrolled in school, the majority of whom continue to be girls. The high cost of schooling continues to be a barrier to enrollment. Problems regarding quality of education and dropout rates continue even in countries where access to education is widespread.

Article 28 of the Convention on the Rights of the Child (CRC) requires that primary education be offered free of cost to all children, that secondary education appropriate to the child's interests and abilities (i.e., vocational or college preparatory) be made available and accessible, and that higher education be made accessible. The lack of requirement for secondary education does not mean that it is viewed as less important, but rather that it is beyond the means of some countries to make it free and compulsory to all (UNICEF, 2007).

It is not sufficient for education to be offered; countries must actively work to remove barriers and to encourage regular attendance and reduce dropout rates. Any discipline within the school must be delivered in a manner that maintains the child's dignity and his or her right to be free of all forms of violence. In summary, the child has the right to the following: access to education, a quality education, and respect in the learning environment (UNICEF, 2007).

Education in Western and non-Western societies has traditionally been conceptualized differently. Reagan (1996) explains some of these general differences as follows. He states that there is a conflating of formal schooling and education in Western societies that is not generally found in non-Western societies. Similarly, there has traditionally been less focus on educational specialists in non-Western societies, and education is more community-based and communal. Reflective of the communal focus of many of these societies (in contrast to the more individualistic focus of typical Western societies), there is more focus in education on helping the children acquire the skills to become good adults and members of society, as well as a focus on helping children acquire the skills to be economically productive in their society. However, regardless of the environment, it is essential for children to receive the education necessary for their ability to achieve their full potential as adults within their society. Thus, two of the United Nations Millennium Development Goals focus on education.

Millennium Development Goals

The Millennium Development Goals were developed in 2000 based on the Millennium Declaration of the United Nations. This declaration affirmed a collective responsibility for global equality and equity and was signed by 189 nations (United Nations Development Programme [UNDP], n.d.). The Millennium Development Goals set clear and precise targets for achieving the commitments made in the Millennium Declaration by 2015. While in the past, development goals tended to focus on economic growth, the Goals placed social development at the heart of the objectives (UNDP, 2003).

One of the Millennium Development Goals focuses specifically on education. Goal Two is to achieve universal primary education—that by 2015 all children, both boys and girls, will complete primary school.

UNDP (2009) reports that as of 2007, almost all regions of the world have shown progress toward this goal, Eastern Asia being the only exception (which decreased from 99% to 95%). Sub-Saharan Africa has made substantial progress, increasing the proportion enrolled from 53% to 74%, but it still has low enrollment.

Although sub-Saharan Africa as a whole has made progress, fewer than half of the children in Burkina Faso, Djibouti, Eritrea, Ethiopia, Mali, or Niger are enrolled in school, underlining the importance of examining diversity within a region. Additional inequalities include those based on residence and sex. Eighty-two percent of children not in school in countries in the Global South live in rural areas. This is typically due to poverty; the children's income from labor is needed, and families often lack the funds to afford school. On a macro level, the country's poverty will limit the number of schools available and there may be no school close enough even if the child is able to attend.

Millennium Development Goal 3 assesses gender parity in primary education and was supposed to be met by 2005, which it was not (UNICEF, 2004). As of 2009, 6 of the 10 regions had achieved parity and 2 more were on track to achieve it by 2015. However, Oceania was considered unlikely to achieve it by 2015 and sub-Saharan Africa is at risk not to meet this goal as well (United Nations Millennium Goals Indicators, 2009). Girls are much more likely to be out of school than boys, especially in southern Asia, western Asia, and Oceania.

Barriers to Education

Certain groups of children are more at risk for not obtaining an education, including girls, children affected by war, and child laborers (the impact of work, as well as conflict, on education was discussed in previous chapters, but it is appropriate to be mentioned here as well). Working children often face discrimination by teachers when they are able to attend school. Their knowledge from their labor is not regarded as important and they face stereotypes and labeling. Dyer's research in Yemen (2007) found that teachers stereotyped working children as dirty, lazy, and always late and felt that they did not belong in a regular school. Children who are working find it difficult to attend school because school is typically held during their working hours. Even if they are able to attend, they have little time to complete homework and are often too tired in the classroom to attend to the lesson properly. Lack of access to education increases child labor by reducing options for these children and their families.

This can also hold true for children, especially girls, who spend a great deal of time on household chores. For example, in Yemen, 90% of the population does not have an adequate supply of water and 69% have inadequate access to safe drinking water. It is the responsibility of rural girls and women to walk long distances to fetch water for the household. A project that provided access to public water sources increased school enrollment by 9 percentage points for all children and 11 points for girls (Dyer, 2007). Additionally, children who work on their family's farms are typically absent during the harvest. If the school schedule does not allow for these absences, the children will miss a great deal of instruction. If they then do return, they are typically unable to pass the end-of-year exams and are held back (Groves, 2004; Valerio, Bardasi, Chambal, & Lobo, 2006).

Education is often affected for children whose lives have been impacted by conflict. As of 2007, 43 million children were out of school due to armed conflict (UNICEF, 2008). Children who are recruited into armed groups are unable to access education, while other children avoid schools due to the danger of getting there or because schools are often targets of violence. For example, the violence in the far south of Thailand has forced hundreds of schools to close, while Afghanistan has seen hundreds of schools close due to violent attacks, especially schools for girls (Bearak, 2007; "Civilians complain," 2007; Human Rights Watch, 2007; United Nations Security Council, 2007). In one Afghani province, there were 224 schools in 2003, but in 2008 only 54 were functioning, most of them for boys ("Attacks deprive," 2008). Children in Afghani households in which they had experienced a "security incident" in the past year were less likely to attend school than those who had not (Guimbert, Miwa, & Nguyen, 2007).

As discussed in Chapter Five, children who are displaced within their own nation are affected by difficulties in accessing education. For example, in the camps for displaced persons outside of Khartoum, Sudan, 90% of the children do not attend school due to a combination of lack of facilities and a need for child labor for survival (Abdelmoneium, 2005). In Pakistan, many families in the Swat Valley in 2009 fled to the city of Lahore to escape the fighting. However, the expense of the journey exhausted their savings, and the children then needed to work upon reaching the city to provide income for the family's survival ("IDP children," 2009).

Children may also have been forced to relocate to a foreign country where they must learn a new language and culture in order to receive an education. Syria has given all Iraqi refugee children access to education, but the huge number of refugee children has overwhelmed the Syrian schools. Schools have doubled in enrollments and are being forced to operate in shifts. Also, Syrian children begin learning English in first grade, which creates difficulties for Iraqi children entering at later ages ("Classrooms in Syria," 2008).

Prejudice and lack of acceptance toward refugees can impact the quality of these services (McBrien, 2005). The trauma leading to their refugee status is typically unknown or unaddressed in the classroom. This trauma can also affect parental support for their education. If the child's parents are overwhelmed by the trauma or have difficulties in adjustment to the new nation, they will be less able to offer support to their child. This lack of parental support has been identified as a contributing factor in dropout rates. Parents may also be accustomed to a different type of school system. For example, in the United States, parental involvement in their child's education is viewed not only as expected but necessary. In other cultures, parents should not be involved in schooling. Self-consciousness about their English language proficiency also inhibits immigrant parents in the United States from being involved in their children's education (Hu, 2008). Additionally, for children coming from cultures that are more collectivist in nature and where working together and for the good of others is the norm, the competitive nature of American high schools can be a difficult adjustment (McBrien, 2005).

Lack of citizenship in a country can be a barrier to receiving an education. Under Chinese law, any child born in China with at least one Chinese citizen as a parent is entitled to citizenship and thus access to education. However, children who are born to a North Korean mother often face difficulties despite having a Chinese father. Since these women have migrated without proper documents (North Korea rarely allows emigration), if their children are registered under the name of both parents, the Chinese government will arrest them and return them to North Korea, where they face harsh labor camps and possible death for emigrating without permission. Therefore, many of these children are kept out of school because the law will deprive them of either their education or their mother (Human Rights Watch, 2008). In Lebanon, Lebanese women are unable to pass their nationality to their children. Additionally, in the event of marital separation, it is the father who receives automatic custody. These laws have resulted in a score of children who are denied access to education, as well as health care and residency, due to their lack of citizenship.

Natural disasters can also affect access to education and its quality. The drought in Kenya not only increased familial poverty, resulting in lowered attendance, but affected the schools themselves because they did not have access to water (Nybo, 2006). Additionally, children have to spend time searching for water for survival rather than attending school ("Drought forcing," 2008). This has been found to occur in Afghanistan, where children may spend many hours searching for water, prohibiting them from attending school. Even those who can attend are affected because they often do not have the time or energy to do homework ("Drought, poverty" 2008). Cyclone Nargis in Myanmar severely disrupted education. Around the capitol of Yangon, almost half of the public school buildings were partially or totally damaged. In the delta region, 43% of schools were affected. Even those children who were able to physically return to school faced concentration difficulties, impeding their ability to learn ("Children and teachers," 2008).

HIV and AIDS are having a devastating impact on education. Children whose parents or other caregivers are sick will often stay home to care for them. They may also quit school in order to work and replace the income no longer generated by the adult. Once death occurs, these responsibilities only increase. Schools may be unable to meet the needs of these pupils. In some communities, school officials lack information not only on how many orphans (single or double) are in the community but also on how many are enrolled in their school (Valerio et al., 2006). In Malawi, children who have lost their mother or both parents are less likely to continue in school (Ueyama, 2007).

Education of Girls

The majority of children who are not enrolled in school are girls. For every 100 boys not in primary school, there are 117 girls who are not enrolled. This gap becomes even wider in secondary school (UNICEF, 2006). Therefore, the majority of illiterate adults in the world are female (United Nations Girls' Education Initiative [UNGEI], 2006). As stated earlier, Goal 3 of the UN Millennium Development Goals is to promote gender equality and empower women, focusing specifically on eliminating gender disparity in all levels of education. Education of girls pays off throughout their lives in ways that benefit the society as a whole (UNFPA, 2005). Research has concluded that the education of women has a greater positive impact on social and economic development of a country than education of men (e.g., Balatchandirane, 2003; UNFPA, 2005). Educated women have increased economic capabilities, are more able to play a role in society, and have a voice in their life. Education of girls has been found to reduce deaths due to childbirth, to lower child mortality and fertility rates, as well as to delay marriage; girls who have received an education are also more likely to send their children to school (Nishimura, Yamano, & Sasaoka, 2008; UNICEF, 1999, 2004; USAID, 2008).

Despite this, girls face numerous barriers to education, including structural barriers. Structural factors such as co-education and low numbers of female teachers have been identified as barriers to higher enrollment of girls in school (Abdelmoneium, 2005; Guimbert et al., 2007). Certain cultures do not believe it is appropriate for male teachers to be teaching female students or for female students to attend classes with male students, especially once puberty is reached (see section entitled "Safety").

Additionally, many schools in rural Africa do not have private toilet facilities. In some schools in Sudan, there is nowhere for girls to relieve themselves, and they will drop out of school rather than embarrass themselves in front of their male classmates by leaving the premises (Abdelmoneium, 2005). This only gets worse after girls experience their first menstrual cycle; there is no private place for them to tend to these needs and again they will drop out of school rather than be shamed (LaFraniere, 2005). In Malawi, there was a substantial rise in the enrollment of girls after a primary school's "sanitation club" together with UNICEF installed a water supply and 10 toilets for boys and girls ("Improved sanitation," 2008).

Cultural Impacts

Certain cultural beliefs may also act to limit girls' education. Some cultures believe it is not useful to educate girls because they will "only" grow up to marry and have children. Other girls may start school, but they may not be able to finish due to early marriage or the need to help with the housework at home. Other barriers include gender roles that assign girls to household chores and caretaking of younger children, concerns about the safety of girls attending school, and the belief that education is wasted on girls because they will not be employed for wages as adults. Familial poverty may also influence school attendance because girls are seen as being valuable at home, where they can assist with household chores; therefore, it can be perceived as more expensive to send a girl to school than a boy in terms of lost labor (United Nations, 2005). In China, due to the governmental limit on the number of children a family may have (as discussed in Chapter Seven), some families choose not to register the birth of a daughter so that they may try again for a son. However, this lack of official status can prevent a girl from being allowed to attend school (Parrot & Cummings, 2006).

In some cases, girls are allowed to go to school, but they must attend school while still remaining responsible for their multiple tasks at home. In Ethiopia, it was found that domestic responsibilities cause girls to have little time at home for studying and completing homework, causing them to be unprepared for class. These chores also often caused girls to arrive late at school. The school gates are closed at the time school starts to discourage tardiness, but they open again after a few periods. Therefore, the girls must wait in the street for admittance to the school grounds, leaving them vulnerable to assault (Save the Children Denmark, Ministry of Education & Ministry of Women's Affairs, 2008). Thus, safety concerns can have an impact on the ability of girls to access education.

Safety

Safety concerns can be a barrier to school attendance, including dangers walking to school and harassment at school. The attacks by the Taliban in Afghanistan have made going to school too dangerous, and many families are keeping girls home to ensure their safety ("Attacks deprive," 2008). In Ethiopia, if a girl is abducted by a man and raped, she will then be married to him because her honor has been ruined. This attack (known as *telefa*) is committed primarily while girls are walking back and forth to school, raising their fears about this journey (Save the Children Denmark et al., 2008).

Teachers sometimes sexually assault girls, promising them good grades in exchange (Save the Children Denmark et al., 2008). In some areas, due to a lack of qualified teachers, young, low-qualified men are hired, which has led to an increase in sexual harassment of female students (Valerio et al., 2006). In Africa, the term for this is "sexually transmitted grades." Data are not widely collected, but research indicates that the problem is widespread in both the number of incidents and where it occurs. For example, in both South Africa and Ecuador, approximately one-third of sexual violence against girls is perpetrated by teachers. In the Netherlands, 27% of students reported being sexually harassed by school staff (Plan International, 2008).

Increasing Girls' Access to Education

In an effort to reduce the disparity in education, the United Nations has started a program specifically focused on increasing the proportion of girls enrolled in school. The UN Girls' Education Initiative [UNGEI] aims to equalize the proportion of girls and boys enrolled in school. Innovative programs have begun to address access to education. In Afghanistan, home-based schools have developed due to the lack of government schools in some regions. The International Rescue Committee (IRC) started these one-room classrooms, which are located in a room in a home, a mosque, or outdoors. Girls are educated with other girls or young boys, while teachers are either female or a local man who is trusted by the community. Many of these teachers are untrained, and the IRC works hard with the Afghan government to provide ongoing training and support. While not ideal, and not intended to be permanent, it helps meet the current need (Kirk & Winthrop, 2006). In some cases, foreign nongovernmental organizations (NGOs) have focused on educational imbalances and have sought to help overcome them. The Cambodian Arts and Scholarship Fund (http://www.cambodianscholarship.org), based in Maine, sends females in Cambodia to high school and university at the minimal cost of U.S.$360 per student each year.

As noted by USAID (2008), when discussing educational parity, the conversation should not focus solely on access but on retention, quality, and results as well. Perceptions of girls as lower quality students pervade many schools, impacting girls' ability to learn and achieve.

The stereotype stems largely from the many responsibilities that girls have at home, impeding them from adequate preparation for school. One project that educated their male classmates about these burdens found the judgments of female students becoming more positive, and boys began helping their female classmates with their homework (USAID, 2008).

Poverty

Poverty is the largest barrier to attending school in the Global South (UNICEF, 2008). Three-quarters of the children not in primary school in the Global South are from the poorest 60% of households (UNICEF, 2006). Poverty inhibits schooling in two fashions. First, children may be needed to stay home and assist the family in earning a living. Second, many countries charge fees for school attendance. As of 2005, 92 countries (out of 192) charged fees for education (United Nations, 2005). In the 1990s the World Bank encouraged fees for textbooks and other school expenses in its debtor nations to reduce the amount of money spent on social and educational services in these countries. However, this substantially reduced the number of children able to attend school and in 2002, the World Bank reversed its policy (Dugger, 2004). In fact, research in sub-Saharan Africa has supported the fact that schooling leads to an increase in national economic growth (Gutema & Bekele, 2004). However many nations continue to charge a tuition fee for school, as well as fees for books, uniforms, and paper. Typically, these countries are unable to bear the costs of education without these fees. In Mozambique, research found that adding these extra costs to the basic tuition fee increased costs almost 500% (Valerio et al., 2006). In Cambodia, children may also be forced to pay "informal fees" to supplement poor salaries and low funding, leading many to drop out ("Children miss out," 2008).

The poverty of a nation inhibits the building of schools, and the lack of a school nearby can discourage enrollment. Guimbert et al. (2007) found that in Afghanistan, proximity of the school was an important determinant of enrollment. The availability of secondary schools had an impact on primary school enrolment as well. In Zimbabwe, the financial instability of the nation, combined with an increased need in South Africa for teachers, caused such a mass exodus of teachers that a number of schools across the nation were forced to close for lack of staff, and students were asked not to report to school ("Schools close," 2007; "Schools turn," 2008). In 2009, 94% of rural schools failed to open ("94 percent," 2009). To try to solve this problem, the government reduced school fees for students and told teachers their children would not need to pay any school fees ("Making schools work," 2009).

Education is seen as vital for escaping poverty, but those who receive a quality education are more likely to be those who are already in the upper income strata. In the United States, students who attend schools where a significant percentage of the students are poor have teachers who have fewer years of experience and lower levels of certification. Additionally, they have classrooms with fewer materials than students in low-poverty schools. Students who are non-White are more likely to attend these high-poverty schools due to the significant correlation between race and poverty in the United States (Fram, Miller-Cribbs, & Van Horn, 2007). In South Africa and the nations of Latin America, those with access to secondary education are the children from wealthier families, and there are movements to make secondary school free for all children ("A call for action," 2008; "Country needs," 2008). Romani children in Slovakia have been found to be segregated into substandard education through special "Roma-only" schools with an inferior education or through disproportionate placement in schools for children with disabilities or other "special needs" (Amnesty International, 2007).

In the Global North, the focus is more on post-secondary education than primary or secondary as the ticket to economic success. Parental post-secondary education in the Global North impacts the learning of the children and their economic mobility. In the United States, students born into the lowest fifth of earners who earn a college degree have a 19% chance of rising to the highest fifth of earners and a 62% chance of joining the middle class. Without a college degree, only 5% will make it. However, in recent years, 11% of children from the poorest families have earned college degrees in contrast to 53% from the top fifth. There are widening gaps in higher education not only between rich and poor but also between Whites and non-Whites. The report's authors conclude that it is more difficult for people who are born into the poorest families to gain the ability to rise out of poverty (Isaacs, Sawhill, & Haskins, 2008).

In Brazil, the number of students attending post-secondary educational facilities more than doubled in the 1990s. However, this did not result in an increase in the percentage of non-White students and was still only reaching less than 10% of the young adult population (Schwartzman, 2004). Problems in Brazil's educational system remain, including quality, equity, and appropriate use of resources (Schwartzman, 2003).

School Leavers/Dropouts

While increasing the number of children entering school has been successful, attention must also be paid to helping students to continue in school and not leave before graduation. This problem occurs around the world. In Australia, it is estimated that one-quarter of students leave school without having earned their senior secondary certificate due primarily to the need to earn an income or a lack of interest in schoolwork (Teese, 2004). Chronic absenteeism (missing more than 20 days of school) has been found to be very high in New York City with 20% of elementary school students, 24% of middle school students, and 40% of high school students being chronically absent, which is typically a precursor to dropping out (Medina, 2008).

While the dropout rate in the United States is estimated by the national Department of Education at only 9% for 2006 (U.S. Department of Education, 2008), a variety of independent researchers have placed it at approximately one-third (Barton, 2005). The Education Trust (2008) stated that the United States is the only country in the Global North where current students are less likely to graduate from high school than their parents. Currently, in a number of states, any improvement in the graduation rate is considered acceptable progress, even if it is 0.01%. At that rate, it would take the African American students in Maryland until the year 3117 to achieve the goal of 90% graduation rate from the current 79%.

There are a number of reasons why children will drop out of school. Poor-quality education, familial need for child labor, teenage pregnancy/marriage, and corporal punishment in schools have all been cited as reasons why children will leave school. Corporal punishment of students is widespread. It is currently allowed by 90 countries and is common even in some countries where it is banned such as China and Cameroon (Plan International, 2008). It is more commonly experienced by boys, while girls are more likely to suffer sexual violence. In Pakistan it has been estimated that 35,000 high school students drop out of school each year due to corporal punishment by their teachers. While regional governments have banned corporal punishment in schools, they are widely ignored. A 2005 UNICEF survey of over 3500 Pakistani children found that 100% stated they had been beaten at school, and 7% of these children suffered severe injuries as a result ("Corporal punishment," 2008). Corporal punishment has also been noted as a factor in school dropout rates in Nepal and Sudan, where teacher frustration from low salaries, poor teaching materials, and high enrollments can contribute to the use of physical violence against students (Abdelmoneium, 2005; "Training the teachers," 2008).

Low-quality education can also result in children leaving school. In fact, it has been argued that teacher quality is by far the most important cause of educational outcomes (Rowe, 2003). Even in countries in Africa that have been implementing free primary education, children still choose not to attend (Avenstrup, 2006). In Bangladesh, the enrollment of children in primary school has been dropping, even in the midst of a campaign to improve education. Children take an average of 6½ years to complete 5 years of primary school, and when they do, they typically have not mastered the basic competencies. Approximately 70% of primary school graduates in Bangladesh cannot read, write, or count properly ("Report blasts," 2009). This raises concern that even those who are attending are not learning basic information. With the drive in the United States for standardized testing in mathematics and reading, focus on other areas has waned. A nationwide survey of American 17 year olds found that fewer than half could identify the correct half-century in which the American Civil War was fought and more than one-quarter thought Christopher Columbus sailed after 1750 (as opposed to 1492). There was a significant difference between the scores of those children who had at least one college-educated parent and those students who had none (Hess, 2008).

It is believed that poor-quality facilities and the lack of qualified teachers contribute heavily to issues of educational quality and school dropouts ("Primary-school dropout," 2007). In Afghanistan, 85% of educators are "nonprofessional" ("Almost half," 2007), and the number of "contract teachers" (as opposed to permanent teachers) was found to have a negative impact on enrollment in school (Guimbert et al., 2008). In Yemen, 40% of teachers had completed secondary school and 60% had only a basic education. Teachers focused on student memorization and copying as learning methods and the material that teachers wrote on the board for students to copy contained numerous errors. Due to the focus on memorization, the teachers themselves had not learned the material well and were thus unable to teach it effectively (Dyer, 2007). In sub-Saharan Africa, an additional 1.6 million teachers are needed to staff anticipated needs at the primary level; 60% of teachers in some African nations have no formal training (Burnett, 2008). The Gambia has been effective at raising enrollment rates, but it lacks qualified teachers and fewer than half of students are passing national exams. Previously, many teachers would pay someone to take the entrance exam for them, resulting in teachers who themselves had difficulty in basic skills. There is now an interview process to eliminate this problem, but The Gambia is finding it difficult to attract qualified candidates due to low pay ("Poor teaching," 2008).

Effective training of teachers is seen as essential to address these issues. There is concern that due to the rapidly growing need for teachers, programs are being shortened to hurry teachers through to the classroom. It is also necessary to change the training of teachers to reflect the Education for All paradigm (see next section)—that it is not only the elite who are in the classroom. There will be children of all social groups, languages, and abilities who will be in the classroom. Classes are larger than previously and there may be adult learners as well. Additionally, teachers themselves should reflect the growing diversity of learners, including those with physical disabilities, females, and people from linguistic or ethnic minorities (Mpokosa & Ndaruhutse, 2008). However, this can be difficult to achieve.

To try to help address these issues in Nepal, a train-the-trainer model was used to help educate teachers about effective classroom management. Teachers faced special difficulties there due to the long-running civil conflict. Local social workers were trained, and they in turn trained the teachers. Teachers learned how to listen to children, analyze the problems the children were having, including their reasons for dropping out, and work to help them return to school. Teachers were also educated about creating a positive classroom climate that did not use physical discipline or belittling of students. As a result, retention rates have improved ("Training the teachers," 2008).

There is also concern about the policies of the International Monetary Fund (IMF) that require borrowing nations to reduce their social service spending, including on education, in order to control inflation. Many nations have had to freeze recruitment of teachers and pay low wages to those already working, impacting the ability to offer students a quality education. While the IMF has allowed individual nations to be flexible in their education spending, problems continue ("IMF policies," 2007).

Education for All

In 2000, 164 countries at the World Education Forum agreed to the "Education for All" movement in an effort to rapidly increase access to, and improve the quality of, education by 2015. The goals developed were as follows:

1. Expanding and improving comprehensive early childhood care and education, especially for the most vulnerable and disadvantaged children
2. Ensuring that by 2015 all children, particularly girls, children in difficult circumstances, and those belonging to ethnic minorities, have access to and complete, free, and compulsory primary education of good quality
3. Ensuring that the learning needs of all young people and adults are met through equitable access to appropriate learning and life-skills programs
4. Achieving a 50% improvement in levels of adult literacy by 2015, especially for women, and equitable access to basic and continuing education for all adults
5. Eliminating gender disparities in primary and secondary education by 2005, and achieving gender equality in education by 2015, with a focus on ensuring girls' full and equal access to and achievement in basic education of good quality
6. Improving all aspects of the quality of education and ensuring excellence of all so that recognized and measurable learning outcomes are achieved by all, especially in literacy, numeracy, and essential life skills (UNESCO, 2000)

UNESCO produced a midterm report in 2007 that assessed progress to date. They found that enrollment had increased, especially in sub-Saharan Africa and South and West Asia. They found that the combination of political support within a country and international donor support can lead to rapid improvements and cited such countries as

India and Yemen as examples. However, they also found that there was much more progress that needed to be made. At the current rate, 25 of the nations will not achieve any of the goals by 2015. The cost of schooling remained a huge barrier to education and gender parity had only been reached in both primary and secondary schooling by an additional three nations since 1999. Poor-quality education continued to be widespread, as was illiteracy. International aid increased sharply between 2000 and 2004, but then dropped significantly in 2005.

The report stated that a number of donor countries give a relatively low percentage of aid to education—Japan, Germany, and the United States being primary among them. Other nations give a relatively low percentage of their education aid to basic education, as opposed to post-secondary, with France, Germany, and Japan all allocating less than one-third to basic education (18%, 19%, and 27%, respectively). In contrast, the United States and United Kingdom allocate approximately 85% to basic education (UNESCO, 2007). The fund received a large boost in September 2008 when a coalition of donors from business, sports organizations, nonprofit organizations, faith groups, and governments gathered at the United Nations to pledge U.S.$4.5 billion between 2008 and 2011 to help achieve the Education for All goals (Karwal, 2008).

Additionally, progress has been uneven on the goals. While much progress has been made on UPE and gender parity at the primary school level, attention to early childhood education (Goal 1) and adult education (Goal 4) has been comparatively rare (Burnett, 2008).

Universal Primary Education

Countries realized that the goal of UPE could only be reached by making primary education free. Costs to families could include not only tuition, but uniforms, textbooks, examination fees, and more (Avenstrup, 2006). A number of countries, such as Kenya, Malawi, Uganda, and Ghana, have now eliminated primary school fees in an effort to move toward UPE (UNICEF, n.d.c). Kenya's previous "cost-sharing" program under the World Bank structural adjustment plan, where families were expected to "share" the costs of education, resulted in higher rates of dropouts and students repeating a grade, while simultaneously lowering graduation rates (Nafula, 2001). In contrast, there was rapid enrollment growth under UPE.

In Uganda, enrollment rose 240% over 6 years (Avenstrup, 2006). Not only have enrollments increased greatly, but delayed enrollments have decreased and more children are completing grades. Girls in poor households in particular have experienced these positive benefits. Only about 10% of children not in primary school state that the cost is the main barrier to attendance (even though tuition is no longer charged, there are still costs for supplies and uniforms). However, this rises sharply for secondary school, which is not free. In addition, more girls drop out during secondary school due to marriage or pregnancy (Nishimura et al., 2008).

The risk associated with eliminating fees is that the rapid increase in students can overwhelm the system. The rapidly rising enrollments associated with UPE led to overcrowded classrooms; running classes in shifts; acute shortages of teachers, textbooks, and other materials; as well as the problem of over-age students in the classrooms (Avenstrup, 2006). In 2008, the government of Togo announced that primary education would become free to all. However, school administrators were caught by surprise by the announcement and were uncertain how they would pay bills without these funds ("School year," 2008).

In Lesotho, Malawi, and Uganda, the enrollments were much greater than anticipated, while in Kenya they were just under the anticipated number. However, even in Kenya, the schools were inundated with students upon the introduction of UPE. Over 1 million students sought enrollment at school, in some cases almost literally beating down the door to get in. Kenya had to make an international appeal for aid because their class sizes soared to 90 students and supplies such as texts and chalk were limited (Chinyama, n.d.). These problems only worsened after the election violence in 2008 as students fled their rural districts to the comparatively safe urban areas. Students in some schools were sitting five to a desk, while their home schools were empty. This increased burden resulted in inadequate sanitation, food, and materials in the schools educating these internally displaced children ("Classroom crush," 2008). Unfortunately, the previously mentioned drought in Kenya has decreased these high enrollment numbers.

Nigeria has been having difficulties as a result of the resounding success of its UPE program. The number of primary school graduates has more than doubled, causing a large increase in the number of students wishing to attend secondary school. However, there is room to educate only 60% of those who wish to attend. Therefore, some students must wait a year to be admitted, while those who are admitted face hugely overcrowded classrooms ("Classrooms shortages," 2008). In Burkina Faso, this pressure continues at the university level, leading to a lack of teachers, classrooms, and research space ("Progress on MDG," 2009). In India, the perceived weakness of the public government schools has created huge competition for the slots in private schools. One principal received over 2000 applications for approximately 100 kindergarten slots. Attending a choice school is seen as imperative for upward economic mobility, and which school children attend at this age is seen as critical to their lifelong educational fate (Sengupta, 2008).

Enrollment is also not the same as attendance. Barriers previously discussed such as gender roles, household chores, and the need for income may limit actual attendance at school despite enrollment. Also, enrolling in primary school is no guarantee that the child will complete it (Burnett, 2008; Shepherd, 2009).

Thus, moving toward UPE is not an easy task. Consideration of the role of outside funders, language of instruction, and the impact of UPE on quality of instruction and secondary education must all be carefully considered. A study of the process in Uganda named four factors as critical in its implementation (Penny, Ward, Read, & Bines, 2008, p. 269):

- Political commitment to reform, especially to UPE and decentralization
- Facilitative/coordinated institutional and financial frameworks
- A comprehensive approach to UPE (access, quality, and financing)
- Early engagement with the reform of post-primary education and training

UNICEF (2007) notes that increased enrollments without concurrent increases in budget can result in a lower quality of education through higher student-to-teacher ratios, lack of materials, and lack of adequate school buildings. Governments may be tempted to lower costs through fewer village schools and clumping children by primary language. While these measures may seem cost efficient on the surface, they typically result in reduced access to education. Children, especially girls, may not be able to travel long distances to a centralized school. Segregation of students by language typically results in unequal access of quality education (UNICEF, 2007).

Money is still a barrier to education for some students. Children may not attend school because they need to work to raise money for the family's survival. Other barriers can include additional "fees" that are mandatory for schooling. In Thailand, there were complaints that free education was not really free due to additional fees for computer usage, the library, and even the restrooms. Some students were even charged for the school landscaping. As a result, the fees could be more than twice the tuition fee that was waived ("Free school," 2006). The impact of HIV/AIDS must also be negotiated because it creates a loss of teachers (either from illness or death—their own or their family members). There will be financial costs from pensions and sick leave. Also, there is a growing number of orphans, who are at higher risk for not receiving an education (Avenstrup, 2006).

To help alleviate some of these problems, the nonprofit organization Innovation for Poverty Action gave 5000 Kenyan sixth-grade girls a free uniform (which would have cost U.S.$6) if they would stay in school; if they stayed in school for the next 18 months, they received another free uniform. Over the next 3 years, they saw the dropout rate and the pregnancy rate both reduce by a third. The same organization has also given scholarships to 682 secondary school children in Ghana, half of them girls, and is tracking their progress (Duflo, 2009).

The Brazilian *Bolsa Familia* program, mentioned in Chapter Two, is perceived as another effective intervention to help impoverished children attend school. Their families receive a stipend of R$70.00 (about U.S.$35) if the children attend school and receive regular health checkups. This money helps offset the money lost to the family by the child not working. This program is seen as widely effective because it targets aid to those most in need, especially those who have not benefited from other social programs (World Bank, 2007). As of 2007, it covered 46 million people. Preliminary data support that it is assisting children in poor families to remain in school (Viana, Carepa, & Camilo, 2009). Mexico's *Progresa-Oportunidades* and Colombia's *Familias en Acción* operate in a similar fashion (UNESCO, 2007).

Balancing the Right to Education with the Right to Play

While it is important that every child receive a quality education, care must be taken not to go too far and have attention solely focused on children's academics to the exclusion of their rights to play and leisure. In the United States and the United Kingdom, schools have been shortening the time allotted for recess and free play. This has been found to have negative effects on both children's academic achievement as well as their social skills. After breaks in academics, children have been found to return to lessons with heightened attention and ability to concentrate. Additionally, free play with peers allows children to develop social competencies (Pellegrini & Bohn, 2005). This is supported by additional research that found a positive correlation between scores on standardized academic tests and fitness tests (Chomitz et al., 2009).

Educational pressure is considered to be very high in certain Asian countries such as Japan and the Republic of Korea. In Korea, parents focused on the child's academic achievement as a means to achieve future success and wealth. Typically, this achievement came at the expense of the child's right to leisure, play, and rest (Yang & Shin, 2008). Similar academic pressure was found in Japan, where education at a good school is considered vital to career success and the preparation to be able to attend such schools starts early. Supplemental schools known as "Juku" are common, with 71.8% of junior high school students and 36.9% of primary school students attending. There are even Juku for children as young as 2 and 3 years old (Tett, 2004). The Confucian value of diligence is also very important and a student who does not perform well academically may be stigmatized (Tett, 2004). The pressure has even resulted in some students committing suicide. Therefore, the government of Japan has introduced some reforms, including educating teachers to assist students in distress (Bossy, 2000). The country also transitioned from a 6-day school week to a 5-day school week in 2002 (Web Japan, n.d.).

Conclusion

Much more needs to be done to secure children's right to an education. While a growing number of countries are moving towards UPE, it can overwhelm their fragile systems and lower the quality of education for everyone. In addition, increasing the number of children who graduate from primary school increases the desire for secondary school, to which countries must adapt. Thus, every country around the world has work to ensure that children have access to quality education in an environment where they are treated with respect.

8

Issues Particularly Affecting the Female Child

The previous chapters in this book have discussed many threats to children's well-being all over the world. However, girls face additional threats because of the subordinate status of females in most world societies. The United Nations has noted some of these threats to include early marriage (and its attendant risk of obstetric fistula), female genital cutting, trafficking, and violence against girls (United Nations, 2007).

The prejudice against females runs so deeply in some cultures that it is estimated that there are 60 million "missing" females—girls who were aborted prior to birth due to their sex or killed at birth. This life-affecting unequal treatment for girls continues into early childhood. Male children in the family are often shown preferential treatment: they are given more and better food and are more likely to receive medical care than female children. As a result, these male children are more likely to live to their fifth birthday than female children (Amnesty International, 2004). Even for those girls who do live, they are less likely to receive an education, learn to read, or have access to the same economic opportunities as their male counterparts.

Due to these unique burdens borne by females and their vulnerable position in many societies, a human rights document focusing specifically on the rights of women was adopted by the United Nations in 1979—the Convention on the Elimination of All Forms of Discrimination against Women (CEDAW). The document defines what constitutes discrimination against women and what nations must do in order to eliminate it. Discrimination includes both intentional discrimination as well as acts that have a discriminatory effect (Association of Women's Rights in Development, 2002). Countries are also required to work to eradicate harmful practices based on discriminatory attitudes toward women, such as female genital cutting and lack of access to education (Dauer, 2001). As of 2009, CEDAW had been ratified by 185 countries, over 90% of the membership of the United Nations (United Nations, 2009). Only eight member nations have not ratified it, and only one in the Global North: the United States. The United States signed CEDAW in 1980 but has not ratified it; it is the only country in this situation (United Nations, 2009).

Despite ratification, a country is allowed to post reservations to certain parts of the document. CEDAW has more substantive reservations posted than any other international treaty, with countries claiming that pieces of it violate their cultural norms (Merry, 2001). The United Nations has expressed concern that a number of countries were expressing reservations to Articles 2 and 16 concerning the equality of men and women under the law and in marriage. As these are considered to be core principles of CEDAW, they are regarded as "impermissible reservations" (United Nations, 2006).

Sex-Selective Abortion and Infanticide

Preference for males over females begins even before birth. Male children are preferred over female children in some countries to the extent that if the parents are able to afford an ultrasound, they may choose to abort the fetus if it shows the fetus is female. Sex-selective abortion is less likely to result in criminal prosecution of the parents and may be less traumatizing than infanticide (Parrot & Cummings, 2006). Two countries where this occurs are China and India. A recent study in India concluded that 10 million girls were "missing" over the last 20 years due to sex-selective abortion (Jha et al., 2006), although this procedure has been illegal since 1994 (Sheth, 2006). Wealthy couples in India will even fly to the United States, one of the few countries where it is legal to test for the sex of embryos prior to implantation, in order to be sure to have a son (Kaur, 2006). Male preference is more common in the rural areas of India and China due to a greater need for physical labor and stronger belief in traditional gender roles (Parrot & Cummings, 2006).

In China, access to ultrasound and other technologies has increased the number of female fetuses that are aborted, although sex-selective abortion is also illegal in that nation. Infanticide is now quite rare, but there continue to be excess boys to girls, which appears to be due to sex-selective abortions (Zhu, Lu, & Hesketh, 2009). Research has found that across all child age groups and locations (urban/rural), there are high rates of boys to girls, primarily due to a widely distorted ratio for second births, especially in areas where families are allowed a second child if the first one is a girl. Boys are seen as needed to care for parents in their old age and if the family already has a girl, they feel an increased need for a boy (Zhu et al., 2009). This discrepancy among latter-born children has also been found in the United States among families originating from India, China, and Korea. The gender ratio for first children is equal, but if there is no son in the family, the ratio for second children increases to 1.17 and to 1.5 for the third child. The authors believe this is due to prenatal sex selection and note this continues despite the lack of in-country cultural factors noted earlier demonstrating the power of these cultural beliefs (Almond & Edlund, 2008).

Once the child is born, some poorer families in India may still resort to infanticide rather than bear the expense of raising a female child. The tradition of paying a dowry upon the marriage of a female child in India has grown to the extent that simply paying the expected dowry can impoverish a family. If a family already has several daughters, the anticipated expense of raising another girl and then paying for her wedding and dowry can lead parents to the hard decision that they are not able to afford to raise her. Girls are also seen as a burden to the family because they are perceived as needing constant protection. A son is needed in a family because only a male successor can light the funeral pyre of his father—an important cultural tradition (Devraj, 2003).

Sex-selective abortion and female infanticide are primarily seen among families living in deep poverty who cannot afford the expense of another child. In a number of cultures, the female moves to her husband's family upon marriage. Thus, she does not contribute any money to her parents' household, but only costs money. Impoverished families cannot bear the expense to raise her, particularly if they already have a daughter. In China, the number of children born to most families is limited. While wealthy families are able to pay the fine for having "excess" children, this is not true for poorer families.

In order to try to help alleviate these practices, governments in both India and Pakistan have been placing cradles outside of police stations, hospitals, and charity organizations. Trying to increase the number of women who give birth in hospitals is also seen as an effective method to identify babies at risk and rescue them. Committees have also been formed in local villages for this same purpose. Relating to the lower educational level of women, efforts are being made to increase the female literacy rate in order to increase the value of females in society. This can also empower mothers to be able to protect their daughters because they will be more self-sufficient and have increased economic options on their own (Parrot & Cummings, 2006). China has changed laws regarding inheritance by females and is conducting a social marketing campaign for gender equality (Zhu et al., 2009). In South Korea, the birth ratio has been approaching equity with growing economic development and changing gender roles (Chun & Gupta, 2009).

Female Genital Cutting

Another type of violence that girls may experience is Female Genital Cutting. This procedure involves partial or total removal of a female's external genitalia for cultural or nonmedical reasons (UNICEF, n.d.). While this has been known as female circumcision in the past, that term draws a parallel with male circumcision. However, as will be described, the practice is not equivalent at all. Thus, currently it is more commonly referred to as Female Genital Cutting (FGC) or Female Genital Mutilation.

Approximately 70 million women living today have undergone the procedure (UNICEF, 2009). The majority of girls undergo FGC between 4 and 14 years of age, but it is sometimes performed on infants as well (UNICEF, n.d.). In Yemen, it is typically conducted 7 to 10 days after birth ("Government body," 2008). It is practiced in about two dozen countries in Africa, as well as countries with immigrants from those countries (Bruni, 2004). Female genital cutting is most common in northeast Africa, where prevalence rates range from 80% to 97% in countries such as Egypt and Eritrea (UNICEF, 2005). However, it also spreads into southwest Asian countries such as Yemen and Iraq (Kurdistan areas) (von der Osten-Sacken & Uwer, 2007).

While many of those in the Global North are horrified by the procedure, it is important to note the historic use of it in those countries as well. Clitoridectomy was used in countries of the Global North as a cure for epilepsy, kleptomania, and depression during the nineteenth century and into the twentieth century. Currently, some Western women undergo plastic surgery to make their genitalia more aesthetically pleasing or to restore their hymen (Parrot & Cummings, 2006).

There are three basic types of FGC, differentiated by the extent of the cutting: clitoridectomy (Type I), excision (Type II), and infibulation (Type III). Type I involves the removal of the clitoral hood and may include the removal of part or all of the clitoris. Type II is the removal of the clitoral hood, the clitoris, and part or all of the labia minora. The most severe form, Type III, is the removal of part or all of the external genitalia (clitoris, labia minora, and labia majora) with a stitching or narrowing of the vaginal opening. Only a very narrow opening is left (about the diameter of a matchstick) for the passage of urine and menstrual blood (American Academy of Pediatrics, 1998).

The reason that FGC is not equivalent to male circumcision, nor considered a cultural tradition that should be protected as such, is the extensive damage that can result from the procedure. The procedure is traditionally performed not in a medical facility by medical personnel, but by traditional practitioners with nonsterile instruments, although it is becoming more medicalized in recent years (UNICEF, 2005). Outcomes can include painful sexual intercourse and menstruation, increased susceptibility to HIV and other sexually transmitted diseases, infertility, increased risk during childbirth, hemorrhaging, and death (UNICEF, n.d.). One study found that women who have experienced FGC are more than 50% more likely to die, or have their infants die, during childbirth than women who have not experienced the procedure. Women who had undergone more severe forms of FGC were more at risk than women who had experienced less severe types. The authors of the study believe that the results actually underestimate the risk to women because only births in hospitals were included in their study; women giving birth at home are more at risk than women giving birth in the hospital due to lower levels of medical care and higher levels of poverty (World Health Organization, 2006).

Female genital cutting may be conducted for several reasons. A primary one is to increase chastity among women and to reduce sexual pleasure for them. It is believed this will help curb promiscuity, as well as protect against sexual assault. Additionally, the procedure is often seen as an important rite of passage in some cultures. The external female genitalia are seen as unhygienic and unsightly in certain societies and thus their removal is seen as beautifying and hygienic (Parrot & Cummings, 2006; UNICEF, n.d.). Although often seen in Muslim countries, FGC is not based in that religion, and in fact predates it. However, some community leaders will state that it is based in the Koran.

Due to the widespread practice and acceptance of FGC in some cultures, it can be very difficult for a girl to be married if she has not undergone the procedure. For this reason, females, including the girl herself and her mother, can be some of the stronger supporters of the procedure. In certain places, a woman who is unmarried is shunned and is barred from employment, thus making survival near impossible (Parrot & Cummings, 2006). Thus, a girl may have the procedure even if she and her mother are against the idea because if she does not, it could be social suicide or a literal death. Therefore, some have chosen to flee their country and seek asylum elsewhere to avoid these consequences, as the following example illustrates:

> *Fauziya Kassindja was a 16-year-old girl in Togo when her father died. A progressive man, he had not forced her to be circumcised. He sent all his daughters to school and allowed them to marry the man of their choice. However, after his death, her aunt took over the family; according to custom, a man's property reverts to his birth family upon his death. Her aunt tried to force her to marry an older man who already had three wives and to undergo FGC. Fauziya fled the country rather than submit, eventually seeking asylum in the United States. No one had ever been granted refuge on this basis before. Asylum laws were established originally to protect political and civil rights and were based on a male model of dissent. She was placed in prison during the evaluation of her appeal. After spending 16 months in prison, she was eventually granted asylum with the help of an American law student and a women's advocacy group. It was determined that having one's clitoris cut off against her will is an act of persecution. She tells her story in the book* Do They Hear You When You Cry?
>
> *(Kassindja & Bashir, 1998)*

While in some places, efforts have been made to reduce these potential negative outcomes by performing the procedure in a medical facility, many of the risks remain. Thus, most countries are looking to eradicate the procedure. However, this must be done in a culturally sensitive fashion. One attempt in Uganda showed an ethnic group a graphic video of a mass cutting ceremony. The people were angered to learn that their culture was considered barbaric and 2 years later, twice as many girls chose to undergo the procedure in order to demonstrate their ethnic pride (Parrot & Cummings, 2006). Ford (2005) also notes that a community-wide approach must be taken because individuals will face stigma if they alone choose to abandon the practice. Additionally, as noted earlier, many mothers will choose to continue the practice, even against their own wishes, if they believe they will not be able to find a husband for their daughters if FGC is not performed. Thus, all the families within the communities where intermarriages occur must abandon the practice together.

In Senegal, a grassroots movement developed in the native language of the Senegalese (as opposed to English or French) has been successful in lowering the rate of FGC. The campaign was developed at the wishes of the local women and in conjunction with local religious leaders. Culturally sensitive terms were used for FGC and through relationships with other villages in the intermarrying community, all agreed to abandon the practice (Easton, Monkman, & Miles, 2003).

In Kenya, an alternative initiation rite was developed that replaced the cutting with information about reproduction. In Ethiopia, national prevalence has dropped markedly, from 61% in 1997 to 46% in 2008, following a national campaign ("More parents," 2008). Burkina Faso has instituted laws that fine and/or imprison practitioners as well as family members who request the procedure ("Dial SOS," 2005). Burkina Faso has also trained religious and community leaders, as well as police and the media, about the dangers associated with FGC and established a national hotline where anyone can report if they suspect it is going to occur ("Girl's death," 2007).

One of the major targets for revising public opinions has been men. Men must be willing to marry a woman who has not undergone the procedure, and fathers must believe it is not necessary in order to maintain family honor (Slackman, 2007). Involving religious leaders to counter the belief that it is necessary for religious purposes is also important. In 2007, Egypt started a nationwide campaign against the practice after tacitly allowing it despite a 1996 law. Top religious leaders have declared it *haram,* or prohibited by Islam, and a national television campaign has been conducted to attempt to lower its occurrence (Slackman, 2007).

It has been found that women with higher levels of education are less likely to have the procedure performed on their daughters, again demonstrating the power of education for women (Hayford, 2005). It is important that educational campaigns be conducted effectively in order to inform people as to why FGC is so dangerous; otherwise the procedure may simply be driven underground. In Burkina Faso, the age at which girls undergo FGC has lowered to infancy in order to hide it, which increases the danger to the girl ("Cutters turn," 2009). Regional strategies are developed because otherwise people will cross borders into a country with less strict laws to have the procedure performed ("Cross-border," 2008). Interventions must also help design alternative methods of income for the women who perform the procedure to encourage them to abandon the practice ("Two thousand," 2007).

Clitoral reconstructive surgery is becoming a possibility for females in West Africa. In 2009, construction began on a hospital in Bobo-Dioulasso, in Burkina Faso, funded by Clitoraid, a U.S. nongovernmental organization (NGO). Money was raised through their campaign called "Adopt a clitoris." Upon completion it will offer free reconstructive surgery to women across West Africa who wish to have it. Prior to this, there were very few surgeons who offered this option, and prices were prohibitive. Five months from expected completion of the facility, there was already a waiting list of 100 women for the procedure ("Pleasure hospital," 2009).

Education

As noted in Chapter Eight, girls face more numerous barriers to achieving an education than boys. For every 100 boys not in primary school, there are 117 girls who are not enrolled. This gap becomes even wider in secondary school (UNICEF, 2006). As stated in Chapter Eight, educated women have increased economic capabilities, and they are more able to play a role in society and to have a voice in their life. Education of girls has been found to reduce deaths due to childbirth, to lower child mortality and fertility rates, as well as to delay marriage; educated women are also more likely to send their children to school (Nishimura, Yamano, & Sasaoka, 2008; UNICEF, 1999, 2004; USAID, 2008).

The barriers to girls' education discussed in Chapter Eight are briefly summarized here. In addition to barriers of poverty and conflict that boys face, girls also face barriers related specifically to their gender and its assigned gender role. Structural barriers can include a lack of female teachers, schools for girls, as well as adequate sanitation facilities (Abdelmoneium, 2005; Guimbert, Miwa, & Nguyen, 2007). Girls are expected to complete household chores that can inhibit their ability to attend school, as well as limit their time to study and do homework. They also face threats to their safety due to attending school. In some nations, they are at risk for kidnapping and/or assault as they walk to school. They are also at risk for assault by their teachers or peers once they reach school (Save the Children Denmark, Ministry of Education & Ministry of Women's Affairs, 2008).

The Taliban, a radically conservative Islamic group, believe that education of females is prohibited by Islam; they target schools for girls and the schoolgirls themselves. In one province in Afghanistan, there were 224 schools in 2003, but in 2008 only 54 were functioning ("Attacks deprive," 2008). Schools for girls are especially at risk for being targets (United Nations Security Council, 2007). In Kandahar, Afghanistan, 15 female students and teachers were the victims of an acid attack in November 2008 ("Acid attack," 2008). In the Swat Valley of Pakistan, the Taliban caused an uprising during the winter of 2008–2009 and approximately 200 schools for girls were torched or bombed. Education of girls was prohibited. In February, the militants stated education for girls up to grade 5 would be allowed and the government promised all schools would reopen ("Origins," 2009). However, the fighting increased, causing schools to close and people to flee. As a result, schools did not reopen until August 2009.

Early Marriage

Girls in Global South countries are susceptible to being married off at very early ages. More than 60 million women aged 20–24 years worldwide were married before the age of 18 years. Rates vary between counties, but South Asia accounts for about half of these girls, with 45% of females married before they reach 18 years of age (UNICEF, 2007).

Sixty-five percent of girls in India are married before they are 18 years old (UNICEF, 2008). Sub-Saharan Africa follows as the region with the next highest rate: 40% (UNICEF, 2007).

While many countries have laws against child marriage, they are often weak or ineffectively enforced. In Nepal, there is confusion in the law regarding the age of a "child." One section states 14 years, another states 16 years, while the Convention on the Rights of the Child (CRC), which has been ratified by Nepal, establishes 18 years as the age of adulthood. Additionally, the case must be filed within 3 months of the marriage and if the perpetrators were unaware of the age of the child at the time of the marriage, they are not guilty. Even if they are found guilty, the punishment is minimal. In the United States, some states allow marriage with girls as young as 14 years old with parental permission (UNICEF, 2008). Guatemala's standard age for marriage is 18 years, but it is allowed at 16 years for boys and 14 years for girls if there is a pregnancy or if parental consent is given (World Vision, 2008).

Yemen has a very high number of child brides, due in part to its lack of a minimum age for marriage. Currently girls' average age at marriage is 12 to 13 years (Worth, 2008). Legislators have been working to establish age 17 years as the minimum; however, some legislators claim that the establishment of a minimum age violates Sharia (Islamic law) because there is no minimum age established in the Koran. Yemen and Saudi Arabia are the only Arab countries without a legal minimum age. There are also fears that rural residents will be able to circumvent the law due to lack of birth registration ("Threat to legislation," 2009).

In some countries, there also exist mechanisms for "temporary marriages," some of which may last only a few hours and are used as a method to legalize intercourse with a child (Mikhail, 2002). Young women also face abduction by militias, where they are forced into what the gangs also calls "temporary marriages." However, these abductions lack even the paperwork associated with "temporary marriages", and are nothing more than sexual violence (Mikhail, 2002).

Overall, the lower status of females leads to early marriage. Education is typically not considered as important for girls, and they are valued for their ability to bear and raise children as well as perform housework. The work of females and their role in society are denigrated, which lowers self-confidence among women and girls. Females typically have few options outside of marriage and thus are forced to accept early marriage, forced intercourse in the marriage, as well as domestic violence (World Vision, 2008).

There are a number of factors that increase the likelihood of child marriage, but poverty is a primary one. For women in the lowest quintile of income worldwide, 56% of them were married as children as compared to 16% in the highest quintile (UNICEF, 2007). If the girl can be married at an early age, her parents no longer have to bear the expense of raising her. In addition, if a bride price is offered, she can be the source of income for the family. In fact, one author has compared child marriage to child prostitution due to this economic transaction (Mikhail, 2002). In Zimbabwe, with its runaway inflation, parents were increasing the normal bride price by huge amounts in order to try to generate income ("Daughters fetch," 2007). Orphanhood is also a reason why girls may marry early. If there is no one to provide for them, and they have no mechanism to provide for themselves, they will seek a marriage for survival (World Vision, 2008).

In Central America, the primacy of family influences early childbearing. If a girl starts her childbearing early, she is more likely to experience more generations of her family (World Vision, 2008). Additionally, if a girl is married early, this reduces the likelihood of her having sex outside of marriage (UNICEF, 2008). Becoming pregnant outside of wedlock is the worst shame a girl can bring to her family, and early marriage is used to prevent this from occurring ("Early marriage," 2008). Additionally, as the mechanisms of HIV infection become more widely known, younger girls are sought because it is believed they are less likely to be infected.

If girls are married early, they face a host of potential negative outcomes. They face a higher risk of domestic violence than those who marry at later ages (UNICEF, 2008). In Afghanistan, a local NGO estimated that up to 70% of known cases of domestic violence had early marriage as one of their root causes ("Widespread child marriage," 2007). In Nigeria, some girls have fled their abusive husbands and wound up working in the sex trade because that was their only option for survival ("Early marriage," 2008).

Girls typically have to leave school once they are married. In Northern Nigeria, local NGOs note that 75% of girls do not have any education past primary school and that many girls drop out due to marriage. There is a law that prohibits child marriages, but enforcement is lacking ("Early marriage," 2008). If they do not drop out upon marriage, they will usually do so when they become pregnant, which typically soon follows. These early pregnancies cause other serious problems as well.

An early pregnancy has a higher risk of maternal death or injury during childbirth. Girls aged 10–14 years are five times more likely to die as a result of childbirth or pregnancy than those aged 20–24 years, and girls aged 15–19 years are more than twice as likely to die (UNFPA, n.d.a). One of the primary risks is the development of an obstetric fistula. Typically experienced by young mothers, especially those who are small (as is typically seen by females who are poor and undernourished throughout their lives), it occurs during extended labor. During contractions, the tissue between the uterus and the bowel, as well as between the uterus and bladder, rub against each other. When labor is protracted, this friction can result in tissue tearing, creating an opening between the two organs. It is more common in smaller women because the baby will be too large comparatively for the birth to proceed easily. Due to the lack of access to medical facilities, the tear is not repaired, resulting in the woman becoming incontinent. The leakage of urine and/or excrement causes a severe rash on the woman as well as a foul odor. As a result, she is typically cast off from her husband and her village. If she does not receive surgery to repair the tear, she will often live a shortened life as a result of this societal neglect.

It is estimated that approximately 2 million women are currently living with a fistula, and 50,000 to 100,000 new cases occur every year. These numbers are based on women seeking treatment, and thus the actual numbers are likely much higher (UNFPA, 2006). The problem is concentrated in sub-Saharan Africa due to a combination of reasons—poverty, lack of access to modern health care, the tradition of home birth, and early pregnancy—but also occurs in other nations where these factors cluster, such as Bangladesh and Afghanistan (LaFraniere, 2005; Leidl, 2006; Ryan, 2006).

The surgery to repair the fistula is relatively easy. It has about a 90% success rate and costs U.S.$300 for the surgery and postoperative care (UNFPA, n.d.b). However, it is typically difficult to obtain because few doctors perform it. To this end, UNFPA has launched the Global Campaign to End Fistula and has been working in a number of countries around the world to work on both prevention and treatment of fistulas (UNFPA, n.d.c).

Because child marriage has a host of negative outcomes, UNICEF (2008) has developed the following suggestions for its elimination: make child marriage illegal and render prior marriages void; establish penalties; make both marriage registration and birth registration compulsory; and increase educational opportunities for girls. Thus, it must be illegal, there must be clear consequences for violating the law, and methods that allow the law to be circumvented must be eliminated. As one example of this, India passed a law in 2006 that outlawed child marriage and voided those that had already occurred. Child marriage protection officers will be hired and the state will help support these former child brides until their remarriage (UNICEF, 2008).

In addition to increasing educational opportunities, economic opportunities for young women must also increase (International Center for Research on Women [ICRW], 2007). Increasing economic opportunities would help them to earn money for their families, lowering the need for the bride price as well as increasing options for her to be able to support herself. It would also increase her self-confidence, which can help lower the incidence of domestic violence.

In order for these efforts to be successful, it is necessary to work on changing the cultural norms that have supported early marriage, much as norms around FGC have been changing. In most countries, there is a "tipping point" at which most marriages occur. In most countries, this is about age 13 or 14 years. Therefore, the families and communities of girls who are younger than this age should be targeted for education about the dangers of early marriage (ICRW, 2007). This will also benefit the country as a whole because girls who marry early have higher fertility rates, which increases population pressures in impoverished countries ("Child marriage," 2009).

Conclusion

At the Fourth World Conference on Women in Beijing in 1995, the plight of the girl child was a special focus. The following strategic objectives were established (United Nations, 1995):

- Eliminate all forms of discrimination against the girl child.
- Eliminate negative cultural attitudes and practices against girls.
- Promote and protect the rights of the girl child and increase awareness of her needs and potential.
- Eliminate discrimination against girls in education, skills development, and training.

- Eliminate discrimination against girls in health and nutrition.
- Eliminate the economic exploitation of child labor and protect young girls at work.
- Eradicate violence against the girl child.
- Promote the girl child's awareness of and participation in social, economic, and political life.
- Strengthen the role of the family in improving the status of the girl child.

Girls must be a focus of any social development approach because progress is impossible if half of the population is excluded. This is especially true when it is the half whose gender role charges it with raising and socializing the next generation. Currently, one in every eight people in the world is a female aged 10–24 years (Levine et al., 2008). Therefore, the World Bank has developed The Adolescent Girls Initiative. Stating that closing the gender gap in education could increase per capita income up to 3% and future income can increase 10%–20% for each additional year of secondary school, they are attempting to increase the quality and quantity of employment for young women (World Bank, n.d.). It is hoped that through this initiative, among others, the status and opportunities for girls will improve, thus improving society as a whole.

Conclusion

A World Fit for Children

This book has examined threats to child welfare and well-being all around the world. Although the situations in all nations were not included, the goal was to include a broad variety of nations. While the plight of children in the Global South is worse for many issues than in the Global North, citizens of the Global North should not use this as an excuse to engage in cultural superiority. Violations of children's rights occur in all nations, and therefore all countries still have work to do to make "a world fit for children," to use UNICEF's term.

The rights guaranteed to children in the Convention on the Rights of the Child are the *minimum* necessary in order for children to achieve their full adult potential. Therefore, we all have a stake in these outcomes. If the world is to continue to improve its developmental conditions, the well-being of children is essential. Intervention with children (or that increase the well-being of children) can have some of the largest impacts of all social development interventions because the impacts continue throughout the child's life.

As stated in Mapp (2008), certain groups are at higher risk for being denied their rights. Those who are impoverished, experience discrimination, and lack education are more likely to experience the conditions described in this book and many others. The three risk factors are intertwined; those who experience one are also likely to experience the other two. Thus, striking at the heart of these issues, using the Millennium Development Goals (MDGs) as a guide, can reap benefits for citizens of all nations.

The MDGs were designed to address the root causes of many human rights violations. They were developed in 2000 from the Millennium Declaration of the United Nations, which affirmed a collective responsibility for global equality and equity. The MDGs set clear and precise targets for achieving the commitments made in the Millennium Declaration and are to be accomplished by 2015. While in the past, development goals tended to focus on economic growth, the Goals placed social development at the heart of the objectives. The majority of the Goals directly impact child well-being.

Goal 1 is *to eradicate extreme poverty and hunger*. While this is aimed at people of all ages, its implications for children are evident. Children who grow up in families whose incomes are sufficient to meet their needs will do better than children in impoverished families. Children require proper nutrition to achieve optimal growth, including cognitive growth. Goal 2 is *to achieve universal primary education*. As stated throughout this book, there are numerous barriers to education, but if they can be overcome, the lifelong benefits are tremendous.

Goal 3, *to promote gender equality and empower women*, is measured through eliminating gender disparity in all levels of education. As detailed in Chapters Seven and Eight, girls face even greater barriers to education than boys in many parts of the world. However, as also explained, the long-term impacts of educating girls are numerous. *To reduce child mortality* is Goal 4. While child survival was not directly addressed in this book, it is clear that if a child dies, he or she is unable to achieve his or her potential or to exercise his or her rights.

The reduction of maternal mortality is how Goal 5, *to improve maternal health*, is assessed. Even if a child survives, if the child's mother does not, his or her life will be negatively impacted. This is also true for Goal 6, *to combat HIV/AIDS, malaria, and other diseases*. If the child's mother or father is infected, the parent's ill health and eventual death will negatively impact the child even if the child is not infected.

Goal 7 seeks *to ensure environmental sustainability*. The first target under this goal is to integrate the policies of sustainable development into the policies and programs of countries and to reverse the loss of environmental resources. The degradation of the planet will have long-term impacts for children if the soil becomes so poor they cannot raise crops in it, if the air is so poor that it causes respiratory problems, or if the seas rise from climate change and flood their traditional lands. The second target under this goal more directly impacts children because it aims to halve the proportion of people without sustainable access to safe drinking water and basic sanitation. Without access to these necessities, children are at risk for a host of diseases. The last target under this goal is to achieve a "significant improvement" in the lives of at least 100 million slum dwellers by 2020.

Goal 8 addresses the role wealthy nations in the MDGs through *developing a global partnership for development*. As seen through the recent economic crisis, the well-being of nations is increasingly linked. People in all nations benefit when the rights guaranteed in the CRC are realized. If children grow up having their needs met, they will be better able to reach their potential and become contributing members of society.

This book has discussed some of the efforts made around the world to increase child welfare and well-being, but much more work remains. In no country have all children achieved the rights of the CRC. Citizens of countries in the Global North, the primary audience of this book, can work in their own nations, as well as alongside those in Global South countries, to help more children achieve their potential. While one could become overwhelmed with the number of issues to be addressed, one's view could be reoriented to see numerous opportunities to help children.

Homan (2004) discusses a list of factors that can prevent someone from taking action to create macro-level change. Examples include "it's so large and I'm only one person," "I really don't know enough about the situation," and "I really don't know what to do." While it is true that a single person cannot solve all the problems of the world, people gathered together to create change can be extraordinarily effective. As systems theory teaches us, a system is greater than the sum of its subsystems. While some people have started organizations, such as Brittany's Hope discussed in Chapter Six, or Greg Mortenson in the book *Three Cups of Tea*, others can make a difference on a smaller level. This can include donating to an effective charity, traveling to a nation to provide labor for a project, or volunteering in one's own neighborhood.

Basing these efforts on the principle of child participation from the CRC can create even larger impacts. As children learn that they can create change in not only their own lives but also the lives of other children, doors open for lifelong learning and community change. Working together with children to create change does not have to involve large sums of money because the gift of time can be even more valuable.

Helping in a mentoring and reading program, for example, opens countless doors to children throughout their life that would otherwise remain closed. Every small step moves us closer to a world where all children can realize their rights and reach their full potential—resulting in a better world for us all.

Appendix

The Convention on the Rights of the Child

Adopted and opened for signature, ratification, and accession by General Assembly resolution 44/25 on 20 November 1989

Entry into force 2 September 1990, in accordance with article 49

Preamble

The States Parties to the present Convention,

Considering that, in accordance with the principles proclaimed in the Charter of the United Nations, recognition of the inherent dignity and of the equal and inalienable rights of all members of the human family is the foundation of freedom, justice and peace in the world,

Bearing in mind that the peoples of the United Nations have, in the Charter, reaffirmed their faith in fundamental human rights and in the dignity and worth of the human person, and have determined to promote social progress and better standards of life in larger freedom,

Recognizing that the United Nations has, in the Universal Declaration of Human Rights and in the International Covenants on Human Rights, proclaimed and agreed that everyone is entitled to all the rights and freedoms set forth therein, without distinction of any kind, such as race, colour, sex, language, religion, political or other opinion, national or social origin, property, birth or other status,

Recalling that, in the Universal Declaration of Human Rights, the United Nations has proclaimed that childhood is entitled to special care and assistance,

Convinced that the family, as the fundamental group of society and the natural environment for the growth and well-being of all its members and particularly children, should be afforded the necessary protection and assistance so that it can fully assume its responsibilities within the community,

Recognizing that the child, for the full and harmonious development of his or her personality, should grow up in a family environment, in an atmosphere of happiness, love and understanding,

Considering that the child should be fully prepared to live an individual life in society, and brought up in the spirit of the ideals proclaimed in the Charter of the United Nations, and in particular in the spirit of peace, dignity, tolerance, freedom, equality and solidarity,

Bearing in mind that the need to extend particular care to the child has been stated in the Geneva Declaration of the Rights of the Child of 1924 and in the Declaration of the Rights of the Child adopted by the General Assembly on 20 November 1959 and recognized in the Universal Declaration of Human Rights, in the International Covenant on Civil and Political Rights (in particular in articles 23 and 24), in the International Covenant on Economic, Social and Cultural Rights (in particular in article 10) and in the statutes and relevant instruments of specialized agencies and international organizations concerned with the welfare of children,

Bearing in mind that, as indicated in the Declaration of the Rights of the Child, "the child, by reason of his physical and mental immaturity, needs special safeguards and care, including appropriate legal protection, before as well as after birth",

Recalling the provisions of the Declaration on Social and Legal Principles relating to the Protection and Welfare of Children, with Special Reference to Foster Placement and Adoption Nationally and Internationally; the United Nations Standard Minimum Rules for the Administration of Juvenile Justice (The Beijing Rules); and the Declaration on the Protection of Women and Children in Emergency and Armed Conflict,
Recognizing that, in all countries in the world, there are children living

in exceptionally difficult conditions, and that such children need special consideration,

Taking due account of the importance of the traditions and cultural values of each people for the protection and harmonious development of the child, Recognizing the importance of international co-operation for improving the living conditions of children in every country, in particular in the developing countries,

Have agreed as follows:

PART I

Article 1

For the purposes of the present Convention, a child means every human being below the age of eighteen years unless under the law applicable to the child, majority is attained earlier.

Article 2

1. States Parties shall respect and ensure the rights set forth in the present Convention to each child within their jurisdiction without discrimination of any kind, irrespective of the child's or his or her parent's or legal guardian's race, colour, sex, language, religion, political or other opinion, national, ethnic or social origin, property, disability, birth or other status.
2. States Parties shall take all appropriate measures to ensure that the child is protected against all forms of discrimination or punishment on the basis of the status, activities, expressed opinions, or beliefs of the child's parents, legal guardians, or family members.

Article 3

1. In all actions concerning children, whether undertaken by public or private social welfare institutions, courts of law, administrative authorities or legislative bodies, the best interests of the child shall be a primary consideration.

2. States Parties undertake to ensure the child such protection and care as is necessary for his or her well-being, taking into account the rights and duties of his or her parents, legal guardians, or other individuals legally responsible for him or her, and, to this end, shall take all appropriate legislative and administrative measures.
3. States Parties shall ensure that the institutions, services and facilities responsible for the care or protection of children shall conform with the standards established by competent authorities, particularly in the areas of safety, health, in the number and suitability of their staff, as well as competent supervision.

Article 4

States Parties shall undertake all appropriate legislative, administrative, and other measures for the implementation of the rights recognized in the present Convention. With regard to economic, social and cultural rights, States Parties shall undertake such measures to the maximum extent of their available resources and, where needed, within the framework of international co-operation.

Article 5

States Parties shall respect the responsibilities, rights and duties of parents or, where applicable, the members of the extended family or community as provided for by local custom, legal guardians or other persons legally responsible for the child, to provide, in a manner consistent with the evolving capacities of the child, appropriate direction and guidance in the exercise by the child of the rights recognized in the present Convention.

Article 6

1. States Parties recognize that every child has the inherent right to life.
2. States Parties shall ensure to the maximum extent possible the survival and development of the child.

Article 7

1. The child shall be registered immediately after birth and shall have the right from birth to a name, the right to acquire a nationality and. as far as possible, the right to know and be cared for by his or her parents.
2. States Parties shall ensure the implementation of these rights in accordance with their national law and their obligations under the relevant international instruments in this field, in particular where the child would otherwise be stateless.

Article 8

1. States Parties undertake to respect the right of the child to preserve his or her identity, including nationality, name and family relations as recognized by law without unlawful interference.
2. Where a child is illegally deprived of some or all of the elements of his or her identity, States Parties shall provide appropriate assistance and protection, with a view to re-establishing speedily his or her identity.

Article 9

1. States Parties shall ensure that a child shall not be separated from his or her parents against their will, except when competent authorities subject to judicial review determine, in accordance with applicable law and procedures, that such separation is necessary for the best interests of the child. Such determination may be necessary in a particular case such as one involving abuse or neglect of the child by the parents, or one where the parents are living separately and a decision must be made as to the child's place of residence.
2. In any proceedings pursuant to paragraph 1 of the present article, all interested parties shall be given an opportunity to participate in the proceedings and make their views known.
3. States Parties shall respect the right of the child who is separated from one or both parents to maintain personal relations and direct contact with both parents on a regular basis, except if it is contrary to the child's best interests.

4. Where such separation results from any action initiated by a State Party, such as the detention, imprisonment, exile, deportation or death (including death arising from any cause while the person is in the custody of the State) of one or both parents or of the child, that State Party shall, upon request, provide the parents, the child or, if appropriate, another member of the family with the essential information concerning the whereabouts of the absent member(s) of the family unless the provision of the information would be detrimental to the well-being of the child. States Parties shall further ensure that the submission of such a request shall of itself entail no adverse consequences for the person(s) concerned.

Article 10

1. In accordance with the obligation of States Parties under article 9, paragraph 1, applications by a child or his or her parents to enter or leave a State Party for the purpose of family reunification shall be dealt with by States Parties in a positive, humane and expeditious manner. States Parties shall further ensure that the submission of such a request shall entail no adverse consequences for the applicants and for the members of their family.
2. A child whose parents reside in different States shall have the right to maintain on a regular basis, save in exceptional circumstances personal relations and direct contacts with both parents. Towards that end and in accordance with the obligation of States Parties under article 9, paragraph 1, States Parties shall respect the right of the child and his or her parents to leave any country, including their own, and to enter their own country. The right to leave any country shall be subject only to such restrictions as are prescribed by law and which are necessary to protect the national security, public order (ordre public), public health or morals or the rights and freedoms of others and are consistent with the other rights recognized in the present Convention.

Article 11

1. States Parties shall take measures to combat the illicit transfer and non-return of children abroad.

2. To this end, States Parties shall promote the conclusion of bilateral or multilateral agreements or accession to existing agreements.

Article 12

1. States Parties shall assure to the child who is capable of forming his or her own views the right to express those views freely in all matters affecting the child, the views of the child being given due weight in accordance with the age and maturity of the child.
2. For this purpose, the child shall in particular be provided the opportunity to be heard in any judicial and administrative proceedings affecting the child, either directly, or through a representative or an appropriate body, in a manner consistent with the procedural rules of national law.

Article 13

1. The child shall have the right to freedom of expression; this right shall include freedom to seek, receive and impart information and ideas of all kinds, regardless of frontiers, either orally, in writing or in print, in the form of art, or through any other media of the child's choice.
2. The exercise of this right may be subject to certain restrictions, but these shall only be such as are provided by law and are necessary:
   (a) For respect of the rights or reputations of others; or
   (b) For the protection of national security or of public order (ordre public), or of public health or morals.

Article 14

1. States Parties shall respect the right of the child to freedom of thought, conscience and religion.
2. States Parties shall respect the rights and duties of the parents and, when applicable, legal guardians, to provide direction to the child in the exercise of his or her right in a manner consistent with the evolving capacities of the child.
3. Freedom to manifest one's religion or beliefs may be subject only to such limitations as are prescribed by law and are necessary to

protect public safety, order, health or morals, or the fundamental rights and freedoms of others.

Article 15

1. States Parties recognize the rights of the child to freedom of association and to freedom of peaceful assembly.
2. No restrictions may be placed on the exercise of these rights other than those imposed in conformity with the law and which are necessary in a democratic society in the interests of national security or public safety, public order (ordre public), the protection of public health or morals or the protection of the rights and freedoms of others.

Article 16

1. No child shall be subjected to arbitrary or unlawful interference with his or her privacy, family, or correspondence, nor to unlawful attacks on his or her honour and reputation.
2. The child has the right to the protection of the law against such interference or attacks.

Article 17

States Parties recognize the important function performed by the mass media and shall ensure that the child has access to information and material from a diversity of national and international sources, especially those aimed at the promotion of his or her social, spiritual and moral well-being and physical and mental health.

To this end, States Parties shall:

(a) Encourage the mass media to disseminate information and material of social and cultural benefit to the child and in accordance with the spirit of article 29;
(b) Encourage international co-operation in the production, exchange and dissemination of such information and material from a diversity of cultural, national and international sources;

(c) Encourage the production and dissemination of children's books;
(d) Encourage the mass media to have particular regard to the linguistic needs of the child who belongs to a minority group or who is indigenous;
(e) Encourage the development of appropriate guidelines for the protection of the child from information and material injurious to his or her well-being, bearing in mind the provisions of articles 13 and 18.

Article 18

1. States Parties shall use their best efforts to ensure recognition of the principle that both parents have common responsibilities for the upbringing and development of the child. Parents or, as the case may be, legal guardians, have the primary responsibility for the upbringing and development of the child. The best interests of the child will be their basic concern.
2. For the purpose of guaranteeing and promoting the rights set forth in the present Convention, States Parties shall render appropriate assistance to parents and legal guardians in the performance of their child-rearing responsibilities and shall ensure the development of institutions, facilities and services for the care of children.
3. States Parties shall take all appropriate measures to ensure that children of working parents have the right to benefit from child-care services and facilities for which they are eligible.

Article 19

1. States Parties shall take all appropriate legislative, administrative, social and educational measures to protect the child from all forms of physical or mental violence, injury or abuse, neglect or negligent treatment, maltreatment or exploitation, including sexual abuse, while in the care of parent(s), legal guardian(s) or any other person who has the care of the child.
2. Such protective measures should, as appropriate, include effective procedures for the establishment of social programmes to provide necessary support for the child and for those who have the care

of the child, as well as for other forms of prevention and for identification, reporting, referral, investigation, treatment and follow-up of instances of child maltreatment described heretofore, and, as appropriate, for judicial involvement.

Article 20

1. A child temporarily or permanently deprived of his or her family environment, or in whose own best interests cannot be allowed to remain in that environment, shall be entitled to special protection and assistance provided by the State.
2. States Parties shall in accordance with their national laws ensure alternative care for such a child.
3. Such care could include, inter alia, foster placement, kafalah of Islamic law, adoption or if necessary placement in suitable institutions for the care of children. When considering solutions, due regard shall be paid to the desirability of continuity in a child's upbringing and to the child's ethnic, religious, cultural and linguistic background.

Article 21

States Parties that recognize and/or permit the system of adoption shall ensure that the best interests of the child shall be the paramount consideration and they shall:

(a) Ensure that the adoption of a child is authorized only by competent authorities who determine, in accordance with applicable law and procedures and on the basis of all pertinent and reliable information, that the adoption is permissible in view of the child's status concerning parents, relatives and legal guardians and that, if required, the persons concerned have given their informed consent to the adoption on the basis of such counselling as may be necessary;

(b) Recognize that inter-country adoption may be considered as an alternative means of child's care, if the child cannot be placed in a foster or an adoptive family or cannot in any suitable manner be cared for in the child's country of origin;

(c) Ensure that the child concerned by inter-country adoption enjoys safeguards and standards equivalent to those existing in the case of national adoption;

(d) Take all appropriate measures to ensure that, in inter-country adoption, the placement does not result in improper financial gain for those involved in it;

(e) Promote, where appropriate, the objectives of the present article by concluding bilateral or multilateral arrangements or agreements, and endeavour, within this framework, to ensure that the placement of the child in another country is carried out by competent authorities or organs.

Article 22

1. States Parties shall take appropriate measures to ensure that a child who is seeking refugee status or who is considered a refugee in accordance with applicable international or domestic law and procedures shall, whether unaccompanied or accompanied by his or her parents or by any other person, receive appropriate protection and humanitarian assistance in the enjoyment of applicable rights set forth in the present Convention and in other international human rights or humanitarian instruments to which the said States are Parties.
2. For this purpose, States Parties shall provide, as they consider appropriate, co-operation in any efforts by the United Nations and other competent intergovernmental organizations or non-governmental organizations co-operating with the United Nations to protect and assist such a child and to trace the parents or other members of the family of any refugee child in order to obtain information necessary for reunification with his or her family. In cases where no parents or other members of the family can be found, the child shall be accorded the same protection as any other child permanently or temporarily deprived of his or her family environment for any reason, as set forth in the present Convention.

Article 23

1. States Parties recognize that a mentally or physically disabled child should enjoy a full and decent life, in conditions which ensure

dignity, promote self-reliance and facilitate the child's active participation in the community.

2. States Parties recognize the right of the disabled child to special care and shall encourage and ensure the extension, subject to available resources, to the eligible child and those responsible for his or her care, of assistance for which application is made and which is appropriate to the child's condition and to the circumstances of the parents or others caring for the child.
3. Recognizing the special needs of a disabled child, assistance extended in accordance with paragraph 2 of the present article shall be provided free of charge, whenever possible, taking into account the financial resources of the parents or others caring for the child, and shall be designed to ensure that the disabled child has effective access to and receives education, training, health care services, rehabilitation services, preparation for employment and recreation opportunities in a manner conducive to the child's achieving the fullest possible social integration and individual development, including his or her cultural and spiritual development
4. States Parties shall promote, in the spirit of international cooperation, the exchange of appropriate information in the field of preventive health care and of medical, psychological and functional treatment of disabled children, including dissemination of and access to information concerning methods of rehabilitation, education and vocational services, with the aim of enabling States Parties to improve their capabilities and skills and to widen their experience in these areas. In this regard, particular account shall be taken of the needs of developing countries.

Article 24

1. States Parties recognize the right of the child to the enjoyment of the highest attainable standard of health and to facilities for the treatment of illness and rehabilitation of health. States Parties shall strive to ensure that no child is deprived of his or her right of access to such health care services.

2. States Parties shall pursue full implementation of this right and, in particular, shall take appropriate measures:
   (a) To diminish infant and child mortality;
   (b) To ensure the provision of necessary medical assistance and health care to all children with emphasis on the development of primary health care;
   (c) To combat disease and malnutrition, including within the framework of primary health care, through, inter alia, the application of readily available technology and through the provision of adequate nutritious foods and clean drinking-water, taking into consideration the dangers and risks of environmental pollution;
   (d) To ensure appropriate pre-natal and post-natal health care for mothers;
   (e) To ensure that all segments of society, in particular parents and children, are informed, have access to education and are supported in the use of basic knowledge of child health and nutrition, the advantages of breastfeeding, hygiene and environmental sanitation and the prevention of accidents;
   (f) To develop preventive health care, guidance for parents and family planning education and services.
3. States Parties shall take all effective and appropriate measures with a view to abolishing traditional practices prejudicial to the health of children.
4. States Parties undertake to promote and encourage international co-operation with a view to achieving progressively the full realization of the right recognized in the present article. In this regard, particular account shall be taken of the needs of developing countries.

Article 25

States Parties recognize the right of a child who has been placed by the competent authorities for the purposes of care, protection or treatment of his or her physical or mental health, to a periodic review of the treatment provided to the child and all other circumstances relevant to his or her placement.

Article 26

1. States Parties shall recognize for every child the right to benefit from social security, including social insurance, and shall take the necessary measures to achieve the full realization of this right in accordance with their national law.
2. The benefits should, where appropriate, be granted, taking into account the resources and the circumstances of the child and persons having responsibility for the maintenance of the child, as well as any other consideration relevant to an application for benefits made by or on behalf of the child.

Article 27

1. States Parties recognize the right of every child to a standard of living adequate for the child's physical, mental, spiritual, moral and social development.
2. The parent(s) or others responsible for the child have the primary responsibility to secure, within their abilities and financial capacities, the conditions of living necessary for the child's development.
3. States Parties, in accordance with national conditions and within their means, shall take appropriate measures to assist parents and others responsible for the child to implement this right and shall in case of need provide material assistance and support programmes, particularly with regard to nutrition, clothing and housing.
4. States Parties shall take all appropriate measures to secure the recovery of maintenance for the child from the parents or other persons having financial responsibility for the child, both within the State Party and from abroad. In particular, where the person having financial responsibility for the child lives in a State different from that of the child, States Parties shall promote the accession to international agreements or the conclusion of such agreements, as well as the making of other appropriate arrangements.

Article 28

1. States Parties recognize the right of the child to education, and with a view to achieving this right progressively and on the basis of equal opportunity, they shall, in particular:
   (a) Make primary education compulsory and available free to all;
   (b) Encourage the development of different forms of secondary education, including general and vocational education, make them available and accessible to every child, and take appropriate measures such as the introduction of free education and offering financial assistance in case of need;
   (c) Make higher education accessible to all on the basis of capacity by every appropriate means;
   (d) Make educational and vocational information and guidance available and accessible to all children;
   (e) Take measures to encourage regular attendance at schools and the reduction of drop-out rates.
2. States Parties shall take all appropriate measures to ensure that school discipline is administered in a manner consistent with the child's human dignity and in conformity with the present Convention.
3. States Parties shall promote and encourage international cooperation in matters relating to education, in particular with a view to contributing to the elimination of ignorance and illiteracy throughout the world and facilitating access to scientific and technical knowledge and modern teaching methods. In this regard, particular account shall be taken of the needs of developing countries.

Article 29

1. States Parties agree that the education of the child shall be directed to:
   (a) The development of the child's personality, talents and mental and physical abilities to their fullest potential;
   (b) The development of respect for human rights and fundamental freedoms, and for the principles enshrined in the Charter of the United Nations;

(c) The development of respect for the child's parents, his or her own cultural identity, language and values, for the national values of the country in which the child is living, the country from which he or she may originate, and for civilizations different from his or her own;
(d) The preparation of the child for responsible life in a free society, in the spirit of understanding, peace, tolerance, equality of sexes, and friendship among all peoples, ethnic, national and religious groups and persons of indigenous origin;
(e) The development of respect for the natural environment.

2. No part of the present article or article 28 shall be construed so as to interfere with the liberty of individuals and bodies to establish and direct educational institutions, subject always to the observance of the principle set forth in paragraph 1 of the present article and to the requirements that the education given in such institutions shall conform to such minimum standards as may be laid down by the State.

Article 30

In those States in which ethnic, religious or linguistic minorities or persons of indigenous origin exist, a child belonging to such a minority or who is indigenous shall not be denied the right, in community with other members of his or her group, to enjoy his or her own culture, to profess and practise his or her own religion, or to use his or her own language.

Article 31

1. States Parties recognize the right of the child to rest and leisure, to engage in play and recreational activities appropriate to the age of the child and to participate freely in cultural life and the arts.
2. States Parties shall respect and promote the right of the child to participate fully in cultural and artistic life and shall encourage the provision of appropriate and equal opportunities for cultural, artistic, recreational and leisure activity.

Article 32

1. States Parties recognize the right of the child to be protected from economic exploitation and from performing any work that is likely to be hazardous or to interfere with the child's education, or to be harmful to the child's health or physical, mental, spiritual, moral or social development.
2. States Parties shall take legislative, administrative, social and educational measures to ensure the implementation of the present article. To this end, and having regard to the relevant provisions of other international instruments, States Parties shall in particular:

   (a) Provide for a minimum age or minimum ages for admission to employment;
   (b) Provide for appropriate regulation of the hours and conditions of employment;
   (c) Provide for appropriate penalties or other sanctions to ensure the effective enforcement of the present article.

Article 33

States Parties shall take all appropriate measures, including legislative, administrative, social and educational measures, to protect children from the illicit use of narcotic drugs and psychotropic substances as defined in the relevant international treaties, and to prevent the use of children in the illicit production and trafficking of such substances.

Article 34

States Parties undertake to protect the child from all forms of sexual exploitation and sexual abuse. For these purposes, States Parties shall in particular take all appropriate national, bilateral and multilateral measures to prevent:

(a) The inducement or coercion of a child to engage in any unlawful sexual activity;
(b) The exploitative use of children in prostitution or other unlawful sexual practices;
(c) The exploitative use of children in pornographic performances and materials.

Article 35

States Parties shall take all appropriate national, bilateral and multilateral measures to prevent the abduction of, the sale of or traffic in children for any purpose or in any form.

Article 36

States Parties shall protect the child against all other forms of exploitation prejudicial to any aspects of the child's welfare.

Article 37

States Parties shall ensure that:

(a) No child shall be subjected to torture or other cruel, inhuman or degrading treatment or punishment. Neither capital punishment nor life imprisonment without possibility of release shall be imposed for offences committed by persons below eighteen years of age;

(b) No child shall be deprived of his or her liberty unlawfully or arbitrarily. The arrest, detention or imprisonment of a child shall be in conformity with the law and shall be used only as a measure of last resort and for the shortest appropriate period of time;

(c) Every child deprived of liberty shall be treated with humanity and respect for the inherent dignity of the human person, and in a manner which takes into account the needs of persons of his or her age. In particular, every child deprived of liberty shall be separated from adults unless it is considered in the child's best interest not to do so and shall have the right to maintain contact with his or her family through correspondence and visits, save in exceptional circumstances;

(d) Every child deprived of his or her liberty shall have the right to prompt access to legal and other appropriate assistance, as well as the right to challenge the legality of the deprivation of his or her liberty before a court or other competent, independent and impartial authority, and to a prompt decision on any such action.

Article 38

1. States Parties undertake to respect and to ensure respect for rules of international humanitarian law applicable to them in armed conflicts which are relevant to the child.
2. States Parties shall take all feasible measures to ensure that persons who have not attained the age of fifteen years do not take a direct part in hostilities.
3. States Parties shall refrain from recruiting any person who has not attained the age of fifteen years into their armed forces. In recruiting among those persons who have attained the age of fifteen years but who have not attained the age of eighteen years, States Parties shall endeavour to give priority to those who are oldest.
4. In accordance with their obligations under international humanitarian law to protect the civilian population in armed conflicts, States Parties shall take all feasible measures to ensure protection and care of children who are affected by an armed conflict.

Article 39

States Parties shall take all appropriate measures to promote physical and psychological recovery and social reintegration of a child victim of: any form of neglect, exploitation, or abuse; torture or any other form of cruel, inhuman or degrading treatment or punishment; or armed conflicts. Such recovery and reintegration shall take place in an environment which fosters the health, self-respect and dignity of the child.

Article 40

1. States Parties recognize the right of every child alleged as, accused of, or recognized as having infringed the penal law to be treated in a manner consistent with the promotion of the child's sense of dignity and worth, which reinforces the child's respect for the human rights and fundamental freedoms of others and which takes into account the child's age and the desirability of promoting the

child's reintegration and the child's assuming a constructive role in society.

2. To this end, and having regard to the relevant provisions of international instruments, States Parties shall, in particular, ensure that:
   (a) No child shall be alleged as, be accused of, or recognized as having infringed the penal law by reason of acts or omissions that were not prohibited by national or international law at the time they were committed;
   (b) Every child alleged as or accused of having infringed the penal law has at least the following guarantees:
      (i) To be presumed innocent until proven guilty according to law;
      (ii) To be informed promptly and directly of the charges against him or her, and, if appropriate, through his or her parents or legal guardians, and to have legal or other appropriate assistance in the preparation and presentation of his or her defence;
      (iii) To have the matter determined without delay by a competent, independent and impartial authority or judicial body in a fair hearing according to law, in the presence of legal or other appropriate assistance and, unless it is considered not to be in the best interest of the child, in particular, taking into account his or her age or situation, his or her parents or legal guardians;
      (iv) Not to be compelled to give testimony or to confess guilt; to examine or have examined adverse witnesses and to obtain the participation and examination of witnesses on his or her behalf under conditions of equality;
      (v) If considered to have infringed the penal law, to have this decision and any measures imposed in consequence thereof reviewed by a higher competent, independent and impartial authority or judicial body according to law;
      (vi) To have the free assistance of an interpreter if the child cannot understand or speak the language used;
      (vii) To have his or her privacy fully respected at all stages of the proceedings.
3. States Parties shall seek to promote the establishment of laws, procedures, authorities and institutions specifically applicable to

children alleged as, accused of, or recognized as having infringed the penal law, and, in particular:

(a) The establishment of a minimum age below which children shall be presumed not to have the capacity to infringe the penal law;
(b) Whenever appropriate and desirable, measures for dealing with such children without resorting to judicial proceedings, providing that human rights and legal safeguards are fully respected.

4. A variety of dispositions, such as care, guidance and supervision orders; counselling; probation; foster care; education and vocational training programmes and other alternatives to institutional care shall be available to ensure that children are dealt with in a manner appropriate to their well-being and proportionate both to their circumstances and the offence.

Article 41

Nothing in the present Convention shall affect any provisions which are more conducive to the realization of the rights of the child and which may be contained in:

(a) The law of a State party; or
(b) International law in force for that State.

PART II

Article 42

States Parties undertake to make the principles and provisions of the Convention widely known, by appropriate and active means, to adults and children alike.

Article 43

1. For the purpose of examining the progress made by States Parties in achieving the realization of the obligations undertaken in the present Convention, there shall be established a Committee on the Rights of the Child, which shall carry out the functions hereinafter provided.

2. The Committee shall consist of eighteen experts of high moral standing and recognized competence in the field covered by this Convention. The members of the Committee shall be elected by States Parties from among their nationals and shall serve in their personal capacity, consideration being given to equitable geographical distribution, as well as to the principal legal systems.
3. The members of the Committee shall be elected by secret ballot from a list of persons nominated by States Parties. Each State Party may nominate one person from among its own nationals.
4. The initial election to the Committee shall be held no later than six months after the date of the entry into force of the present Convention and thereafter every second year. At least four months before the date of each election, the Secretary-General of the United Nations shall address a letter to States Parties inviting them to submit their nominations within two months. The Secretary-General shall subsequently prepare a list in alphabetical order of all persons thus nominated, indicating States Parties which have nominated them, and shall submit it to the States Parties to the present Convention.
5. The elections shall be held at meetings of States Parties convened by the Secretary-General at United Nations Headquarters. At those meetings, for which two thirds of States Parties shall constitute a quorum, the persons elected to the Committee shall be those who obtain the largest number of votes and an absolute majority of the votes of the representatives of States Parties present and voting.
6. The members of the Committee shall be elected for a term of four years. They shall be eligible for re-election if renominated. The term of five of the members elected at the first election shall expire at the end of two years; immediately after the first election, the names of these five members shall be chosen by lot by the Chairman of the meeting.
7. If a member of the Committee dies or resigns or declares that for any other cause he or she can no longer perform the duties of the Committee, the State Party which nominated the member shall appoint another expert from among its nationals to serve for the remainder of the term, subject to the approval of the Committee.
8. The Committee shall establish its own rules of procedure.
9. The Committee shall elect its officers for a period of two years.

10. The meetings of the Committee shall normally be held at United Nations Headquarters or at any other convenient place as determined by the Committee. The Committee shall normally meet annually. The duration of the meetings of the Committee shall be determined, and reviewed, if necessary, by a meeting of the States Parties to the present Convention, subject to the approval of the General Assembly.
11. The Secretary-General of the United Nations shall provide the necessary staff and facilities for the effective performance of the functions of the Committee under the present Convention.
12. With the approval of the General Assembly, the members of the Committee established under the present Convention shall receive emoluments from United Nations resources on such terms and conditions as the Assembly may decide.

Article 44

1. States Parties undertake to submit to the Committee, through the Secretary-General of the United Nations, reports on the measures they have adopted which give effect to the rights recognized herein and on the progress made on the enjoyment of those rights
   (a) Within two years of the entry into force of the Convention for the State Party concerned;
   (b) Thereafter every five years.
2. Reports made under the present article shall indicate factors and difficulties, if any, affecting the degree of fulfillment of the obligations under the present Convention. Reports shall also contain sufficient information to provide the Committee with a comprehensive understanding of the implementation of the Convention in the country concerned.
3. A State Party which has submitted a comprehensive initial report to the Committee need not, in its subsequent reports submitted in accordance with paragraph 1 (b) of the present article, repeat basic information previously provided.
4. The Committee may request from States Parties further information relevant to the implementation of the Convention.
5. The Committee shall submit to the General Assembly, through the Economic and Social Council, every two years, reports on its activities.

6. States Parties shall make their reports widely available to the public in their own countries.

Article 45

In order to foster the effective implementation of the Convention and to encourage international co-operation in the field covered by the Convention:

(a) The specialized agencies, the United Nations Children's Fund, and other United Nations organs shall be entitled to be represented at the consideration of the implementation of such provisions of the present Convention as fall within the scope of their mandate. The Committee may invite the specialized agencies, the United Nations Children's Fund and other competent bodies as it may consider appropriate to provide expert advice on the implementation of the Convention in areas falling within the scope of their respective mandates. The Committee may invite the specialized agencies, the United Nations Children's Fund, and other United Nations organs to submit reports on the implementation of the Convention in areas falling within the scope of their activities;
(b) The Committee shall transmit, as it may consider appropriate, to the specialized agencies, the United Nations Children's Fund and other competent bodies, any reports from States Parties that contain a request, or indicate a need, for technical advice or assistance, along with the Committee's observations and suggestions, if any, on these requests or indications;
(c) The Committee may recommend to the General Assembly to request the Secretary-General to undertake on its behalf studies on specific issues relating to the rights of the child;
(d) The Committee may make suggestions and general recommendations based on information received pursuant to articles 44 and 45 of the present Convention. Such suggestions and general recommendations shall be transmitted to any State Party concerned and reported to the General Assembly, together with comments, if any, from States Parties.

PART III

Article 46

The present Convention shall be open for signature by all States.

Article 47

The present Convention is subject to ratification. Instruments of ratification shall be deposited with the Secretary-General of the United Nations.

Article 48

The present Convention shall remain open for accession by any State. The instruments of accession shall be deposited with the Secretary-General of the United Nations.

Article 49

1. The present Convention shall enter into force on the thirtieth day following the date of deposit with the Secretary-General of the United Nations of the twentieth instrument of ratification or accession.
2. For each State ratifying or acceding to the Convention after the deposit of the twentieth instrument of ratification or accession, the Convention shall enter into force on the thirtieth day after the deposit by such State of its instrument of ratification or accession.

Article 50

1. Any State Party may propose an amendment and file it with the Secretary-General of the United Nations. The Secretary-General shall thereupon communicate the proposed amendment to States Parties, with a request that they indicate whether they favour a conference of States Parties for the purpose of considering and voting upon the proposals. In the event that, within four months

from the date of such communication, at least one third of the States Parties favour such a conference, the Secretary-General shall convene the conference under the auspices of the United Nations. Any amendment adopted by a majority of States Parties present and voting at the conference shall be submitted to the General Assembly for approval.

2. An amendment adopted in accordance with paragraph 1 of the present article shall enter into force when it has been approved by the General Assembly of the United Nations and accepted by a two-thirds majority of States Parties.
3. When an amendment enters into force, it shall be binding on those States Parties which have accepted it, other States Parties still being bound by the provisions of the present Convention and any earlier amendments which they have accepted.

Article 51

1. The Secretary-General of the United Nations shall receive and circulate to all States the text of reservations made by States at the time of ratification or accession.
2. A reservation incompatible with the object and purpose of the present Convention shall not be permitted.
3. Reservations may be withdrawn at any time by notification to that effect addressed to the Secretary-General of the United Nations, who shall then inform all States. Such notification shall take effect on the date on which it is received by the Secretary-General.

Article 52

A State Party may denounce the present Convention by written notification to the Secretary-General of the United Nations. Denunciation becomes effective one year after the date of receipt of the notification by the Secretary-General.

Article 53

The Secretary-General of the United Nations is designated as the depositary of the present Convention.

Article 54

The original of the present Convention, of which the Arabic, Chinese, English, French, Russian and Spanish texts are equally authentic, shall be deposited with the Secretary-General of the United Nations. In witness thereof the undersigned plenipotentiaries, being duly authorized thereto by their respective Governments, have signed the present Convention.

References

Chapter One

Ali, S. S. (2007). A comparative perspective of the Convention on the Rights of the Child and the principles of Islamic law. In UNICEF (Ed.), *Protecting the world's children: Impact of the Convention on the Rights of the Child in diverse legal systems* (pp. 142–208). New York: Cambridge University Press.

Amnesty International. (1999). *Children's rights: The future starts here.* Retrieved May 5, 2008, from the Child Rights Information Network Web site: http://www.crin.org/resources/InfoDetail.asp?ID=493

Banks, C. (2007). The discourse of children's rights in Bangladesh: International norms and local definitions. *International Journal of Children's Rights, 15*, 391–414.

Burr, R. (2004). Children's rights: International policy and lived practice. In M. J. Kehily (Ed.), *An introduction to childhood studies* (pp. 145–159). Berkshire, England: Open University Press.

Cunningham, H. (1995). *Children & childhood in western society since 1500.* New York: Addison Wesley Longman.

Edmonds, B. C., & Fernekes, W. R. (1996). *Children's rights: A reference handbook.* Santa Barbara, CA: ABC-CLIO.

Ensalaco, M. (2005). The right of the child to development. In M. Ensalaco & L. C. Majka (Eds.), *Children's human rights: Progress and challenges for children worldwide* (pp. 9–29). New York: Rowman & Littlefield.

Fuchs, E. (2007). Children's rights and global civil society. *Comparative Education, 43*(3), 393–412.

Gerschutz, J. M., & Karns, M. P. (2005). Transforming visions into reality: The Convention on the Rights of the Child. In M. Ensalaco & L. C. Majka (Eds.), *Children's human rights: Progress and challenges for children worldwide* (pp. 31–51). New York: Rowman & Littlefield.

Gittins, D. (2004). The historical construction of childhood. In M. J. Kehily (Ed.), *An introduction to childhood studies* (pp. 25–38). Berkshire, England: Open University Press.

Goonesekere, S. (2007). Introduction and overview. In UNICEF (Ed.), *Protecting the world's children: Impact of the Convention on the Rights of the Child in diverse legal systems* (pp. 1–33). New York: Cambridge University Press.

Grover, S. (2004). On recognizing children's universal rights: What needs to change in the Convention on the Rights of the Child. *The International Journal of Children's Rights, 12,* 259–271.

Groves, L. (2004). Implementing ILO Child Labour Convention 182: Lessons from Honduras. *Development in Practice, 14*(1/2), 171–182.

Grugel, J., & Peruzzotti, E. (2007). Claiming rights under global governance: Children's rights in Argentina. *Global Governance, 13,* 199–216.

Harris-Short, S. (2003). International human rights law: Imperialist, inept and ineffective? Cultural relativism and the UN Convention on the Rights of the Child. *Human Rights Quarterly, 25,* 130–181.

Hashemi, K. (2007). Religious legal traditions, Muslim states and the Convention on the Rights of the Child: An essay on the relevant UN documentation. *Human Rights Quarterly, 29,* 194–227.

Kabašinskaitė, D., & Bak, M. (2006). Lithuania's children's policy in the period of transition. *International Journal of Social Welfare, 15,* 247–256.

King, M. L. (2007). Concepts of childhood: What we know and where we might go. *Renaissance Quarterly, 60,* 371–407.

McAdam, J. (2006). Seeking asylum under the Convention on the Rights of the Child: A case for complementary protection. *The International Journal of Children's Rights, 14,* 251–274.

McTernan, E., & Godfrey, A. (2006). Children's services planning in Northern Ireland: Developing a planning model to address rights and needs. *Child Care in Practice, 12*(3), 219–240.

Méndez, E. G. (2007). Law reform in selected civil law countries. In UNICEF (Ed.), *Protecting the world's children: Impact of the Convention on the Rights of the Child in diverse legal systems* (pp. 100–141). New York: Cambridge University Press.

Njungwe, E. N. (2001). *International protection of children's rights: An analysis of African attributes in the African Charter on the Rights and Welfare of the Child*. Retrieved May 5, 2008, from the Progressive Initiative for Cameroon Web site: http://www.picam.org/Articles/African%20Attributes%20in%20the%20African%20Children's%20Charter.pdf

Obama, B. (2008). *Question 12: Human Rights*. Retrieved May 18, 2009, from http://debate.waldenu.edu/video/question-12/

Odongo, G. O. (2004). The domestication of international standards on the rights of the child: A critical and comparative evaluation of the Kenyan example. *The International Journal of Children's Rights, 12*, 419–430.

Office of High Commissioner for Human Rights. (1993). *Fact sheet No. 10 (Rev. 1): The rights of the child*. Retrieved May 8, 2008, from http://www.ohchr.org/Documents/Publications/FactSheet10Rev.1en.pdf

Omokhodion, F. O., Omokhodion, S. I., & Odusote, T. O. (2006). Perceptions of child labour among working children in Ibadan, Nigeria. *Child: Care, Heath & Development, 32*(3), 281–286.

Onyango, P., & Lynch, M. A. (2006). Implementing the right to child protection: A challenge for developing countries. *The Lancet, 367*, 693–694.

Pardeck, J. T. (2006). *Children's rights: Policy and practice* (2nd ed.). New York: Haworth.

Polakoff, E. G. (2007). Globalization and child labor: Review of issues. *Journal of Developing Societies, 23*(1-2), 259–283.

Powley, E. (2008). *Defending children's rights: The legislative priorities of Rwandan women parliamentarians*. Retrieved June 4, 2008, from the Hunt Alternatives Fund Web site: http://www.huntalternatives.org/download/1077_defending_childrens_rights.pdf

Rios-Kohn, R. (2007). Law reform in selected common law countries. In UNICEF (Ed.), *Protecting the world's children: Impact of the Convention on the Rights of the Child in diverse legal systems* (pp. 34–99). New York: Cambridge University Press.

Rogers, W. S. (2004). Promoting better childhoods: Constructions of child concern. In M. J. Kehily (Ed.), *An introduction to childhood studies* (pp. 125–144). Berkshire, England: Open University Press.

Roose, R., & De Bie, M. (2008). Children's rights: A challenge for social work. *International Social Work, 51*(1), 37–46.

Sloth-Nielson, J., & Mezmur, B. D. (2008). 2 + 2 = 5? Exploring the domestication of the CRC in South African jurisprudence. *The International Journal on the Rights of the Child, 16*, 1–28.

Smith, A. B. (2007). Children and young people's participation rights in education. *International Journal of Children's Rights, 15*, 147–164.

Southwick, E. M. (2001, February 1). *Statement by Ambassador E. Michael Southwick, Deputy Assistant Secretary of State for International Organization Affairs, in the Preparatory Committee for the General Assembly Special Session on the Children's World Summit*. Retrieved June 24, 2006, from http://www.un.int/usa/01_015.htm

Tang, K. (2003). Implementing the United Nations Convention on the Rights of the Child: The Canadian experience. *International Social Work, 46*(3), 277–288.

Timmerman, G. (2009). Youth policy and participation: An analysis of pedagogical ideals in municipal youth policy in the Netherlands. *Children and Youth Services Review, 31*, 572–576.

UNICEF Innocenti Research Centre. (2004). *Study on the impact of the implementation of the Convention on the Rights of the Child*. Retrieved May 13, 2008, from http://www.unicef-irc.org/publications/pdf/CRC_Impact_summaryreport.pdf

UNICEF. (n.d.). *Convention on the Rights of the Child*. Retrieved June 5, 2006, from http://www.unicef.org/crc/index_30166.html

Walker, N. E., Brooks, C. M., & Wrightsman, L. S. (1999). *Children's rights in the United States: In search of a national policy*. Thousand Oaks, CA: Sage.

World Bank. (2004). *Development policy lending replaces adjustment lending*. Retrieved May 9, 2008, from http://web.worldbank.org/WBSITE/EXTERNAL/NEWS/0,contentMDK:20237378~menuPK:34457~pagePK:64003015~piPK:64003012~theSitePK:4607,00.html

Chapter Two

Abdelmoneium, A. O. (2005). Challenges facing children in education and labour: Case study of displaced children in Khartoum-Sudan. *The Ahfad Journal, 22*(2), 64–76.

Ajayi, A. O., & Torimiro, D. O. (2004). Perspectives on child abuse and labour: Global ethical ideals versus African cultural realities. *Early Child Development and Care, 174*(2), 183–191.

Akimov, M. (2000, June). *Risk factors of victimization: Street children in Saint-Petersburg, Russia*. Paper presented at the Family Research Laboratory's 7th Annual International Research Conference on the Victimization of Children and Youth, Durham, NH.

Ashayagachat, A. (2006, May 5). Child labour situation here improving: But young migrants pose new challenge. *Bangkok Post*. Retrieved May 5, 2006, from http://www.bangkokpost.com

Attitudes to child labour changing. (2007, November 19). *IRIN News*. Retrieved November 20, 2007, from http://www.irinnews.org/Report.aspx?ReportId=75384

Bales, K. (2004). *Disposable people: New slavery in the global economy*. Los Angeles: University of California Press.

Bower, B. (2005). Childhood's end. *Science News, 168*(13), 200–201.

Child labour on the rise as poverty increases. (2007, June 12). *IRIN News*. Retrieved June 15, 2007, from http://www.irinnews.org/Report.aspx?ReportId=72683

Child Workers in Asia. (2007). *Understanding bonded child labour in Asia*. Retrieved May 14, 2007, from the Child Rights Information Network Web site: http://www.crin.org/docs/CWA_%20UnderstandingBondedChildLabour.pdf

Children eke out a living on the streets. (2008, October 10). *IRIN News*. Retrieved October 13,2008, from http://www.irinnews.org/Report.aspx?ReportId=80845

Children of former bonded labourers face hardship. (2008, January 28). *IRIN News*. Retrieved January 31, 2008, from http://www.irinnews.org/Report.aspx?ReportId=76457

Children work in brick factories to help pay off family debts. (2008, April 8). *IRIN News*. Retrieved April 16, 2008, from http://www.irinnews.org/Report.aspx?ReportId=77662

Children work the streets to support families. (2007, January 16). *IRIN News*. Retrieved May 14, 2007, from http://www.irinnews.org/Report.aspx?ReportId=64363

Code of conduct to fight child labour launched. (2007, July 10). *IRIN News*. Retrieved July 16, 2007, from http://www.irinnews.org/Report.aspx?ReportId=73152

Co-op America. (2006). *Responsible shopper profile: Disney*. Retrieved September 8, 2006, from http://www.coopamerica.org/programs/rs/profile.cfm?id=213

Cunningham, H., & Stromquist, S. (2005). Child labor and the rights of children: Historical patterns of decline and persistence. In B. H. Weston (Ed.), *Child labor and human rights: Making children matter* (pp. 55–83). Boulder, CO: Lynne Rienner Publishers.

Cyclone orphans forced to work. (2008, October 31). *IRIN News*. Retrieved October 31, 2008, from http://www.irinnews.org/Report.aspx?ReportId=81219

Dybicz, P. (2005). Interventions for street children: An analysis of best practices. *International Social Work, 48*(6), 763–771.

Efforts too small to curb child labour on cocoa farms. (2008, February 18). *IRIN News*. Retrieved March 5, 2008, from http://www.irinnews.org/Report.aspx?ReportId=76798

Gem slaves: Tanzanite's child labour. (2006, September 6). *IRIN News*. Retrieved May 29, 2007, from http://www.irinnews.org/Report.aspx?ReportId=61004

Gentleman, A. (2007, March 4). Stricter law fails to diminish the demand for child laborers in India. *New York Times*. Retrieved March 6, 2007, from http://www.nytimes.com

Global March Against Child Labour. (2006a). *Review of child labour, education and poverty agenda: India country report 2006*. Retrieved August 16, 2007, from http://www.globalmarch.org/images/India-report.pdf

Global March Against Child Labour. (2006b). *Review of child labour, education and poverty agenda: Bangladesh country report 2006*. Retrieved August 16, 2007, from http://www.globalmarch.org/images/Bangladesh-report.pdf

Godoy, A. S. (1999). "Our right is the right to be killed": Making rights real on the streets of Guatemala City. *Childhood, 6*(4), 423–442.

Goodman, A. (2008, February 14). *"Chocolate's bittersweet economy": Cocoa industry accused of greed, neglect for labor practices in Ivory Coast*. Retrieved May 6, 2008, from the International Labor Rights Forum Web site: http://www.laborrights.org/stop-child-labor/cocoa-campaign/1099

Government could do more to tackle child labour. (2007, July 18). *IRIN News*. Retrieved August 16, 2007, from http://www.irinnews.org/Report.aspx?ReportId=73288

Government intensifies campaign against child labour. (2007, November 30). *IRIN News*. Retrieved December 3, 2007, from http://www.irinnews.org/Report.aspx?ReportId=75626

Groves, L. (2004). Implementing ILO Child Labour Convention 182: Lessons from Honduras. *Development in Practice, 14*(1/2), 171–182.

Groves, L. (2005). Implementing ILO Child Labour Convention 182: Lessons from the gold-mining sector in Burkina Faso. *Development in Practice, 15*(1), 49–59.

Harris, B. (2000). Suffer the little children. *The Lancet, 355*, 1805.

Human Rights Watch. (1994). *Generation under fire: Children and violence in Colombia*. Retrieved July 2, 2006, from http://www.hrw.org/reports/pdfs/c/crd/colombia94n.pdf

Human Rights Watch. (1996). *Police abuse and killings of street children in India*. Retrieved July 2, 2006, from http://www.hrw.org/reports/1996/India4.htm

Human Rights Watch. (1997a). *Police brutality in urban Brazil.* Retrieved July 2, 2006, from http://www.hrw.org/reports/1997/brazil

Human Rights Watch. (1997b). *Guatemala's forgotten children: Police violence and abuses in detention*. Retrieved July 2, 2006, from http://www.hrw.org/reports/1997/guat1

Human Rights Watch. (2000). Fingers to the bone: United States failure to protect child farm workers. Retrieved May 8, 2008, from http://www.hrw.org/reports/2000/frmwrkr

Human Rights Watch. (2001). *Underage and unprotected: Child labor in Egypt's cotton fields*. Retrieved May 8, 2008, from http://www.hrw.org/reports/2001/egypt/

Human Rights Watch. (2002). *Tainted harvest: Child labor and obstacles to organizing on Ecuador's banana plantations*. Retrieved May 8, 2008, from http://hrw.org/reports/2002/ecuador/

Human Rights Watch. (2003). *Small change: Bonded child labor in India's silk industry*. Retrieved June 18, 2006, from http://www.hrw.org/reports/2003/india

Human Rights Watch. (2006). *What future: Street children in the Democratic Republic of the Congo*. Retrieved April 18, 2006, from http://hrw.org/reports/2006/drc0406

Hunte, P., & Hozyainova, A. (2008). *Factors influencing decisions to use child labour: A case study of poor households in rural Badakhshan*. Retrieved May 6, 2009, from www.areu.org.af/index.php?option=com_docman&task=doc_download&gid=594&Itemid=26

International Labour Organization. (2006a). *Global child labour trends 2000 to 2004*. Retrieved April 16, 2008, from http://www.ilo.org/dyn/declaris/DECLARATIONWEB.DOWNLOAD_BLOB?Var_DocumentID=6233

International Labour Organization. (2006b). *Child labour in gold mining: The problem*. Retrieved April 21, 2008, from http://www.ilo.org/ipec/areas/Miningandquarrying/MoreaboutCLinmining/lang–en/index.htm

International Labour Organization. (2006c). *Child labour in salt mining: The problem*. Retrieved April 21, 2008, from http://www.ilo.org/ipec/areas/Miningandquarrying/MoreaboutCLinmining/lang–en/index.htm

International Labour Organization. (2006d). *Child labour in stone quarrying: The problem*. Retrieved April 21, 2008, from http://www.ilo.org/ipec/areas/Miningandquarrying/MoreaboutCLinmining/lang–en/index.htm

International Labour Organization. (2003). *Investing in every child: An economic study of the costs and benefits of eliminating child labour*. Retrieved April 24, 2008, from http://www.ilo.org/ipecinfo/product/viewProduct.do?productId=175

International Labour Organization. (2004). *Child labour: A textbook for university students*. Retrieved April 24, 2008, from http://www.ilo.org/ipecinfo/product/viewProduct.do?productId=174

International Labour Organization. (n.d.a). *Facts on children working in the street*. Retrieved June 20, 2006, from http://www.ilo.org/public/english/standards/ipec/publ/download/factsheets/fs_streetchildren_0303.pdf

International Labour Organization. (n.d.b). *Facts on child labour in agriculture*. Retrieved from http://www.ilo.org/ipec/areas/Agriculture/lang–en/index.htm

International Programme on the Elimination of Child Labour. (2006). *Global child labour trends 2000 to 2004*. Retrieved March 5, 2008, from http://www.ilo.org/ipecinfo/product/viewProduct.do;?productId=2299

International Programme on the Elimination of Child Labour. (n.d.a). *Facts on children working in the streets*. Retrieved June 20, 2006 from http://www.ilo.org/public/English/standards/ipec/publ/download/factsheets/fs_streetchildren_0303.pdf

International Programme on the Elimination of Child Labour. (n.d.b). *Facts on education's role in combating child labour*. Retrieved June 20, 2006, from http://www.ilo.org/public/English/standards/ipec/publ/download/factsheets/fs_educationforall_0303.pdf

Karabanow, J. (2003). Creating a culture of hope: Lessons from street children agencies in Canada and Guatemala. *International Social Work, 46*(3), 369–386.

Kerfoot, M., Koshyl, V., Roganov, O., Mikhailichenko, K., Gorbova, I., & Pottage, D. (2007). The health and well-being of neglected, abused and exploited children: The Kyiv Street Children Project. *Child Abuse & Neglect, 31*(1), 27–37.

Kombarakaran, F. A. (2004). Street children of Bombay: Their stresses and strategies of coping. *Children and Youth Services Review, 26*, 853–971.

Kudrati, M., Plummer, M. L., & Yousif, N. D. H. (2008). Children of the sug: A study of the daily lives of street children in Khartoum, Sudan, with intervention recommendations. *Child Abuse & Neglect, 32*, 439–448.

LaFraniere, S. (2007, November 15). African crucible: Cast as witches, then cast out. *New York Times*. Retrieved November 15, 2007, from http://www.nytimes.com

Lalor, K. (1999). Street children: A comparative perspective. *Child Abuse & Neglect, 23*(8), 759–770.

Lalor, K. (2000). The victimization of juvenile prostitutes in Ethiopia. *International Social Work, 43*(2), 227–242.

Lam, D., & Cheng, F. (2008). Chinese policy reaction to the problem of street children: An analysis from the perspective of street children. *Children & Youth Services Review, 30*, 575–584.

More children on the streets. (2008, July 24). *IRIN News*. Retrieved July 28, 2008, from http://www.irinnews.org/Report.aspx?ReportId=79423

Mull, L. D., & Kirkhorn, S. R. (2005). Child labor in Ghana cocoa production: Focus on agricultural tasks, ergonomic exposures, and associated injuries and illness. *Public Health Reports, 120*, 649–655.

Murphy, P. (2007, December 3). Most Ivorian child cocoa workers not slaves–govt. *Reuters AlertNet*. Retrieved May 8, 2008, from http://www.alertnet.org/thenews/newsdesk/L03654399.htm

Ngamkham, W. (2006, November 3). Schoolgirls "selling sex for easy money." *Bangkok Post*. Retrieved November 3, 2006, from http://www.bangkokpost.com

Omokhodion, F. O., Omokhodion, S. I., & Odusote, T. O. (2006). Perceptions of child labour among working children in Ibadan, Nigeria. *Child: Care, Heath & Development, 32*(3), 281–286.

Orme, J., & Seipel, M. M. O. (2007). Survival strategies of street children in Ghana: A qualitative study. *International Social Work, 50*(4), 489–499.

Parenti, C. (2008, February 15). *Chocolate's bittersweet economy*. Retrieved May 6, 2008, from the CNN Web site: http://money.cnn.com/2008/01/24/news/international/chocolate_bittersweet.fortune

Parker, D. L. (2002). Street children and child labour around the world. *The Lancet, 360.*, 2067–2071.

Payson Center for International Development and Technology Transfer–Tulane University. (2007). *Oversight of public and private initiatives to eliminate the worst forms of child labor in the cocoa sector in Cote D'Ivoire and Ghana*. Retrieved May 6, 2008, from the Global Exchange Web site: http://www.globalexchange.org/campaigns/fairtrade/cocoa/tulanereport07.pdf

Plummer, M. L., Kudrati, M., & Yousif, N. D. E. H. (2007). Beginning street life: Factors contributing to children working and living on the streets of Khartoum, Sudan. *Children and Youth Services Review*, *29*, 1520–1536.

Polakoff, E. G. (2007). Globalization and child labor: A review of the issues. *Journal of Developing Societies*, *23*(1–2), 259–283.

Poverty at root of commercial sex work. (2008, July 24). *IRIN News*. Retrieved July 28, 2008, from http://www.irinnews.org/Report.aspx?ReportId=79441

Poverty driving Palestinian children onto the streets. (2007, June 12). *IRIN News*. Retrieved June 15, 2007, from http://www.irinnews.org/Report.aspx?ReportId=72677

Profile of a child sex worker. (2008, March 20). *IRIN News*. Retrieved March 24, 2008, from http://www.irinnews.org/Report.aspx?ReportId=77388

Response to "thriving" child sex industry too weak. (2008, March 20). *IRIN News*. Retrieved March 24, 2008, from http://www.irinnews.org/Report.aspx?ReportId=77389

Save the Children. (2003). *Save the Children's position on children and work*. Retrieved June 30, 2006, from http://www.savethechildren.net/alliance/resources/publications.html

Save the Children UK. (2007). *The small hands of slavery*. Retrieved May 2, 2008, from the Child Rights Information Network Web site: http://www.crin.org/docs/ChildSlaveryBrieffinal.pdf

Schwinger, M. (2007). Empowering families as an alternative to foster care for street children in Brazil. *Development in Practice*, *17*(6), 800–806.

Silva, T. L. (2002). Preventing child exploitation in the Philippines. *The Lancet*, *360*, 1507–1508.

Singer, P. W. (2005). *Children at war*. New York: Pantheon Books.

Skills education for working children. (2008, June 17). *IRIN News*. Retrieved June 18, 2008, from http://www.irinnews.org/Report.aspx?ReportId=78778

South Africa draws child migrants. (2007, September 20). *IRIN News*. Retrieved September 25, 2007, from http://www.irinnews.org/Report.aspx?ReportId=74400

Street children sniff glue to beat hunger pangs. (2007, October 22). *IRIN News*. Retrieved October 23, 2007, from http://www.irinnews.org/Report.aspx?ReportId=74899

UNICEF. (2001). *Adult wars, child soldiers*. Retrieved June 28, 2006, from http://www.unicef.org/publications/pub_adultwars_en.pdf

UNICEF. (2006a). *The state of the world's children 2006*. Retrieved April 29, 2008, from http://www.unicef.org/sowc06/profiles/street.php

UNICEF. (2006b). *Commercial sexual exploitation*. Retrieved June 28, 2006, from http://www.unicef.org/protection/files/sexual_exploitation.pdf

UNICEF. (2007). *Progress for children: A world fit for children statistical review, number 6*. Retrieved April 16, 2008, from http://www.unicef.org/publications/files/Progress_for_Children_No_6_revised.pdf

U.S. Department of State. (2005). *The facts about child sex tourism*. Retrieved June 28, 2006, from http://www.state.gov/documents/organization/51459.pdf

Willis, B. M., & Levy, B. S. (2002). Child prostitution: Global health burden, research needs, and interventions. *The Lancet, 359*, 1417–1422.

World Bank. (2007). *Bolsa Familia: Changing the lives of millions in Brazil*. Retrieved December 4, 2007, from http://web.worldbank.org/WBSITE/EXTERNAL/COUNTRIES/LACEXT/BRAZILEXTN/0,contentMDK:21447054~pagePK:141137~piPK:141127~theSitePK:322341,00.html

Zelaya, R., & Larson, D. (2004). Honduras. In C. L. Schmitz, E. K. Traver & D. Larson (Eds.), *Child labor: A global view* (pp 91–99). Westport, CT: Greenwood Press.

Chapter Three

Adepoju, A. (2005). Review of research and data on human trafficking in sub-Saharan Africa. In F. Laczko & E. Gozdziak (Eds.), *Data and research on human trafficking: A global survey* (pp. 75–98). Geneva, Switzerland: International Organization for Migration.

Ali, A. K. M. M. (2005). Treading along a treacherous trail: Research on trafficking in persons in South Asia. In F. Laczko & E. Gozdziak (Eds.), *Data and research on human trafficking: A global survey* (pp. 141–164). Geneva, Switzerland: International Organization for Migration.

Bales, K. (2004). *Disposable people: New slavery in the global economy*. Los Angeles: University of California Press.

Barboza, D. (2008, May 1). China says abusive child labor ring is exposed. *New York Times*. Retrieved May 1, 2008, from http://www.nytimes.com

Barboza, D. (2008, May 10). Chinese factories, flouting labor laws, hire children from poor, distant villages. *New York Times*, pp. A5, A7.

Bernstein, N. (2008, March 12). Foes of sex trade are stung by a champion's fall. *New York Times*, pp. A1, A20.

Bokhari, F. (2008). Falling through the gaps: Safeguarding children trafficked into the UK. *Children & Society, 22*, 201–211.

Boxill, N. A., & Richardson, D. J. (2007). Ending sex trafficking in Atlanta. *Affilia, 22*(2), 138–149.

Buck, T. (2008). "International criminalization and child welfare protection": The Optional Protocol to the Convention on the Rights of the Child. *Children & Society, 22*, 167–178.

Centre for Child Rights. (2006). *A report of fact finding team on children rescued from zari industry, Delhi and restored in their families in various districts in Bihar*. Retrieved March 14, 2008, from the HAQ: Centre for Child Rights Web site: http://www.haqcrc.org/fileadmin/Publication/Fact_Finding_Reports/Fact_Finding_Report_on_Children_Rescued_from__Zari_Industry.pdf

Children found to be making clothes for Gap. (2007, October 29). *San Francisco Chronicle*, p. A14.

Council of Europe. (2008a). *Council of Europe Convention on the Protection of Children against Sexual Exploitation and Sexual Abuse*. Retrieved May 8, 2008, from http://conventions.coe.int/Treaty/Commun/ChercheSig.asp?NT=201&CM=1&DF=4/1/2008&CL=ENG

Council of Europe. (2008b). *Action against trafficking in human beings*. Retrieved May 29, 2008, from http://www.coe.int/t/dg2/trafficking/campaign/default_en.asp

Craig, G., Gaus, A., Wilkinson, M., Skrivankova, K., & McQuade, A. (2007). *Contemporary slavery in the UK: Overview and key issues*. Retrieved April 4, 2008, from the Child Rights Information Network Web site: http://www.crin.org/docs/JRF_uk_slavery.pdf

de Lange, A. (2007). Child labour migration and trafficking in rural Burkina Faso. *International Migration, 45*(2), 147–167.

Department for Children, Schools and Families. (2007). *Safeguarding children who may have been trafficked*. Retrieved March 26, 2008, from the Child Rights Information Network Web site: http://www.crin.org/docs/safeguarding_trafficked_children.pdf

Derks, A., Henke, R., & Ly, V. (2006). *A review of a decade of research on trafficking in persons, Cambodia*. Retrieved February 25, 2008, from the Asia Foundation Web site: http://www.asiafoundation.org/pdf/CB_TIPreview.pdf

De Sas Kropiwnicki, Z. (2007). *Children speak out: Trafficking risk and resilience in Southeast Europe*. Retrieved March 27, 2008, from http://www.savethechildren.net/alliance/where_we_work/europegrp_pubs.html

DeStefano, A. M. (2007). *The war on human trafficking: U.S. policy assessed*. New Brunswick, NJ: Rutgers University Press.

Dottridge, M. (2002). Trafficking in children in West and Central Africa. *Gender and Development, 10*(1), 38–42.

Dottridge, M. (2006). *Action to prevent child trafficking in South Eastern Europe: A preliminary assessment*. Retrieved March 27, 2008, from the UNICEF Web site: http://www.unicef.org/ceecis/Assessment_report_June_06.pdf

Dottridge, M. (2008). *Young people's voices on child trafficking: Experiences from South Eastern Europe*. Retrieved May 13, 2009, from the UNICEF Web Site http://www.unicef-irc.org/publications/pdf/iwp_2008_05.pdf

ECPAT. (2006). *Informe global de monitoreo de las acciones en contra de la explotación sexual comercial de niños, niñas y adolescentes: Colombia.* [Global monitoring report on actions against the commercial sexual exploitation of boys, girls and adolescents]. Retrieved April 4, 2008, from http://www.ecpat.net/eng/A4A_2005/PDF/Americas/Global_Monitoring_Report-COLOMBIA.pdf

ECPAT UK. (2007). Missing out: A study of child trafficking in the North-West, North-East and West Midlands. Retrieved September 4, 2007, from http://www.savethechildren.org.uk/en/docs/missing_out.pdf

Ekberg, G. (2004). The Swedish law that prohibits the purchase of sexual services: Best practices for prevention of prostitution and trafficking in human beings. *Violence Against Women, 10*(10), 1187–1218.

Estes, R., & Weiner, N. A. (2002). *The commercial sexual exploitation of children in the U.S., Canada and Mexico*. Retrieved March 19, 2008, from the University of Pennsylvania, Penn School of Social Policy & Practice Web site: http://www.sp2.upenn.edu/~restes/CSEC.htm

First sentencing for 'sex tourism.' (2005, June 3). *New York Times*, p. A6.

French, H. W. (2007, June 16). Reports of forced labor at brick kilns unsettle China. *New York Times*, p. A3.

French, H. W. (2007, June 21). Fast-growing China says little of child slavery's role. *New York Times*, p. A4.

Gjermeni, E., Van Hook, M. P., Gjipali, S., Xhillari, L., Lungu, F., & Hazizi, A. (2008). Trafficking of children in Albania: Patterns of recruitment and reintegration. *Child Abuse & Neglect, 32*, 941–948.

Goździak, E. M. (2008). *On challenges, dilemmas, and opportunities in studying trafficked children*. Retrieved March 7, 2008, from Oblates of Mary Immaculate Web site: http://www.omiusajpic.org/docs/corporateresponsibility/study_of_child_trafficking_jan08.htm

Group battles child, female exploitation in Tanzania. (2008, January 9). Retrieved March 5, 2008, from the Child Rights Information Network Web site: http://www.crin.org/resources/infoDetail.asp?ID=16149

Grover, S. (2006). Denying the right of trafficked minors to be classed as Convention refugees: The Canadian case example. *The International Journal of Children's Rights, 14*, 235–249.

Haviland, C. (2007). Desperate plight of Nepal 'slave girls.' *BBC News*. Retrieved March 11, 2008, from http://news.bbc.co.uk/go/pr/fr/-/2/hi/south_asia/6405373.stm

Healing the children. (2008, February 26). *IRIN News*. Retrieved February 27, 2008, from http://www.irinnews.org/Report.aspx?ReportId=76948

Hodge, D. R., & Lietz, C. A. (2007). The international sexual trafficking of women and children: A review of the literature. *Affilia, 22*(2), 163–174.

Hughes, W. (2008). Operational perspective on trafficking in women and children in the United Kingdom. In O. N. I. Ebbe & D. K. Das (Eds.), *Global trafficking in women and children* (pp. 195–205). New York: CRC Press.

Human Rights Watch. (2003). *Borderline slavery: Child trafficking in Togo*. Retrieved February 25, 2008, from http://hrw.org/reports/2003/togo0403/togo0403.pdf

Human Rights Watch. (2007). *Bottom of the ladder: Exploitation and abuse of girl domestic workers in Guinea*. Retrieved March 12, 2008, from http://hrw.org/reports/2007/guinea0607/guinea0607text.pdf

International Labour Office. (2004). *Helping hands or shackled lives? Understanding child domestic labor and responses to it*. Retrieved from www.ilo.org/wcmsp5/groups/public/—ed_norm/—ipec/documents/publication/kd00098.pdf

International Labour Office. (2005). *A global alliance against forced labour*. Retrieved on March 19, 2008, from http://www.ilo.org/wcmsp5/groups/public/—ed_norm/—declaration/documents/publication/wcms_081882.pdf

International Labour Organization. (2007). *Child trafficking: The ILO's response through IPEC*. Retrieved March 6, 2008, from http://www.ilo.org/ipecinfo/product/viewProduct.do?productId=6484

International Labour Organization. (2008). *Vienna forum to fight human trafficking*. Retrieved May 18, 2009, from http://www.ilo.org/global/About_the_ILO/Media_and_public_information/Feature_stories/lang–en/WCMS_090351/index.htm

International Labor Organization. (2010). *Convention No. C182*. Retrieved January 29, 2010, from http://www.ilo.org/ilolex/cgi-lex/ratifce.pl?C182

International Organization for Migration. (2003). *Seduction, sale & slavery: Trafficking in women and children for sexual exploitation in Southern Africa*. Retrieved March 26, 2008, from http://www.iom.org.za/site/media/docs/TraffickingReport3rdEd.pdf

Jordan, A. D. (2002). Human rights or wrongs: The struggle for a rights-based response to trafficking in human beings. *Gender and Development, 10*(1), 28–37.

Kelly, L. (2005). "You can find anything you want": A critical reflection on research on trafficking in persons within and into Europe. In F. Laczko & E. Gozdziak (Eds.), *Data and research on human trafficking: A global survey* (pp. 235–265). Geneva, Switzerland: International Organization for Migration.

Khan, N. (2005). *A report into the child trafficking phenomena in Zimbabwe*. Zimbabwe: The Child and Law Foundation.

KIWOHEDO's research into sex trafficking. (2007). Retrieved March 11, 2008, from http://www.kiota.org/news/62

Langberg, L. (2005). A review of recent OAS research on human trafficking in the Latin American and Caribbean region. In F. Laczko & E. Gozdziak (Eds.), *Data and research on human trafficking: A global survey* (pp. 129–139). Geneva, Switzerland: International Organization for Migration.

Lee, J. J. H. (2005). Human trafficking in East Asia: Current trends, data collection, and knowledge gaps. In F. Laczko & E. Gozdziak (Eds.),

Data and research on human trafficking: A global survey (pp. 165–201). Geneva, Switzerland: International Organization for Migration.

Liedtke, M. (2007, November 15). *Gap takes steps to stem child labor*. Retrieved November 15, 2008, from http://news.yahoo.com

Loiselle, M., MacDonnell, M., Duncan, J., & Dougherty, M. E. (2006). *Care for trafficked children*. Retrieved March 26, 2008, from the Bridging Refugee Youth & Children's Services Web site: http://www.brycs.org/documents/guidelines_care_for_trafficked_children.pdf

Lyon, A. (2008, February 27). Poverty fuels trafficking of Yemeni children. *International Herald Tribune*. Retrieved March 7, 2008, from http://www.iht.com/articles/reuters/2008/02/27/Africa/OUKWD-UK-YEMEN-CHILDREN-TRAFFICKING.php

Madigan, N. (2004, November 20). Man, 86, convicted under new law against Americans who go abroad to molest minors. *New York Times*, p. A10.

Monzini, P. (2004). Trafficking in women and girls and the involvement of organized crime in Western and Central Europe. *International Review of Victimology, 11I*, 73–88.

Murray, J. (2008). The role of community policing in trafficking in women and children in Australia. In O. N. I. Ebbe & D. K. Das (Eds.), *Global trafficking in women and children* (pp. 207–218). New York: CRC Press.

Mydans, S. (2008, May 18). Myanmar's children face new risks, aid groups say. *New York Times*, p. A8.

New draft law targets sex traffickers. (2008, March 17). *IRIN News*. Retrieved March 28, 2008, from http://www.irinnews.org/Report.aspx?ReportId=77311

No welcome for sex tourism. (2008, October 7). *IRIN News*. Retrieved October 8, 2008, from http://www.irinnews.org/Report.aspx?ReportId=80798

On the child trafficking route. (2007, November 23). *IRIN News*. Retrieved November 26, 2007, from http://www.irinnews.org/Report.aspx?ReportId=75485

Piper, N. (2005). A problem by a different name? A review of research on trafficking in South-East Asia and Oceania. In F. Laczko & E. Gozdziak (Eds.), *Data and research on human trafficking: A global survey* (pp. 203–233). Geneva, Switzerland: International Organization for Migration.

PLUS. (2007). *Dancing boys: Traditional prostitution of young males in India*. Retrieved March 7, 2008, from the Child Rights Information Network Web site: http://www.crin.org/docs/dancing%20boy.pdf

Ritter, K. (2008, March 16). Others eye Sweden's sex-buyer penalties. *Patriot News*, A10.

Robot jockeys to ride Gulf camels. (2005, April 10). *BBC News*. Retrieved March 4, 2008, from http://news.bbc.co.uk/2/hi/middle_east/4430851.stm

Save the Children. (2004). *Responding to child trafficking: An introductory handbook to child rights-based interventions drawn from Save the Children's experience in Southeast Europe*. Retrieved March 27, 2008, from http://www.childcentre.info/projects/traffickin/dbaFile11301.pdf

Save the Children UK. (2006). *Community-based initiatives against trafficking in children in the Mekong sub-region*. Retrieved February 27, 2008, from http://www.savethechildren.org.uk/en/docs/cross-border_project_terminal-report.pdf

Save the Children UK. (2007). *Commercial sexual exploitation of children in Honduras*. Retrieved March 27, 2008, from http://www.crin.org/docs/Save_UK_Honduras.pdf

Schauer, E. J., & Wheaton, E. M. (2006). Sex trafficking into the United States: A literature review. *Criminal Justice Review, 31*(2), 146–169.

Scratching the surface of child trafficking. (2008, April 2). *IRIN News*. Retrieved April 2, 2008, from http://www.irinnews.org/Report.aspx?ReportId=77575

Sex tourism booming on the Caribbean coast. (2008, November 18). *IRIN News*. Retrieved November 19, 2008, from http://www.irinnews.org/Report.aspx?ReportId=81528

Sex tourists exploiting children. (2008, October 30). *IRIN News*. Retrieved November 3, 2008, from http://www.irinnews.org/Report.aspx?ReportId=81205

Silen, J., & Beddoe, C. (2007). *Rights here, rights now: Recommendations for protecting trafficked children*. Retrieved March 5, 2008, from the ECPAT UK Web site: http://www.ecpat.org.uk/downloads/RightsHere_RightsNow.pdf

Tackling child trafficking. (2008, July 16). *IRIN News*. Retrieved July 28, 2008, from http://www.irinnews.org/Report.aspx?ReportId=79284

Terre des Hommes. (2003). *Child trafficking in Nepal: An assessment of the present situation*. Retrieved February 27, 2008, from the ReliefWeb Web site: http://www.reliefweb.int/library/documents/2003/tdh-nep-2jun.pdf

Thomson, A. (2007, November 18). African human traffic is catalyst for child abuse. *Reuters AlertNet*. Retrieved March 5, 2008, from http://www.alertnet.org/thenews/newsdesk/L18213814.htm

Trafficking of children on the rise. (2008, January 21). *IRIN News*. Retrieved January 21, 2008, from http://www.irinnews.org/Report.aspx?ReportId=76109

Trafficking of girls, abuse worsening. (2008, July 7). *IRIN News*. Retrieved July 8, 2008, from http://www.irinnews.org/Report.aspx?ReportId=79118

UNICEF. (2002). *Child trafficking in west Africa: Policy responses*. Retrieved March 5, 2008, from http://www.unicef-irc.org/publications/pdf/insight7.pdf

UNICEF. (2003). *Trafficking in human beings, especially women and children, in Africa*. Retrieved March 25, 2008, from http://www.unicef-irc.org/publications/pdf/insight9e.pdf

UNICEF. (2004). *Launch of "Code of Conduct" for travel industry to protect children from sex tourism*. Retrieved April 20, 2005, from http://www.unicef.org/media/media_20445.html

UNICEF. (2005). *Trafficking for sexual exploitation and other exploitative purposes*. Retrieved January 2, 2008, from http://www.unicef-irc.org/publications/pdf/trafficking-exploitation-eng.pdf

UNICEF. (2006). *Trafficking*. Retrieved June 5, 2006, from http://www.unicef.org/protection/files/trafficking.pdf

UNICEF. (2008). *Stop child trafficking: One of the main objectives in Guinea Bissau*. Retrieved October 22, 2008, from http://www.unicef.org/media/media_46091.html

UNICEF. (n.d.). *Trafficking and sexual exploitation*. Retrieved June 5, 2006, from http://www.unicef.org/protection/index_exploitation.html

United Arab Emirates says all child jockeys sent home. (2006, June 13). *New York Times*. Retrieved June 18, 2006, from http://www.nytimes.com

United Nations. (2009). *Protocol to prevent, suppress and punish trafficking in persons, especially women and children, supplementing the United Nations Convention against Transnational Organized Crime*. Retrieved January 29, 2010, from http://treaties.un.org/Pages/ViewDetails.aspx?src=IND&mtdsg_no=XVIII-12-a&chapter=18&lang=en

United Nations. (2010). *Optional Protocol to the Convention on the Rights of the Child on the sale of children, child prostitution and child pornography. New York, 25 May 2000*. Retrieved January 29, 2010, from http://treaties.un.org/Pages/ViewDetails.aspx?src=TREATY&mtdsg_no=IV-11-c&chapter=4&lang=en

U.S. Department of State. (2005). *The facts about children trafficked for use as camel jockeys*. Retrieved June 3, 2006, from http://www.state.gov/g/tip/rls/fs/2005/ 50940.htm

van de Glind, H., & Kooijmans, J. (2008). Modern-day child slavery. *Children & Society, 22*, 150–166.

Willis, B. M., & Levy, B. S. (2002). Child prostitution: Global health burden, research needs and interventions. *The Lancet, 359*, 1417–1442.

Wilson, D. G., Walsh, W. F., & Kleuber, S. (2008). Trafficking in human beings: Training and services in American law enforcement agencies. In O. N. I. Ebbe & D. K. Das (Eds.), *Global trafficking in women and children* (pp. 145–162). New York: CRC Press.

Women's Commission for Refugee Women and Children. (2007). *The U.S. response to human trafficking: An unbalanced approach*. Retrieved March 26, 2008, from http://www.womenscommission.org/pdf/ustraff.pdf

World Outreach UK. (n.d.). *Trafficking in women for prostitution: Thailand*. Retrieved May 18, 2009, from http://www.wouk.org/rahab_international/pdf_files/Trafficking%20in%20Women%20for%20Prostitution%20-%20Thailand.pdf

Zimbabwean migration camouflages human traffickers. (2009, May 1). *IRIN News*. Retrieved May 5, 2009, from http://www.irinnews.org/Report.aspx?ReportId=84186

Chapter Four

Amnesty International. (2002). *Sri Lanka: Rape in custody*. Retrieved September 2, 2007, from http://web.amnesty.org/library/index/engasa370012002

Amnesty International. (2005). *Uganda: Child "night commuters."* Retrieved June 24, 2006, from http://web.amnesty.org/library/print/ENGAFR590132005

Amnesty International. (2007, March 14). *Sri Lanka: Armed groups infiltrating refugee camps*. Retrieved May 14, 2007, from http://news.amnesty.org/index/ENGASA370072007

Beah, I. (2007). *A long way gone: Memoirs of a boy soldier*. New York: Sarah Crichton Books.

Blattman, C. (2006). *The consequences of child soldiering.* Retrieved January 31, 2007, from the Households in Conflict Web site: http://www.hicn.org/papers/wp22.pdf

Boothby, N. (2006). When former child soldiers grow up: The keys to reintegration and reconciliation. In N. Boothby, A. Strang, & M. Wessells (Eds.), *A world turned upside down: Social ecological approaches to children in war zones* (pp. 155–178). Bloomfield, CT: Kumarian Press.

Briggs, J. (2005). *Innocents lost: When child soldiers go to war.* New York: Basic Books.

Care International. (2008). *Overcoming lost childhoods: Lessons learned from the rehabilitation and reintegration of former child soldiers in Colombia.* Retrieved April 22, 2008, from http://www.childsoldiers.org/Overcoming_Lost_Childhoods_-_Colombia_-_Y_Care_International_-_January_2008.pdf

Challenges of reintegrating former child soldiers. (2007, December 31). *IRIN News.* Retrieved December 31, 2007, from http://www.irinnews.org/Report.aspx?ReportId=73308

Charbonneau, L. (2009, May 23). U.N.'s Ban visits Sri Lankan displaced persons camp. *Reuters.* Retrieved August 4, 2009, from http://www.alertnet.org/thenews/newsdesk/COL457922.htm

Cheney, K. E. (2005). "Our children have known only war": Children's experiences and the uses of childhood in northern Uganda. *Children's Geographies, 3*(1), 23–45.

Coalition to Stop the Use of Child Soldiers. (2007). *Frontiers: Childhood at the borderline.* Retrieved September 4, 2007, from http://www.child-soldiers.org/2007-23-02-Colombia_frontiers_report-FINAL.pdf

Coalition to Stop the Use of Child Soldiers. (2008a). *Child soldiers: Global report 2008.* Retrieved May 29, 2008, from http://www.childsoldiersglobalreport.org

Coalition to Stop the Use of Child Soldiers. (2008b). *Returning home: Children's perspectives on reintegration.* Retrieved May 6, 2009, from http://www.child-soldiers.org/psycho-social/Returning_Home_-_Children_s_perspectives_on_reintegration_-_A_case_study_of_children_abducted_by_the_Lord_s_Resistance_Army_in_Teso_eastern_Uganda_-_February_2008.pdf

Denov, M. (2007). *Girls in fighting forces: Moving beyond victimhood.* Retrieved February 23, 2008, from http://www.crin.org/docs/CIDA_Beyond_forces.pdf

de Silva, H., Hobbs, C., & Hanks, H. (2001). Conscription of children in armed conflict – A form of child abuse. A study of 19 former child soldiers. *Child Abuse Review, 10,* 125–134.

Derluyn, I., Broekaert, E., Schuyten, G., & De Temmerman, E. (2004). Post-traumatic stress in former Ugandan child soldiers. *The Lancet, 363,* 861–863.

"Empowering Hands" for former child soldiers in Uganda. (2007, July 16). Retrieved December 28, 2007, from http://www.unicef.org/infobycountry/Uganda_40339.html

Fonseka, B. (2001). The protection of child soldiers in international law. *Asia*-Pacific *Journal on Human Rights and the Law, 2*(2), 69–89.

Former child soldiers at risk of HIV. (2008, February 15). *IRIN News.* Retrieved February 15, 2008, from http://www.irinnews.org/Report.aspx?ReportId=76781

Fox, M. (2005). Child soldiers and international law: Patchwork gains and conceptual debates. *Human Rights Review, 7*(1), 27–48.

Green, E. C., & Honwana, A. (1999). Indigenous healing of children in Africa. *IK Notes, 10.* Retrieved May 26, 2007, from http://www.worldbank.org/afr/ik/iknt10.pdf

Hogg, C. L. (2007). *Sri Lanka's leader takes a step backwards on human rights.* Retrieved January 11, 2008, from the Human Rights Watch Web site: http://hrw.org/english/docs/2007/08/15/slanka16690.htm

Høiskar, A. H. (2001). Underage and under fire: An enquiry into the use of child soldiers 1994-8. *Childhood, 8*(3), 340–360.

Honwana, A. (2006). *Child soldiers in Africa.* Philadelphia: University of Pennsylvania Press.

Human Rights Watch. (1997). *Voices of child soldiers.* Retrieved June 3, 2006, from http://hrw.org/campaigns/crp/voices.htm

Human Rights Watch. (2003). *"You'll learn not to cry": Child combatants in Colombia.* Retrieved May 29, 2007, from http://hrw.org/reports/2003/colombia0903.htm

Human Rights Watch. (2004). *Living in fear: Child soldiers and the Tamil Tigers in Sri Lanka.* Retrieved May 27, 2007, from http://hrw.org/reports/2004/srilanka1104

Human Rights Watch. (2005). *Colombia: Armed groups send children to war.* Retrieved June 3, 2006, from http://hrw.org/english/docs/2005/02/22/colomb10202.htm

Human Rights Watch. (2007a). *Sold to be soldiers: The recruitment and use of child soldiers in Burma*. Retrieved January 11, 2008, from http://hrw.org/reports/2007/burma1007

Human Rights Watch. (2007b). *Children in the ranks: The Maoists' use of child soldiers in Nepal*. Retrieved August 31, 2007, from http://hrw.org/reports/2007/nepal0207/nepal0207webwcover.pdf

Human Rights Watch. (2007c). *Complicit in crime: State collusion in abductions and child recruitment by the Karuna group*. Retrieved May 29, 2007, from http://hrw.org/reports/2007/srilanka0107/srilanka0107webwcover.pdf

Human Rights Watch. (2008). *US: Respect rights of child detainees in Iraq*. Retrieved June 4, 2008, from http://hrw.org/english/docs/2008/05/20/iraq18886.htm

Kanagaratnam, P., Raundalen, M., & Asbjørnsen, A. E. (2005). Ideological commitment and posttraumatic stress in former Tamil child soldiers. *Scandinavian Journal of Psychology, 46,* 511–520.

Machel, G. (2001). *The impact of war on children*. New York: Palgrave.

Mapp, S. C. (2008). *Human rights and social justice in a global perspective: An introduction to international social work*. New York: Oxford University Press.

McKay, S. (2006). Girlhoods stolen: The plight of girl soldiers during and after armed conflict. In N. Boothby, A. Strang, & M. Wessells (Eds.), *A world turned upside down: Social ecological approaches to children in war zones* (pp. 89–109). Bloomfield, CT: Kumarian Press.

McKay, S., & Mazurana, D. (2004). *Where are the girls? Girls in fighting forces in northern Uganda, Sierra Leone and Mozambique: Their lives during and after war*. Retrieved August 31, 2007, from the Droits et Démocratie Rights & Democracy Web site: http://www.dd-rd.ca/site/_PDF/publications/women/girls_whereare.pdf

Médecins Sans Frontières. (2006). *Living in fear: Colombia's cycle of violence*. Retrieved October 13, 2006, from http://www.msf.org/source/countries/americas/colombia/2006/report/living_in_fear.pdf

Office of the High Commissioner for Human Rights. (2010). *Optional protocol to the Convention on the Rights of the Child on the involvement of children in armed conflict*. Retrieved January 30, 2010, from http://treaties.un.org/Pages/ViewDetails.aspx?src=TREATY&mtdsg_no=IV-11-b&chapter=4&lang=en

Paris Commitments. (2007). Retrieved May 29, 2007, from http://www.unicef.org/media/files/ParisCommitments120207english.pdf

Paris conference on child soldiers concludes with commitment to stop recruitment of children. (2007, February 6). Retrieved December 28, 2007, from http://www.unicef.org/media/media_38231.html

Park, A. S. J. (2006). "Other inhumane acts": Forced marriage, girl soldiers and the special court for Sierra Leone. *Social & Legal Studies, 15*(3), 315–337.

Poverty drives children to work for armed groups. (2007, May 10). *IRIN News*. Retrieved May 29, 2007, from http://www.irinnews.org/Report.aspx?ReportId=72084

Retraining Tiger cubs. (2009, July 16). *Economist*. Retrieved August 4, 2009, from http://www.economist.com/world/asia/displaystory.cfm?story_id=14052240

Santacruz, M. L., & Arana, R. E. (2002). *Experiences and psychosocial impact of the El Salvador civil war on child soldiers*. Retrieved January 2, 2008, from the Coalition to Stop the Use of Child Soldiers Web site: http://www.child-soldiers.org/psycho-social/Linked_English_Santacruz_Arana_2002.pdf

Save the Children. (2005a). *Forgotten casualties of war: Girls in armed conflict*. Retrieved May 14, 2007, from http://www.savethechildren.co.uk/scuk_cache/scuk/cache/cmsattach/2800_Forgottencasualties33395.pdf

Save the Children. (2005b). *Fighting back: Child and community-led strategies to avoid children's recruitment into armed forces and groups in West Africa*. Retrieved July 16, 2007, from http://www.savethechildren.co.uk/scuk_cache/scuk/cache/cmsattach/3487_Fighting_Back.pdf

Senanayake, S. (2006, November 14). Sri Lanka accused on child soldiers. *New York Times*, p. A8.

Singer, P. W. (2005). *Children at war*. New York: Pantheon Books.

Special Representative of the Secretary-General for Children and Armed Conflict. (2007). *Machel study 10*-year *strategic review: Children and conflict in a changing world*. Retrieved October 22, 2007, from http://www.un.org/children/conflict/_documents/machel/MachelReviewReport.pdf

Summerfield, D. (2000). Conflict and health: War and mental health: A brief overview. *BMJ, 321*, 232–235.

Train the soldiers, protect the children. (2008, October 17). *IRIN News*. Retrieved from http://www.irinnews.org/Report.aspx?ReportId=80974

UNICEF. (2001). *Adult wars, child soldiers*. Retrieved June 28, 2006, from http://www.unicef.org/publications/pub_adultwars_en.pdf

UNICEF. (2006a). *Children associated with armed groups*. Retrieved January 2, 2008, from http://www.unicef.org/protection/files/Armed_Groups.pdf

UNICEF. (2006b). *State of the world's children 2006*. Retrieved June 21, 2006, from http://www.unicef.org/publications/index_30398.html

UNICEF. (2007, April 27). *UNICEF says Karuna faction "not serious" about child releases*. Retrieved May 14, 2007, from http://www.unicef.org/media/media_39477.html

UNICEF. (2007). *Cape Town Principles and best practices*. Retrieved from www.unicef.org/emery/files/Cape_Town_Principles(1).pdf

United Nations Security Council. (2006). *Report of the Secretary-General on children and armed conflict in Sri Lanka*. Retrieved May 27, 2007, from http://www.securitycouncilreport.org/atf/cf/%7B65BFCF9B-6D27-4E9C-8CD3-CF6E4FF96FF9%7D/CAC%20S2006%201006.pdf

United Nations Security Council. (2007). *Report of the Secretary-General on children and armed conflict in Sri Lanka*. Retrieved February 23, 2008, from http://www.un.org/children/conflict/english/index.html

U.S. says it is holding 500 youths in Iraq. (2008, May 20). *New York Times*, p. A15.

Wessells, M. (2006a). *Child soldiers: From violence to protection*. Cambridge, MA: Harvard University Press.

Wessells, M. (2006b). A living wage: The importance of livelihood in reintegrating former child soldiers. In N. Boothby, A. Strang, & M. Wessells (Eds.), *A world turned upside down: Social ecological approaches to children in war zones* (pp. 179–197). Bloomfield, CT: Kumarian Press.

World Vision. (2007). *World Vision's work in Uganda*. Retrieved May 27, 2007, from http://www.worldvision.org/worldvision/wvususfo.nsf/stable/globalissues_uganda_wvwork?Open&lid=Uganda_WVwork&lpos=main

Youth again forced to fight in Congo, aid group says. (2007, December 25). *New York Times*, p. A4.

Chapter Five

Abdelmoneium, A. O. (2005). Challenges facing children in education and labour: Case study of displaced children in Khartoum-Sudan. *The Ahfad Journal, 22*(2), 64–76.

Aqtash, N. A., Seif, A., & Seif, A. (2004). Media coverage of Palestinian children and the Intifada. *Gazette: The International Journal for Communication Studies, 66*(5), 383–409.

Attacks deprive 300,000 students of education. (2008, September 22). *IRIN News*. Retrieved September 23, 2008, from http://www.irinnews.org/Report.aspx?ReportId=80506

Baker, A., & Shalhoub-Kevorkian, N. (1999). Effects of political and military traumas on children: The Palestinian case. *Clinical Psychology Review, 19*(8), 935–950.

Baker-Henningham, H., Meeks-Gardner, J., Chang, S., & Walker, S. (2009). Experiences of violence and deficits in academic achievement among urban primary school children in Jamaica. *Child Abuse & Neglect, 33*, 296–306.

Barbarin, O. A., Richter, L., & de Wet, T. (2001). Exposure to violence, coping resources, and psychological adjustment of South African children. *American Journal of Orthopsychiatry, 71*(1), 16–25.

Barenbaum, J., Ruchkin, V., & Schwab-Stone, M. (2004). The psychosocial aspects of children exposed to war: Practice and policy initiatives. *Journal of Child Psychology and Psychiatry, 45*(1), 41–62.

Bayer, C. P., Klasen, F., & Adam, H. (2007). Association of trauma and PTSD symptoms with openness to reconciliation and feelings of revenge among former Ugandan and Congolese child soldiers. *JAMA: The Journal of the American Medical Association, 298*(5), 555–559.

Bearak, B. (2007, July 10). As war enters classrooms, fear grips Afghans. *New York Times*. Retrieved July 16, 2007, from http://www.nytimes.com

Beaumont, P. (2009, March 13). Obama takes US closer to total ban on cluster bombs. *The Guardian*. Retrieved May 19, 2009, from http://www.guardian.co.uk/world/2009/mar/13/us-national-security-obama-administration/print

Benard, C. (2002). *Veiled courage: Inside the Afghan women's resistance*. New York: Broadway Books.

Bhabha, J., & Finch, N. (2006). *Seeking asylum alone: United Kingdom*. Retrieved March 5, 2008, from the Child Rights Information Network Web site: http://www.crin.org/docs/harvard_seeking_as_uk.pdf

Bhabha, J., & Schmidt, S. (2006). *Seeking asylum alone: United States*. Retrieved March 5, 2008, from Harvard University, Committee on Human Rights Studies Web site: http://www.humanrights.harvard.edu/conference/Seeking_Asylum_Alone_US_Report.pdf

Boothby, N., Strang, A., & Wessells, M. (2006). Introduction. In N. Boothby, A. Strang, & M. Wessells (Eds.), *A world turned upside down: Social ecological approaches to children in war zones* (pp. 1–18). Bloomfield, CT: Kumarian Press.

Boynton-Jarrett, R., Ryan, L. M., Berkman, L. F., & Wright, R. J. (2008). Cumulative violence exposure and self-rated health: Longitudinal study of adolescents in the United States. *Pediatrics, 122*, 961–970.

Burns, J. F. (2008, May 29). Britain joins a draft treaty on cluster munitions. *New York Times*. Retrieved May 29, 2008, from http://www.nytimes.com

Burrows, R., & Keenan, B. (2004). Bearing witness: Supporting parents and children in the transition to peace. *Child Care in Practice, 10*(2), 107–125.

Cabral, C., & Speek-Warnery, V. (2005). *Voices of children: Experiences with violence*. Retrieved February 20, 2008, from http://www.sdnp.org.gy/csoc/childviolreport.pdf

Cambridge, P., & Williams, L. (2004). Approaches to advocacy for refugees and asylum seekers: A developmental case study for a local support and advice service. *Journal of Refugee Studies, 17*(1), 97–113.

Camps offer little refuge. (2008, January 28). *IRIN News*. Retrieved February 8, 2008, from http://www.irinnews.org/Report.aspx?ReportId=76454

Catani, C., Schauer, E., & Neuner, F. (2008). Beyond individual war trauma: Domestic violence against children in Afghanistan and Sri Lanka. *Journal of Marital and Family Therapy, 34*(2), 165–176.

Cemlyn, S., & Briskman, L. (2003). Asylum, children's rights, and social work. *Child and Family Social Work, 8*, 163–178.

Centers for Disease Control. (2007). *Youth violence*. Retrieved February 20, 2008, from http://www.cdc.gov/ncipc/dvp/YV_DataSheet.pdf

Children have been the main victims of war. (2006, November 19). *IRIN News*. Retrieved May 28, 2007, from http://www.irinnews.org/Report.aspx?ReportId=61950

Children in clash-prone north highly traumatized—aid workers. (2008, February 18). *IRIN News*. Retrieved February 18, 2008, from http://www.irinnews.org/Report.aspx?ReportId=76801

Civilians complain about impact of fighting on their lives. (2007, July 3). *IRIN News*. Retrieved July 6, 2007, from http://www.irinnews.org/Report.aspx?ReportId=73061

Cluster bomb ban treaty: 138 nations make progress in Vienna—CMC calls for strongest possible treaty. (2007). Retrieved February 5, 2008, from the International Campaign to Ban Landmines Web site: http://www.icbl.org/news/vienna_cmc

Cluster Munition Coalition. (n.d.). *Frequently asked questions about cluster munitions*. Retrieved February 5, 2008, from http://www.stopclustermunitions.org/dokumenti/dokument.asp?id=72&print=1

Coalition to Stop the Use of Child Soldiers. (2007). *Frontiers: Childhood at the borderline*. Retrieved September 4, 2007, from http://www.child-soldiers.org/2007-23-02-Colombia_frontiers_report-FINAL.pdf

Crock, M. (2006). *Seeking asylum alone: Australia*. Retrieved March 5, 2008, from the Child Rights Information Network Web site: http://www.crin.org/docs/harvard_seeking_as_aust.pdf

Delaney-Black, V., Covington, C., Ondersma, S. J., Nordstrom-Klee, B., Templin, T., Ager, J., Sokol, R. J. (2002). Violence exposure, trauma, and IQ and/or reading deficits among urban children. *Archives of Pediatrics and Adolescent Medicine, 156*, 280–285.

DeVoe, E. R., Dean, K., Traube, D., & McKay, M. M. (2005). The SURVIVE community project: A family-based intervention to reduce the impact of violence exposures in urban youth. *Journal of Aggression, Maltreatment & Trauma, 11*(4), 95–116.

Doctors Without Borders/Médecins Sans Frontières. (2005a). *The crushing burden of rape: Sexual violence in Darfur*. Retrieved September 29, 2006, from http://www.doctorswithoutborders.org/publications/reports/2005/sudan03.pdf

Doctors Without Borders/Médecins Sans Frontières. (2005b). *Mental health*. Retrieved September 29, 2006, from http://www.doctorswithoutborders.org/news/mentalhealth.htm

Dolan, S. (2006). *Psychosocial programmes help Palestinian children cope with crisis*. Retrieved February 16, 2008, from the UNICEF Web site: http://www.unicef.org/infobycountry/index_35191.html

Dunkerly,D., Scourfield, J., Maegusuku-Hewett, T., & Smalley, N. (2005). The experiences of frontline staff working with children seeking asylum. *Social Policy & Administration, 39*(6), 640–652.

Dyregrov, A., Gjestad, R., & Raundalen, M. (2002). Children exposed to warfare: A longitudinal study. *Journal of Traumatic Stress, 15*(1), 59–68.

Elbedour, S., Onwuegbuzie, A. J., Ghannam, J., Whitcome, J. A., & Hein, F. A. (2007). Post-traumatic stress disorder, depression and anxiety among Gaza Strip adolescents in the wake of the second Uprising (Intifada). *Child Abuse & Neglect, 31*, 719–729.

Elbert, T., Schauer, M., Schauer, E., Huschka, B., Hirth, M., & Neuner, F. (2009). Trauma-related impairment in children: A survey in Sri Lankan provinces affected by armed conflict. *Child Abuse & Neglect, 33*, 238–246.

Escalating war takes toll on children. (2008, February 20). *IRIN News*. Retrieved February 20, 2008, from http://www.irinnews.org/Report.aspx?ReportId=76845

Experts see big holes in cluster bomb ban. (2008, May 29). Retrieved May 29, 2008, from http://www.nytimes.com.

Farwell, N. (2004). In war's wake: Contexualizing trauma experiences and psychological well-being among Eritrean youth. *International Journal of Mental Health, 32*(4), 20–50.

Frederico, M. M., Picton, C. J., Muncy, S., Ongsiapco, L. M., Santos, C., & Hernandez, V. (2007). Building community following displacement due to armed conflict: A case study. *International Social Work, 50*(2), 171–184.

Funding shortfall threatens cluster bomb demining. (2009, May 14). *IRIN News*. Retrieved May 15, 2009, from http://www.irinnews.org/Report.aspx?ReportId=84384

Gallagher, T. (2004). After the war comes peace? An examination of the impact of the Northern Ireland conflict on young people. *Journal of Social Issues, 60*(3), 629–642.

Garbarino, J. (2001). An ecological perspective on the effects of violence on children. *Journal of Community Psychology, 29*(1), 361–378.

Grover, S. (2006). Denying the right of trafficked minors to be classed as Convention refugees: The Canadian case example. *The International Journal of Children's Rights, 14*, 235–249.

Hadi, F. A., & Llabre, M. M. (1998). The Gulf Crisis experience of Kuwaiti children: Psychological and cognitive factors. *Journal of Traumatic Stress, 11*(1), 45–56.

Hoge, W. (2005, June 22). U.N. relief official condemns use of rape in African wars. *New York Times*, p. A4.

Hoge, W. (2005, July 30). U.N. charges Sudan ignores rape in Darfur by military and police. *New York Times*. Retrieved September 29, 2006, from http://www.nytimes.com.

Human Rights Watch. (1996). *Shattered lives: Sexual violence during the Rwandan genocide and its aftermath*. Retrieved February 20, 2008, from http://www.hrw.org/reports/1996/Rwanda.htm

Human Rights Watch. (2003). *Climate of fear: Sexual violence and abduction of women and girls in Baghdad*. Retrieved October 1, 2006, from http://hrw.org/reports/2003/iraq0703/iraq0703.pdf

IBON Foundation. (2006). *Uncounted lives: Children, women and conflict in the Philippines: A needs assessment of children and women affected by armed conflict*. Retrieved March 13, 2008, from http://www.internal-displacement.org/8025708F004CE90B/(httpDocuments)/4195F736A00885CCC1257289005B3781/$file/Uncounted+Lives+-Oct+2006.pdf

Inter-Agency Standing Committee (IASC) (2007). *IASC guidelines on mental health and psychosocial support in emergency settings*. Retrieved August 4, 2009, from http://www.who.int/hac/network/interagency/news/iasc_guidelines_mental_health_psychososial_upd2008.pdf

International Campaign to Ban Landmines. (2007). *The treaty*. Retrieved January 30, 2010, from http://www.icbl.org/index.php/icbl/Treaties

International Campaign to Ban Landmines. (2009, May 1). *Cluster bomb campaign accepts peace prize in Ireland*. Retrieved May 19, 2009, from http://www.icbl.org/news/cmc_tipperary_award

International Campaign to Ban Landmines. (2009). *Landmine monitor 2009*. Retrieved from http://lm.icbl.org/index.php/publications/display?url=lm/2009

International Campaign to Ban Landmines. (n.d.). *What does the treaty cover?* Retrieved May 19, 2008, from http://www.icbl.org/tools/faq/treaty/cover

International Rescue Committee. (2008). *Mortality in the Democratic Republic of Congo: An ongoing crisis*. Retrieved February 4, 2008, from http://www.theirc.org/resources/2007/2006-7_congomortalitysurvey.pdf

IRIN. (2007). *The shame of war: Sexual violence against women and girls in conflict*. Retrieved February 7, 2008, from http://allafrica.com/peaceafrica/resources/view/00011095.pdf

Is this the end for cluster munitions? (2008, May 17). *IRIN News*. Retrieved May 22, 2008, from http://www.irinnews.org/Report.aspx?ReportId=78270

Kilpatrick, R., & Leitch, R. (2004). Teachers' and pupils' educational experiences and school-based responses to the conflict in Northern Ireland. *Journal of Social Issues, 60*(3), 563–586.

Kohli, R., & Mather, R. (2003). Promoting psychosocial well-being in unaccompanied asylum seeking young people in the United Kingdom. *Child & Family Social Work, 8*(3), 201–212.

Kostelny, K. (2006). A culture-based, integrative approach. In N. Boothby, A. Strang, & M. Wessells (Eds.), *A world turned upside down: Social ecological approaches to children in war zones* (pp. 19–37). Bloomfield, CT: Kumarian Press.

Kuwert, P., Spitzer, C., Träder, A., Freyberger, H. J., & Ermann, M. (2006). Sixty years later: Post-traumatic stress symptoms and current psychopathology in former German children of World War II. *International Psychogeriatrics, 19*(5), 955–961.

Lacey, M. (2005, March 20). Beyond the bullets and blades. *New York Times, Section 4*, p. 1, 14.

Lamberg, L. (2007). Mental health experts work to help youth recover from war's psychic toll. *JAMA: The Journal of the American Medical Association, 298*(5), 501–503.

Landmine Survivors Network. (2007). *Landmine facts*. Retrieved February 22, 2008, from http://www.landminesurvivors.org/what_landmines.php

Landmines, UXO kill, maim hundreds in 2007. (2008, January 21). *IRIN News*. Retrieved January 21, 2008, from http://www.irinnews.org/Report.aspx?ReportId=76344

Lidén, H., & Rusten, H. (2007). Asylum, participation and the best interests of the child: New lessons from Norway. *Children & Society, 21*, 273–283.

Lustig, S. L., Kia-Keating, M., Knight, W. G., Geltman, P., Ellis, H., Kinzie, J. D., et al. (2004). Review of child and adolescent refugee mental health. *Journal of the American Academy of Child & Adolescent Psychiatry, 43*(1), 24–36.

Lynch, M. (2003). Consequences of children's exposure to community violence. *Clinical Child and Family Psychology Review*, 6(4), 265–274.

Machel, G. (1996). *The impact of armed conflict on children*. Retrieved February 7, 2008, from http://www.un.org/documents/ga/docs/51/plenary/a51-306.htm

Machel, G. (2001). *The impact of war on children*. New York: Palgrave.

Martin, S. (2005). *Must boys be boys? Ending sexual exploitation & abuse in UN peacekeeping missions*. Retrieved October 6, 2006, from http://www.refugeesinternational.org/files/6976_file_FINAL_MustBoys.pdf

McAdam, J. (2006). Seeking asylum under the Convention on the Rights of the Child: A case for complementary protection. *The International Journal of Children's Rights, 14*, 251–274.

McCabe, K. M., Lucchini, S. E., Hough, R. L., Yeh, M., & Hazen, A. (2005). The relation between violence exposure and conduct problems among adolescents: A prospective study. *American Journal of Orthopsychiatry, 75*(4), 575–584.

Mine ban treaty facing its acid test. (2008, April 4). *IRIN News*. Retrieved April 4, 2008, from http://www.irinnews.org/Report.aspx?ReportId=77622

Mitchell, F. (2003). The social services response to unaccompanied children in England. *Child and Family Social Work, 8*, 179–189.

Morgan, J., & Behrendt, A. (2008). *Silent suffering*. Retrieved May 6, 2009, from the Plan International Web site: http://plan-international.org/files/global/publications/protection/silent-suffering-english

Muldoon, O. T. (2004). Children of the Troubles: The impact of political violence in Northern Ireland. *Journal of Social Issues, 60*(3), 453–468.

Murphy, M. (2004). When trauma goes on.... *Child Care in Practice, 10*(2), 185–191.

Nader, K. O., Pynoos, R. S., Fairbanks, L. A., Al-Ajell, M., & Al-Asfou, A. (1993). A preliminary study of PTSD and grief among the children of Kuwait following the Gulf crisis. *British Journal of Clinical Psychology, 32*, 407–416.

New law threatens to imprison refugees. (2008, May 27). *IRIN News*. Retrieved May 28, 2008, from http://www.irinnews.org/Report.aspx?ReportId=78414

Okitikpi, T., & Aymer, C. (2003). Social work with African refugee children and their families. *Child and Family Social Work, 8*, 213–222.

O'Loughlin, T. (2007, December 12). *Education suffers amidst political tension and conflict in Gaza*. Retrieved February 16, 2008, from http://www.unicef.org/infobycountry/oPt_42178.html

One-third of conflict victims were children. (2007, May 15). *IRIN News*. Retrieved May 29, 2007, from http://www.irinnews.org/Report.aspx?ReportId=72151

Ozer, E. J. (2005). The impact of violence on urban adolescents: Longitudinal effects of perceived school connection and family support. *Journal of Adolescent Research, 20*(2), 167–192.

Patchin, J. W., Hueber, B. M., McCluskey, J. D., Varano, S. P., & Bynum, T. S. (2006). Exposure to community violence and childhood delinquency. *Crime & Delinquency, 52*(2), 307–332.

Pearn, J. (2003). Children and war. *Journal of Paediatrics and Child Health, 39*, 166–172.

Plight of internally displaced children not improving. (2007, July 11). *IRIN News*. Retrieved July 16, 2007, from http://www.irinnews.org/Report.aspx?ReportId=73190

Punamäki, R. (2001). From childhood trauma to adult well-being through psychosocial assistance of Chilean families. *Journal of Community Psychology, 29*(3), 281–303.

Risser, G. (2007). *Children caught in conflicts: The impact of armed conflict on children in Southeast Asia*. Retrieved March 13, 2008, from the Child Rights Information Network Web site: http://www.crin.org/docs/CIDA_Caught_Conflict.pdf

Save the Children. (2006). *Rewrite the future: Education for children in conflict-affected countries*. Retrieved February 16, 2008, from http://www.savethechildren.org/publications/reports/RewritetheFuture-PolicyReport.pdf

Save the Children. (2007). *Last in line, last in school*. Retrieved February 4, 2008, from http://www.savethechildren.org/publications/rewrite-the-future/RTF_Last_in_Line_Last_in_School_report_FINAL.pdf

Save the Children. (2008a). *Children of West Darfur are getting an education*. Retrieved March 1, 2008, from http://savethechidlren.org/newsroom/2008/rewrite-the-future-darfur-are.html

Save the Children. (2008b). *No one to turn to: The under-reporting on child sexual exploitation and abuse by aid workers and peacekeepers*. Retrieved May 28, 2008, from http://savethechildren.org.uk/en/docs/No_One_to_Turn_To.pdf

Scarpa, A., Haden, S. C., & Hurley, J. (2006). Community violence victimization and symptoms of posttraumatic stress disorder. *Journal of Interpersonal Violence, 21*(4), 446–469.

Schmidt, S. (2005). *Liberian refugees: Cultural considerations for social service providers*. Retrieved March 13, 2008, from http://www.brycs.org/documents/Liberian_Cultural_Considerations.pdf

Schools without teachers. (2007, September 18). *IRIN News*. Retrieved September 19, 2007, from http://www.irinnews.org/Report.aspx?ReportId=74360

Sexual violence continues in IDP camps. (2008, March 4). *IRIN News*. Retrieved March 5, 2008, from http://www.irinnews.org/Report.aspx?ReportId=77102

Sharar, S. A. (2007). UNICEF extends helping hand to traumatized children of Lebanon. *Washington Report on Middle East Affairs, 26*(1), 28–29.

Shaw, J. A. (2003). Children exposed to war/terrorism. *Clinical Child and Family Psychology Review, 6*(4), 237–246.

Shields, N., Nadasen, K., & Pierce, L. (2008). The effects of community violence on children in Cape Town, South Africa. *Child Abuse & Neglect, 32*, 589–601.

Six million schoolchildren to receive landmine training. (2007, November 15). *IRIN News*. Retrieved November 15, 2007, from http://www.irinnews.org/Report.aspx?ReportId=75310

Sossou, M. (2006). Mental-health services for refugee women and children in Africa. *International Social Work, 49*(1), 9–17.

Special Representative of the Secretary-General for Children and Armed Conflict. (2007). *Machel study 10-year strategic review: Children and conflict in a changing world*. Retrieved October 22, 2007, from http://www.un.org/children/conflict/_documents/machel/MachelReviewReport.pdf

Srour, R. W., & Srour, A. (2006). Communal and familial war-related stress factors: The case of the Palestinian child. *Journal of Loss and Trauma, 11*, 289–309.

Stein, B. D., Jaycox, L. H., Kataoka, S., Rhodes, H. J.,& Vestal, K. D. (2003). Prevalence of child and adolescent exposure to community violence. *Clinical Child and Family Psychology Review, 6*(4), 247–264.

Students return to Gaza schools still suffering from lack of heat and electricity. (2008, February 13). Retrieved February 16, 2008, from http://www.unicef.org/infobycountry/oPt_42766.html

Tavernise, S. (2006, June 26). Amid Iraq chaos, schools fill after long declines. *New York Times*, p. A1, A10.

Thabet, A. A., Abu Tawahina, A., El Sarraj, E., Vostanis, P. (2008). Exposure to war trauma and PTSD among parents and children in the Gaza Strip. *European Child & Adolescent Psychiatry, 17*(4). Retrieved March 13, 2008, from http://www.athabet.org/files/shelling%20paper.pdf

Thabet, A. A. M., Abed, Y., & Vostanis, P. (2002). Emotional problems in Palestinian children living in a war zone: A cross-sectional study. *The Lancet, 359*, 1801–1804.

Thabet, A. A. M., Abed, Y., & Vostanis, P. (2004). Comorbidity of PTSD and depression among refugee children during war conflict. *Journal of Child Psychology and Psychiatry, 45*(3), 533–542.

Thabet, A. A. M., & Vostanis, P. (1999). Post-traumatic stress reactions in children of war. *Journal of Child Psychology and Psychiatry, 40*(3), 385–391.

Thompson, T., & Massat, C. R. (2005). Experiences of violence, post-traumatic stress, academic achievement and behavior problems of urban African-American children. *Child and Adolescent Social Work Journal, 22*(5-6), 367–393.

Too scared to tell—sexual violence in Darfur. (2008, February 12). *IRIN* News. Retrieved February 12, 2008, from http://www.irinnews.org/Report.aspx?ReportId=76705

Unexploded mines block development. (2008, January 31). *IRIN* News. Retrieved February 7, 2008, from http://www.irinnews.org/Report.aspx?ReportId=76510

UN suspends Moroccan troops in Cote D'Ivoire. (2007, July 23). *China Daily*, p. 7.

UNICEF. (1996). *State of the world's children 1996*. Retrieved February 6, 2008, from http://www.unicef.org/sowc96/8mlitary.htm

UNICEF. (2005). *The impact of conflict on women and girls in west and central Africa and the UNICEF response*. Retrieved June 30, 2006, from http://www.unicef.org/publications/index_25262.html

UNICEF (2006). *State of the world's children 2006*. Retrieved June 21, 2006, from http://www.unicef.org/publications/index_30398.html

UNICEF. (2007). *Little respite for Iraq's children in 2007*. Retrieved January 21, 2008, from http://www.unicef.org/media/media_42256.html

UNICEF. (2008). *State of the world's children 2008*. Retrieved February 4, 2008, from http://www.unicef.org/sowc08/docs/sowc08.pdf

UNICEF. (n.d.). *Children in conflict and emergencies*. Retrieved February 4, 2008, from http://www.unicef.org/protection/index_armedconflict.html

United Nations High Commissioner for Refugees. (2004). *Trends in unaccompanied and separated children seeking asylum in industrialized countries, 2001-2003*. Retrieved February 7, 2008, from http://www.unhcr.org/statistics/STATISTICS/40f646444.pdf

United Nations High Commissioner for Refugees. (2007). *2006 UNHCR statistical yearbook*. Retrieved February 7, 2008, from http://www.unhcr.org/cgi-bin/texis/vtx/home/opendoc.pdf?id=478ce0d42&tbl=STATISTICS

United Nations Security Council. (2007). *Children and armed conflict: Report of the Secretary-General*. Retrieved February 23, 2008, from http://www.un.org/children/conflict/english/index.html

U.S. State Department. (2004). *New United States policy on landmines: Reducing humanitarian risk and saving lives of United States soldiers*. Retrieved September 29, 2006, from http://www.state.gov/t/pm/rls/fs/30044.htm

Victora, C. G., Adair, L., Fall, C., Hallal, P. C., Martorell, R., Richter, L., & Sachdev, H. S. (2008). Maternal and child undernutrition: Consequences for adult health and human capital. *The Lancet, 371*, 340–357.

Voisin, D. R. (2003). Victims of community violence and HIV sexual risk behaviors among African American adolescent males. *Journal of HIV/AIDS Prevention & Education for Adolescents & Children, 5*(3/4), 87–110.

Wali, S., Gould, E., & Fitzgerald, P. (2005). The impact of political conflict on women: The case of Afghanistan. In P. S. Rothenberg (Ed.), *Beyond borders: Thinking critically about global issues* (pp. 311–315). New York: Worth Publishers.

Wallen, J., & Rubin, R. H. (1997). The role of the family in mediating the effects of community violence on children. *Aggression and Violent Behavior, 2*(1), 33–41.

Walton, J. R., Nuttall, R. L., & Nuttall, E. V. (1997). The impact of war on the mental health of children: A Salvadoran study. *Child Abuse & Neglect, 21*(8), 737–749.

Women's Commission for Refugee Women and Children. (2006). *Education in Darfur: A critical component of humanitarian response*. Retrieved February 20, 2007, from http://www.womenscommission.org/pdf/dfeducrit.pdf

Women's Commission for Refugee Women and Children. (2007). *Ensuring fair treatment of women, children and families seeking asylum in the United States*. Retrieved February 16, 2008, from http://www.womenscommission.org/pdf/DAPgen.pdf

World Health Organization. (2002). *World report on violence and health*. Retrieved February 13, 2008, from http://www.who.int/violence_injury_prevention/violence/world_report/chapters/en/index.html

Živčić, I. (1993). Emotional reactions of children to war stress in Croatia. *Journal of the American Academy of Child and Adolescent Psychiatry, 32*, 709–713.

Zwi, A. B., Grove, N. J., Kelly, P., Gayer, M., Ramos-Jimenez, P., Sommerfield, J. (2006). Child health in armed conflict: Time to think. *The Lancet, 367,* 1886–1888.

Chapter Six

Adoption Council of Canada. (2006). *Country survey reveals status of international adoption.* Retrieved January 24, 2009, from http://www.adoption.ca/news/050730cystatus.htm

Adoptions by U.S. parents come under jeopardy. (2008, March 11). *The Patriot News,* p. A7.

Akpalu, D. A. (2007). Adoption of children and the contribution of the Osu Children's Home in Ghana. *Children and Youth Services Review, 29,* 1070–1084.

Alekseeva, L. S. (2007). Problems of child abuse in the home. *Russian Education and Society, 49*(5), 6–18.

Alyahri, A., & Goodman, R. (2008). Harsh corporal punishment of Yemeni children: Occurrence, type and association. *Child Abuse & Neglect, 32,* 766–773.

Ansah-Koi, A. (2006). Care of orphans: Fostering interventions for children whose parents die of AIDS in Ghana. *Families in Society, 87*(4), 555–564.

Assavanonda, A. (2005, October 18). Child Protection Act "not being enforced." *Bangkok Post.* Retrieved October 18, 2005, from http://www.bangkokpost.com

Bamba, S., & Haight, W. L. (2007). Helping maltreated children find their Ibasho: Japanese perspectives on supporting the well-being of children in state care. *Children and Youth Services Review, 29,* 405–427.

Belluck, P., & Yardley, J. (2006, December 20). China tightens adoptions rules for foreigners. *New York Times.* Retrieved December 20, 2006, from http://www.nytimes.com

Blair, M. (2005). *Assessing U.S. and international regulation of international adoption through the prism of the Cambodian trafficking scandal.* Retrieved April 5, 2008, from the Association of American Law Schools Web site: http://www.aals.org/am2005/fripapers/400blair.pdf

Bross, D. C., Miyoshi, T. J., Miyoshi, P. K., & Krugman, R. D. (2000). *World perspectives on child abuse: The fourth international resource book.* Denver: University of Colorado.

Browne, K. Hamilton-Giachritsis, C., Johnson, R., & Ostergren, M. (2006). Overuse of institutional care for children in Europe. *BMJ: British Medical Journal, 332*, 485–487.

Brummitt, C. (2008, April 29). Vietnam to stop adoptions in U.S. *The Patriot News*, p. A7.

Cambodian League for the Promotion and Defense of Human Rights. (2002). *Abuses related to the international adoption process in Cambodia*. Retrieved April 5, 2008, from http://www.licadho.org/reports/files/31AdoptBPaper.pdf

Chen, J., Dunne, M. P., & Han, P. (2007). Prevention of child sexual abuse in China: Knowledge, attitudes, and communication practices of children of elementary school children. *Child Abuse & Neglect, 31*, 747–755.

China paying more attention to orphans. (2001, February 5). *The Straits Times*. Retrieved June 28, 2006, from http://www.hartford-hwp.com/archives/55/337/html.

China's orphans not adequately looked after: Official. (2006, January 5). *Agence France Presse*. Retrieved June 28, 2006, from LexisNexis Database.

Corbett, S. (2002, June 16). Where do babies come from? *New York Times*. Retrieved from http://www.nytimes.com

Corbillon, M. (2006). France. In M. Colton & M. Williams (Eds.), *Global perspectives on family foster care* (pp. 19–27). Dorset, United Kingdom: Russell House Publishing.

Corso, P. S., Edwards, V. J., Fang, X., & Mercy, J. A. (2008). Health-related quality of life among adults who experienced maltreatment during childhood. *American Journal of Public Health, 98*(6), 1094–1100.

Costa Rica detains 14, including judge, in adoption-for-cash scheme. (2008, March 4). *International Herald Tribune*. Retrieved March 7, 2008, from http://www.iht.com/bin/printfriendly.php?id=10710458

del Valle, J. F., López, M., Montserrat, C., & Bravo, A. (2009). Twenty years of foster care in Spain: Profiles, patterns and outcomes. *Children and Youth Services Review, 31*, 847–853.

Desai, M. (2009). A comparative study of policy approach for child protection in Goa and Singapore. *Children and Youth Services Review, 31*, 32–39.

Dezeo de Nicora, M. (2006). Argentina. In M. Colton & M. Williams (Eds.), *Global perspectives on family foster care* (pp. 1–9). Dorset, United Kingdom: Russell House Publishing.

Domestic violence against children on the rise. (2007, May 24). *IRIN News*. Retrieved May 29, 2007, from http://www.irinnews.org/PrintReport.aspx?ReportId=72350

Dramatic rise in child abuse cases. (2008, August 29). *IRIN News*. Retrieved September 2, 2008, from http://www.irinnews.org/PrintReport.aspx?ReportId=80059

Draper, B., Pfaff, J. J., Pirkis, J., Snowdon, J. Lautenschlager, N. T., Wilson, I, & Almeida, O. P. (2008). Long-term effects of childhood abuse on the quality of life and health of older people: Results from the depression and early prevention of suicide in general practice project. *Journal of the American Geriatrics Society, 56*(2), 262–271.

EveryChild. (2009). *News Centre*. Retrieved May 13, 2009, from http://www.everychild.org.uk/content/News

Finkelhor, D., & Korbin, J. (1988). Child abuse as an international issue. *Child Abuse & Neglect, 12*(1), 3–23.

Foster families give children hope. (2005, October 30). *Bangkok Post*. Retrieved October 30, 2005, from http://www.bangkokpost.com

Gámez-Guadix, M., & Straus, M. (n.d.). Childhood and adolescent victimization and sexual coercion and assault by male and female university students. Retrieved from http://pubpages.unh.edu/~mas2/CP91-%20ID91%20-%20PR91-%20Victimization%20%20Sexual%20Coercion%20-%20Gamez%20%20S.pdf

Glover, R. (2006). China. In M. Colton & M. Williams (Eds.), *Global perspectives on family foster care* (pp. 11–17). Dorset, United Kingdom: Russell House Publishing.

Goriawalla, N., & Telang, K. (2006). India. In M. Colton, & M. Williams (Eds.), *Global perspective on family foster care* (pp. 29–38). Dorset, United Kingdom: Russell House Publishing.

Gross. J., & Connors, W. (2007). Surge in adoptions raise concerns in Ethiopia. *New York Times*. Retrieved October 10, 2007, from http://www.nytimes.com

Hague Conference on Private International Law. (2010). *Convention of 29 May 1993 on Protection of Children and Co-operation in Respect of Intercountry Adoption*. Retrieved from http://hcch.e-vision.nl/index_en.php?act=conventions.status&cid=69

Hard times raise levels of abuse. (2007, August 1). *IRIN News*. Retrieved August 16, 2007, from http://www.irinnews.org/PrintReport.aspx?ReportId=73530

Helpline allows children to report abuse. (2007, June 13). *IRIN News*. Retrieved June 20, 2007, from http://www.irinnews.org/PrintReport.aspx?ReportId=72710

Hojer, I. (2006). Sweden. In M. Colton & M. Williams (Eds.), *Global perspectives on family foster care* (pp. 69–78). Dorset, United Kingdom: Russell House Publishing.

Hollingsworth, L. D. (2003). International adoption among families in the United States: Considerations of social justice. *Social Work, 48*(2), 209–217.

Human Rights Watch. (1996). *Death by default: A policy of fatal neglect in China's state orphanages*. Retrieved June 27, 2006, from http://www.hrw.org/summaries/s.china961.html.

Human Rights Watch. (1998). *Cruelty and neglect in Russian orphanages*. Retrieved from http://www.hrw.org/reports98/russia2/Russ98d-02.htm

Hunt, K. (1990, June 24). Romania's lost children. *New York Times*. Retrieved from http://www.nytimes.com

Huntenburg, B. (2008). Guatemalan adoptions suspended by overseas crackdown. *Council on Hemispheric Affairs*. Retrieved January 24, 2009, from http://www.coha.org/2008/03/guatemalan-adoptions-suspended-by-overseas-crack-down

International Social Services. (2008, April). *Monthly review*. Retrieved July 1, 2008, from http://www.iss-usa.org/files/IRC/Monthly%20Review%20.doc

Iwasaki, K. (2006). Japan. In M. Colton & M. Williams (Eds.), *Global perspectives on family foster care* (pp. 39–46). Dorset, United Kingdom: Russell House Publishing.

Jacobs, A. (2009, April 5). Chinese hunger for sons fuels boys' abductions. *New York Times*. Retrieved April 6, 2009, from http://www.nytimes.com

Johnson, K. (2002). Politics of international and domestic adoption in China. *Law and Society Review, 36*(2), 379–396.

Johnson, K. A. (2004). *Wanting a daughter, needing a son: Abandonment, adoption and orphanage care in China*. St. Paul, MN: Yeong & Yeong Book Company.

Johnson, K., Banghan, H., & Liyao, W. (1998). Infant abandonment and adoption in China. *Population and Development Review, 24*(3), 469–510.

Junger, M., Feder, L., Clay, J., Côté, S. M., Farrington, D. P., Freiberg, K., et al. (2007). Preventing violence in seven countries: Global convergence in policies. *European Journal on Criminal Policy and Research, 13*, 327–356.

Krug, E. G., Dahlberg, L. L., Mercy, J. A., Zwi, A. B., & Lozano, R. (2002). *World report on violence and health*. Retrieved July 5, 2006, from the World Health Organization

Web site: http://www.who.int/violence_injury_prevention/violence/global_campaign/en/chap3.pdf

Laffan, G. (2005). Romania's policy of emptying its orphanages raises controversy. *British Medical Journal, 331*, 1360.

LaFraniere, S. (2006, December 1). Sex abuse of girls is stubborn scourge in Africa. *New York Times*. Retrieved from http://www.nytimes.com

Lalor, K. (2004a). Child sexual abuse in sub-Saharan Africa: A literature review. *Child Abuse & Neglect, 28*, 439–460.

Lalor, K. (2004b). Child sexual abuse in Tanzania and Kenya. *Child Abuse & Neglect, 28*, 833–844.

Lee, B. J. (2009). Residential care in Korea: Past, present, and future. In M. Courtney & D. Iwaniec (Eds.), *Residential care of children: Comparative perspectives* (pp. 120–138). New York: Oxford University Press.

Lombe, M., & Ochumbo, A. (2008). Sub-Saharan Africa's orphan crisis. *International Social Work, 51*(5), 682–698.

Maluccio, A. N., Canali, C., & Vecchiato, T. (2006). Family foster care: Cross-national research perspectives. *Families in Society, 87*(4), 491–495.

Mantra may help kids escape abuse. (2005, October 18). *Bangkok Post*. Retrieved October 18, 2005, from http://www.bangkokpost.com

Mathews, B. & Bross, D. C. (2008). Mandated reporting is still a policy with reason: Empirical evidence and philosophical grounds. *Child Abuse & Neglect, 32*, 511–516.

Maundeni, T. (2009). Residential care for children in Botswana: The past, the present, and the future. In M. Courtney & D. Iwaniec (Eds.), *Residential care of children: Comparative perspectives* (pp. 88–104). New York: Oxford University Press.

McCrann, D., Lalor, K., & Katabaro, J. K. (2006). Childhood sexual abuse among university students in Tanzania. *Child Abuse & Neglect, 30*, 1343–1351.

McRee, N. (2008). Child abuse in blended households: Reports from runaway and homeless youth. *Child Abuse & Neglect, 32*, 449–453.

Mental Disability Rights International. (2006). *Hidden suffering: Romania's segregation and abuse of infants and children with disabilities*. Retrieved from http://www.mdri.org/projects/romania/romania-May%209%20final.pdf

Mildred, J., & Plummer, C. A. (2009). Responding to child sexual abuse in the United States and Kenya: Child protection and children's rights. *Children and Youth Services Review, 31*, 601–608.

Ministry of Children and Family Development. (n.d.). *Adoption—Cambodia alert!* Retrieved January 18, 2009, from http://www.mcf.gov.bc.ca/adoption/alerts_fact_sheets/cambodia.htm

Move to keep orphans out of institutions. (2008, July 29). *IRIN News*. Retrieved July 30, 2008, from http://www.irinnews.org/PrintReport.aspx?ReportId=79488

Mydans, S. (2001, November 5). U.S. interrupts Cambodian adoptions. *New York Times*. Retrieved June 24, 2006, from http://www.nytimes.com

National Conference of State Legislatures. (2006). *State child welfare legislation 2006*. Retrieved April 16, 2008, from http://www.ncsl.org/print/cyf/childwelfarelaws06.pdf

Nelson, C. A., Zeanah, C. H., Fox, N. A., Marshall, P. J., Smyke, A. T., & Guthrie, D. (2007). Cognitive recovery in socially deprived young children: The Bucharest early intervention project. *Science, 318*(5858), 1937–1940.

New Guatemala adoption law approved. (2007, December 11). *New York Times*. Retrieved December 13, 2007, from http://www.nytimes.com

Pereda, N., Guilera, G., Forns, M., & Gómez-Benito, J. (2009). The international epidemiology of child sexual abuse: A continuation of Finkelhor (1994). *Child Abuse & Neglect, 33*, 331–342.

Pew Charitable Trusts. (2007). *Time for reform: Investing in children: Keeping children safe at home*. Retrieved March 5, 2008, from http://kidsarewaiting.org/tools/reports/files/0011.pdf

Phanayanggoor, P. (2005). Calls for more policewomen to handle cases. *Bangkok Post*. Retrieved November 8, 2005, from http://www.bangkokpost.com

Pierce, L., & Bozalek, V. (2004). Child abuse in South Africa: An examination of how child abuse and neglect are defined. *Child Abuse & Neglect, 28*(8), 817–832.

Pinheiro, P. S. (2006). *World report on violence against children*. Geneva, Switzerland: United Nations.

Platt, K. (2000). Children of quake thrive in China's improved orphanage conditions. *Christian Science Monitor, 92*(67), 8.

Pollack, D. (2007). Should social workers be mandated reporters of child maltreatment? An international legal perspective. *International Social Work, 50*(5), 699–705.

Protecting children from orphan-dealers. (2009, May 27). *IRIN News*. Retrieved June 1, 2009, from http://www.irinnews.org/PrintReport.aspx?ReportId=84582

Reza, A., Breiding, M. J., Gulaid, J., Mercy, J. A., Blanton, C., Mthethwa, Z. et al. (2009). Sexual violence and its health consequences for female children in Swaziland: A cluster survey study. *The Lancet, 373*. Retrieved May 13, 2009, from http://www.thelancet.com/journals/lancet/article/PIIS0140-6736(09)60247-6/fulltext?_eventId=login

Roby, J. L., & Shaw, S. A. (2008). Evaluation of a community-based orphan care program in Uganda. *Families in Society, 89*(1), 119–128.

Romania: Closing the door on foreign adoptions. (2006, April 19). *New York Times*, p. A6.

Rosenthal, E. (2005, June 23). Law backfires, stranding orphans in Romania. *The New York Times*, pA1, A6.

Santos, R. (2005). *Voices from the field. Research on home visiting: Implications for early childhood development (ECD) Policy and practice across* Canada. Retrieved January 19, 2009, from the Encyclopedia of Early Childhood Development Web site: http://www.child-encyclopedia.com/pages/PDF/SantosANGps.pdf

Sellick, C. (2006). United Kingdom. In M. Colton & M. Williams (Eds.), *Global perspectives on family foster care* (pp. 79–85). Dorset, United Kingdom: Russell House Publishing.

September, R. L. (2006). The progress of child protection in South Africa. *International Journal of Social Welfare, 15*(Suppl. 1), S65–S72.

Shang, X. (2002). Looking for a better way to care for children: Cooperation between the state and civil society in China. *Social Service Review, 76*, 203–228.

Shulruf, B., O'Loughlin, C., & Tolley, H. (2009). Parenting education and support policies and their consequences in selected OECD countries. *Children and Youth Services Review, 31*, 526–532.

Slonim-Nevo, V., & Mukuka, L. (2007). Child abuse and AIDS-related knowledge, attitudes and behavior among adolescents in Zambia. *Child Abuse & Neglect, 31*, 143–159.

Small, M. F. (1998). *Our babies, ourselves: How biology and culture shape the way we parent*. New York: Anchor Books.

Smith, D. J. (2008). *Love, fear and discipline: Everyday violence toward children in Afghan families*. Retrieved January 10, 2009, from http://www.areu.org.af/index.php?option=com_docman&Itemid=26&task=doc_download&gid=563

So-Kung Tang, C. (1998). The rate of physical child abuse in Chinese families: A community survey in Hong Kong. *Child Abuse & Neglect, 22*(5), 381–391.

Speizer, I. S., Goodwin, M., Whittle, L., Clyde, M., & Rogers, J. (2008). Dimensions of child sexual abuse before age 15 in three Central American countries: Honduras, El Salvador, and Guatemala. *Child Abuse & Neglect, 32*, 455–462.

Stelmaszuk, Z. W. (2006). Poland. In M. Colton & M. Williams (Eds.), *Global perspectives on family foster care* (pp. 47–58). Dorset, United Kingdom: Russell House Publishing.

Stephenson, R., Sheikhattari, P., Assasi, N., Eftekhar, H., Zamani, Q., Maleki, B., & Kiabayan, H. (2006). Child maltreatment among school children in the Kurdistan Province, Iraq. *Child Abuse & Neglect, 30*, 231–245.

Stop sale of children, rights watchdog says. (2008, February 3). *IRIN News*. Retrieved February 8, 2008, from http://www.irinnews.org/PrintReport.aspx?ReportId=76544

Thousands of AIDS orphans destitute in China. (2005, January 14). *National Catholic Reporter*. Retrieved June 30, 2006, from EbscoHost database.

Trying to understand the unspeakable crime. (2008, March 12). *IRIN News*. Retrieved March 13, 2008, from http://www.irinnews.org/PrintReport.aspx?ReportId=77255

UNICEF. (1999). *Innocenti digest: Intercountry adoption*. Retrieved January 30, 2009, from http://www.unicef-irc.org/publications/pdf/digest4e.pdf

UNICEF. (2005). *Violence against children in Europe: A preliminary review of the research*. Retrieved January 9, 2009, from http://www.unicef-irc.org/publications/pdf/violence_against.pdf

UNICEF. (2006). *Africa's orphaned and vulnerable generations: Children affected by AIDS*. Retrieved January 24, 2009, from http://www.unicef.org/publications/files/Africas_Orphaned_Generation_Executive_Summary_Eng.pdf

UNICEF. (2007a). *Progress for children report: A world fit for children statistical review*. Retrieved January 9, 2009, from http://www.unicef.org/progressforchildren/2007n6/files/Progress_for_Children_-_No._6.pdf

UNICEF. (2007b). *Data and analysis on the lives of children in CEE/CIS and Baltic states*. Retrieved May 13, 2009, from http://www.unicef-irc.org/publications/pdf/tm2007_features.pdf

UNICEF. (2009a). *State of the world's children 2009*. Retrieved April 19, 2009, from http://www.unicef.org/sowc09/docs/SOWC09-FullReport-EN.pdf

UNICEF. (2009b). *Child trafficking*. Retrieved from http://www.unicef.org/protection/index_exploitation.html

UNICEF & Terre des Hommes. (2008). *Adopting the rights of the child: A study on intercountry adoption and its influence on child protection in Nepal*. Retrieved January 30, 2009, from the Childtrafficking.com Web site: http://www.childtrafficking.com/Docs/adopting_rights_child_unicef29_08.pdf

U.S. Department of State. (2007). *U.S. embassy in Guatemala adds second DNA test to adoption procedure.* Retrieved April 5, 2008, from http://travel.state.gov/family/adoption/intercountry/intercountry_3751.html

U.S. Department of State. (2008). *Guatemala country information*. Retrieved January 9, 2009, from http://adoption.state.gov/country/guatemala.html

U.S. Department of State. (n.d.). *Total adoptions to the United States*. Retrieved January 31, 2010, from http://adoption.state.gov/news/total_chart.html

van Delft, W. (2006). South Africa. In M. Colton & M. Williams (Eds.), *Global perspectives on family foster care* (pp. 59–68). Dorset, United Kingdom: Russell House Publishing.

War, poverty and ignorance fuel sexual abuse of children. (2007, June 6). *IRIN News*. Retrieved June 15, 2007, from http://www.irinnews.org/PrintReport.aspx?ReportId=72578

Wehrmann, K., Unrau, Y., & Martin, J. (2006). United States. In M. Colton & M. Williams (Eds.), *Global perspectives on family foster care* (pp. 87–97). Dorset, United Kingdom: Russell House Publishing.

WHO calls child abuse major public health problem. (1999, July/August). *Public Health Reports, 114*, 296.

Williamson, D. (2002). *Child abuse found to be a global problem, WHO review reveals*. Retrieved July 2, 2006, from http://www.unc.edu/news/archives/oct02/runyan100302.htm

Wilson, S. L., Weaver, T. L., Cradock, M. M., & Kuebli, J. E. (2008). A preliminary study of the cognitive and motor skills acquisition of young international adoptees. *Children and Youth Services Review, 30*, 585–596.

World Health Organization. (n.d.). *WHO scales up child maltreatment prevention activities*. Retrieved September 4, 2007,

from http://www.who.int/violence_injury_prevention/violence/activities/child_maltreatment/en
Yen, C., Yang, M., Yang., M., Su, Y., Wang, M., & Lan, C. (2008). Childhood physical and sexual abuse: Prevalence and correlates among adolescents living in rural Taiwan. *Child Abuse & Neglect, 32*, 429–438.

Chapter Seven

A call for action on free, compulsory and quality education for all Latin American youth. (2008, October 28). Retrieved November 3, 2008, from http://www.unicef.org/media/media_46186.html
Abdelmoneium, A. O. (2005). Challenges facing children in education and labour: Case study of displaced children in Khartoum-Sudan. *The Ahfad Journal, 22*(2), 64–76.
Almost half of all Afghan children not in school. (2006, November 27). *IRIN News*. Retrieved May 14, 2007, from http://www.irinnews.org/Report.aspx?ReportId=61819
Amnesty International. (2007). *Still separate, still unequal.* Retrieved May 13, 2009, from http://www.amnesty.org/en/library/asset/EUR72/001/2007/en/2bf73037-d374-11dd-a329-2f46302a8cc6/eur720012007en.pdf
Attacks deprive 300,000 students of education. (2008, September 22). *IRIN News*. Retrieved September 23, 2008, from http://www.irinnews.org/Report.aspx?ReportId=80506
Avenstrup, R. (2006). Reducing poverty through free primary education: Learning from the experiences of Kenya, Lesotho, Malawi, and Uganda. In L. Fox & R. Liebenthal (Eds.), *Attacking Africa's poverty: Experiences from the ground* (pp. 227–255). Washington, DC: The World Bank.
Balatchandirane, G. (2003). Gender discrimination in education and economic development: A study of South Korea, China and India. *International Studies, 40*(4), 349–378.
Barton, P. E. (2005). *One-third of a nation: Rising dropout rates and declining opportunities*. Retrieved September 28, 2008, from the Educational Testing Service Web site: http://www.ets.org/Media/onethird.pdf
Bearak, B. (2007, July 10). As war enters classrooms, fear grips Afghans. *New York Times*. Retrieved July 16, 2007, from http://www.nytimes.com

Bossy, S. (2000). Academic pressure and impact on Japanese students. *McGill Journal of Education*, 35. Retrieved October 27, 2008, from http://findarticles.com/p/articles/mi_qa3965/is_200001/ai_n8894769

Burnett, N. (2008). Education for all: An imperative for reducing poverty. *Annals of the New York Academy of Sciences, 1136*, 269–275.

Children and teachers finding it hard to concentrate. (2008, July 3). *IRIN News*. Retrieved July 8, 2008, from http://www.irinnews.org/Report.aspx?ReportId=79082

Children miss out on school because of corruption. (2008, December 5). *IRIN News*. Retrieved December 5, 2008, from http://www.irinnews.org/Report.aspx?ReportId=81825

Chinyama, V. (n.d.). *Kenya's abolition of school fees offers lessons for rest of Africa*. Retrieved April 26, 2006, from http://www.unicef.org/infobycountry/kenya_33391.html

Chomitz, V. R., Slining, M. M., McGowan, R. J., Mitchell, S. E., Dawson, G. F., & Hacker, K. A. (2009). Is there a relationship between physical fitness and academic achievement? Positive results from public school children in the Northeastern United States. *Journal of School Health*, *79*(1), 30–37.

Civilians complain about impact of fighting on their lives. (2007, July 3). *IRIN News*. Retrieved July 6, 2007, from http://www.irinnews.org/Report.aspx?ReportId=73061

Classroom crush. (2008, February 25). *IRIN News*. Retrieved February 27, 2008, from http://www.irinnews.org/Report.aspx?ReportId=76931

Classroom shortages threaten primary education targets. (2008, January 15). *IRIN News*. Retrieved January 16, 2008, from http://www.irinnews.org/Report.aspx?ReportId=76243

Classrooms in Syria crowded with Iraqi children whose families have fled conflict. (2008, September 28). Retrieved October 7, 2008, from http://www.unicef.org/infobycountry/syra_45751.html

Corporal punishment key reason for school dropouts. (2008, May 18). *IRIN News*. Retrieved May 22, 2008, from http://www.irinnews.org/Report.aspx?ReportId=78275

Country needs free universal education. (2008, October 30). *IRIN News*. Retrieved November 3, 2008, from http://www.irinnews.org/Report.aspx?ReportId=81209

Drought forcing children to quit school. (2008, November 12). *IRIN News*. Retrieved November 13, 2008, from http://www.irinnews.org/Report.aspx?ReportId=81429

Drought, poverty lead children to abandon school. (2008, December 2). *IRIN News*. Retrieved December 3, 2008, from http://www.irinnews.org/Report.aspx?ReportId=81769

Duflo, E. (2009, May 10). What do you give the developing world for Mother's Day: An education. *New York Times*, p. wk10.

Dugger, C. W. (2006, April 11). Britain: $15 billion for third world schools. *New York Times*, p. A12.

Dyer, C. (2007). Working children and educational inclusion in Yemen. *International Journal of Educational Development, 27*, 512–524.

Education tops pastoralists' concerns. (2007, July 10). *IRIN News*. Retrieved July 16, 2007, from http://www.irinnews.org/Report.aspx?ReportId=73156

Education Trust. (2008). *Counting on graduation*. Retrieved October 24, 2008, from http://www2.edtrust.org/NR/rdonlyres/6CA84103-BB12-4754-8675-17B18A8582AC/0/CountingonGraduation1008.pdf

Fram, M. S., Miller-Cribbs, J. E., & Van Horn, L. (2007). Poverty, race, and the contexts of achievement: Examining educational experiences of children in the U.S. South. *Social Work, 52*(4), 309–319.

Free school far from it, with many hidden costs, forum told. (2006, July 26). *Bangkok Post*. Retrieved July 26, 2006, from http://www.bangkokpost.com

Groves, L. (2004). Implementing ILO Child Labour Convention 182: Lessons from Honduras. *Development in Practice, 14*(1/2), 171–182.

Guimbert, S., Miwa, K., & Nguyen, D. T. (2008). Back to school in Afghanistan: Determinants of school enrollment. *International Journal of Educational Development, 28*, 419–434.

Gutema, P., & Bekele, M. (2004). Does schooling promote economic growth? *African Development Review, 16*(2), 385–397.

Hess, F. M. (2008). *Still at risk: What students don't know, even now*. Retrieved March 5, 2008, from the Common Core Web site: http://www.commoncore.org/_docs/CCreport_stillatrisk.pdf

Hu, W. (2008, November 12). As Asians excel at L.I. school, district tries to lure parents. *New York Times*. Retrieved November 12, 2008, from http://www.nytimes.com

Human Rights Watch. (2007). *Thailand: Education in the south engulfed in fear*. Retrieved July 16, 2007, from http://hrw.org/English/docs/2007/06/14/thaila16189_txt.htm

Human Rights Watch. (2008). *Denied status, denied education. Children of North Korean women in China*. Retrieved October 26, 2008, from http://hrw.org/reports/2008/northkorea0408/northkorea00408web.pdf

IDP children out of school, obliged to work. (2009, May 11). *IRIN News*. Retrieved May 12, 2009, from http://www.irinnews.org/Report.aspx?ReportId=84324

I'm beginning to see the value of education. (2007, September 28). *IRIN News*. Retrieved October 2, 2007, from http://www.irinnews.org/Report.aspx?ReportId=74535

IMF policies may impact on education quality. (2007, May 30). *IRIN News*. Retrieved May 30, 2007, from http://www.irinnews.org/Report.aspx?ReportId=72457

Improved sanitation keeps more girls in school in Malawi. (2008) . Retrieved October 7, 2008, from http://www.ungei.org/infobycountry/Malawi_1916.html

Isaacs, J. B., Sawhill, I. V., & Haskins, R. (2008). *Getting ahead or losing ground: Economic mobility in America*. Retrieved September 28, 2008, from http://www.brookings.edu/reports/2008/~/media/Files/rc/reports/2008/02_economic_mobility_sawhill/02_economic_mobility_sawhill.pdf

Karwal, R. (2008, September 26). *UN event features $4.5 billion pledge to support 'Education for All'*. Retrieved October 7, 2008, from http://www.unicef.org/girlseducation/index_45763.html

Kirk, J., & Winthrop, R. (2006). Home-based schooling: Access to quality education for Afghan girls. *Journal of Education for International Development*, 2(2). Retrieved October 7, 2008, from the Education Quality Improvement Program Web site: http://www.equip123.net/JEID/articles/3/HomebasedSchoolingforAfghanGirls.pdf

LaFraniere, S. (2005, December 23). Another school barrier for African girls: No toilet. *New York Times*. Retrieved June 26, 2006, from http://www.nytimes.com

Making schools work. (2009, May 4). *IRIN News*. Retrieved May 5, 2009, from http://www.irinnews.org/Report.aspx?ReportId=84226

McBrien, J. L. (2005). Educational needs and barriers for refugee students in the United States: A review of the literature. *Review of Educational Research*, 75(3), 329–364.

Medina, J. (2008, October 21). Report cites chronic absenteeism in city schools. *New York Times*. Retrieved October 21, 2008, from http://www.nytimes.com

Mpokosa, C., & Ndaruhutse, S. (2008). *Managing teachers: The centrality of teacher management to quality education.* Retrieved October 7, 2008, from http://www.vso.org.uk/Images/MT_(v4)_tcm8_17563.pdf

Nafula, N. N. (2001, July). *Achieving sustainable universal primary education through debt relief: The case of Kenya.* Paper presented at the World Institute for Development Economics Research, Helsinki, Finland. Retrieved February 3, 2005, from http://www.wider.unu.edu/conference/conference-2001-2/poster%20papers/Nafula.pdf

94 percent of schools fail to open., 2009 94 percent of schools fail to open. (2009, February 10). *IRIN News.* Retrieved February 11, 2009, from http://www.irinnews.org/Report.aspx?ReportId=82850

Nishimura, M., Yamano, T., & Sasaoka, Y. (2008). Impacts of the universal primary education policy on educational attainment and private costs in rural Uganda. *International Journal of Educational Development, 28,* 161–175.

Nybo, T. (2006, May 30). *Falling behind: In Kenya, drought threatens children's education and dims their hopes.* Retrieved June 5, 2006, from http://www.unicef.org/infobycountry/Kenya_34208.html

Parrot, A., & Cummings, N. (2006). *Forsaken females: The global brutalization of women.* Lanham, MD: Rowman & Littlefield.

Pellegrini, A. D., & Bohn, C. M. (2005). The role of recess in children's cognitive performance and school adjustment. *Educational Researcher, 34,* 13–19.

Penny, A., Ward, M., Read, T., & Bines, H. (2008). Education sector reform: The Ugandan experience. *International Journal of Educational Development, 28,* 268–285.

Plan International. (2008). *Learn without fear. The global campaign to end violence in schools.* Retrieved October 13, 2008, from the Learn Without Fear Web site: http://www.learnwithoutfear.org/downloads/Learn_Without_Fear_English.pdf

Poor teaching quality slows education progress. (2008, November 4). *IRIN News.* Retrieved November 5, 2008, from http://www.irinnews.org/Report.aspx?ReportId=81285

Primary-school dropout rate rises to 47 percent. (2007, November 4). *IRIN News.* Retrieved November 7, 2007, from http://www.irinnews.org/Report.aspx?ReportId=75139

Progress on MDG education goal creates new problems. (2009, January 30). *IRIN News.* Retrieved February 2, 2009, from http://www.irinnews.org/Report.aspx?ReportId=82676

Reagan, T. (1996). *Non-western educational traditions: Alternative approaches to educational thought and practice*. Mahwah, NJ: Erlbaum.

Report blasts primary school education. (2009, February 11). *IRIN News*. Retrieved February 11, 2009, from http://www.irinnews.org/Report.aspx?ReportId=82868

Rowe, K. (2003, October). *The importance of teacher quality as a key determinant of students' experiences and outcomes of schooling.* Keynote address presented at the ACER Research Conference, Melbourne, Australia. Retrieved November 7, 2008, from http://www.acer.edu.au/documents/Rowe_ACER_Research_Conf_2003_Paper.pdf

Save the Children Denmark, Ministry of Education, & Ministry of Women's Affairs. (2008). *A study on violence against girls in primary schools and its impacts on girls' education in Ethiopia*. Retrieved October 7, 2008, from the UNGEI Web site: http://www.ungei.org/resources/files/Study_on_Violence_Against_schoolgfils_final.pdf

School year reopens with free primary schools. (2008, October 6). *IRIN News*. Retrieved October 7, 2008, from http://www.irinnews.org/Report.aspx?ReportId=80776

Schools close as hordes of teachers resign. (2007, October 8). *IRIN News*. Retrieved October 9, 2007, from http://www.irinnews.org/Report.aspx?ReportId=74698

Schools turn children away. (2008, September 25). *IRIN News*. Retrieved October 8, 2008, from http://www.irinnews.org/Report.aspx?ReportId=80596

Schwartzman, S. (2003). *The challenges of education in Brazil.* Retrieved November 21, 2008, from http://www.schwartzman.org.br/simon/pdf/challenges.pdf

Schwartzman, S. (2004). Equity, quality and relevance in higher education in Brazil. *Anais da Academia Brasileira de Ciências*, 76(1). Retrieved November 7, 2008, from http://www.scielo.br/scielo.php?pid=S0001-37652004000100015&script=sci_arttext&tlng=en

Sengupta, S. (2008, February 6). India's school shortage means glut of parental stress. *New York Times*, p. A3.

Shepherd, J. (2009, March 10). Don't look back. *The Guardian*. Retrieved March 12, 2009, from http://www.guardian.co.uk/education/2009/mar/10/schools-worldwide-tanzania

Teese, R. (2004). Early school leavers and VET. In K. Bowman (Ed.), *Equity in vocational education and training* (p.184–193). Retrieved

November 7, 2008, from the National Center for Vocational Education Research Web site: http://www.ncver.edu.au/research/proj/nr2201.pdf

Tett, L. (2004). Parents and school communities in Japan and Scotland: Contrasts in policy and practice in primary schools. *International Journal of Lifelong Education, 23*(3), 259–273.

Training the teachers keeps children in school. (2008, July 7). *IRIN News*. Retrieved July 8, 2008, from http://www.irinnews.org/Report.aspx?ReportId=79117

Ueyama, M. (2007). *Mortality, mobility and schooling outcomes among orphans: Evidence from Malawi*. Retrieved January 22, 2009, from http://www.ifpri.org/pubs/dp/IFPRIDP00710.pdf

UNESCO. (2000). *The Dakar framework for action*. Retrieved September 27, 2008, from http://unesdoc.unesco.org/images/0012/001211/121147e.pdf

UNESCO. (2007). *Education for All by 2015: Will we make it?* Retrieved September 27, 2008, from http://unesdoc.unesco.org/images/0015/001547/154743e.pdf

United Nations Girls' Education Initiative [UNGEI]. (2006). *UNGEI fact sheet*. Retrieved from http://www.ungei.org/resources/files/ungei_fact_sheet.pdf

UNICEF. (1999). *The state of the world's children 1999: Education*. Retrieved from http://www.unicef.org/publications/files/pub_sowc99_en.pdf

UNICEF. (2008). *Annual report 2007*. Retrieved November 8, 2008, from http://www.unicef.org/publications/files/Annual_Report_2007.pdf

UNICEF. (n.d.a). *Fact sheet*. Retrieved June 5, 2006, from http://www.unicef.org/voy/explore/education/explore_166.html

United Nations. (2005). *Creating an enabling environment for girls' and women's participation in education*. Retrieved July 24, 2006, from http://www.un.org/womenwatch/daw/egm/enabling-environment2005/docs/EGM-WPD-EE-2005-EP.8%20%20A.pdf

United Nations Development Programme. (2003). *Human development report 2003*. New York: Oxford University Press.

United Nations Development Programme. (2009). *The Millennium Development Goals report 2009*. Retrieved from http://mdgs.un.org/unsd/mdg/Resources/Static/Products/Progress2009/MDG_Report_2009_En.pdf

United Nations Development Programme. (n.d.). *About the MDGs: Basics*. Retrieved August 12, 2006, from http://www.undp.org/mdg/basics.shtml.

United Nations Millennium Goals Indicators (2009). *Millennium Development Goals: 2009 progress chart*. Retrieved from http://mdgs.un.org/unsd/mdg/Resources/Static/Products/Progress2009/MDG_Report_2009_Progress_Chart_En.pdf

United Nations Population Fund [UNFPA]. (2005). *State of the world population 2005*. Retrieved from http://www.unfpa.org/upload/lib_pub_file/493_filename_en_swp05.pdf

United Nations Security Council. (2007). *Children and armed conflict: Report of the Secretary-General*. Retrieved February 23, 2008, from http://www.un.org/children/conflict/english/index.html

USAID. (2008). *Education from a gender equality perspective*. Retrieved October 16, 2008, from the UNGEI Web site: http://www.ungei.org/resources/files/Education_from_a_Gender_Equality_Perspective.pdf

U. S. Department of Education. (2008). *Fast facts*. Retrieved September 28, 2008, from http://nces.ed.gov/fastfacts/display.asp?id=16

Valerio, A., Bardasi, E., Chambal, A., & Lobo, M. F. (2006). Mozambique: School fees and primary school enrollment and retention. In A. Coudouel, A. A. Dani, & S. Paternostro (Eds.), *Poverty & social impact analysis of reforms: Lessons and examples from implementation* (pp. 93–148). Washington, DC: The World Bank.

Viana, I., Carepa, J., & Camilo, A. (2009, September). *Schooling transitions to evaluate the impact of the Bolsa Família Program in Brazil: Breaking the intergenerational cycle of poverty*. Poster presented at the 26th meeting of the IUSSP International Population Conference, Marrakech, Morocco. Retrieved August 1, 2009, from the Princeton University Web site: http://iussp2009.princeton.edu/download.aspx?submissionId=93015

Web Japan. (n.d.). *Education: Foundation for growth and prosperity*. Retrieved October 27, 2008, from http://web-japan.org/factsheet/pdf/EDUCATIO.pdf

World Bank. (2007). *Bolsa Familia: Changing the lives of millions in Brazil*. Retrieved December 4, 2007, from http://web.worldbank.org/WBSITE/EXTERNAL/COUNTRIES/LACEXT/BRAZILEXTN/0,contentMDK:21447054~pagePK:141137~piPK:141127~theSitePK:322341,00.html

Yang, S., & Shin, C. S. (2008). Parental attitudes towards education: What matters for children's well-being? *Children and Youth Services Review, 30,* 1328–1335.

Chapter Eight

Abdelmoneium, A. O. (2005). Challenges facing children in education and labour: Case study of displaced children in Khartoum-Sudan. *The Ahfad Journal, 22*(2), 64–76.

Acid attack keeps Afghan girls away from school. (2008, November 14). *MSNBC News*. Retrieved March 15, 2009, from http://www.msnbc.msn.com/id/27713077

Almond, D., & Edlund, L. (2008). Son-biased sex ratios in the 2000 United States Census. *PNAS: Proceedings of the National Academy of Sciences, 105*(15), 5681–5682.

American Academy of Pediatrics. (1998). Female genital mutilation. *Pediatrics, 102*(1), 153–156.

Amnesty International. (2004). *Making violence against women count*. Retrieved August 25, 2006, from http://web.amnesty.org/library/pdf/ACT770362004ENGLISH/$File/ACT7703604.pdf

Association for Women's Rights in Development. (2002). *The Convention on the Eliminations of All Forms of Discrimination Against Women and the Optional Protocol*. Retrieved September 11, 2006, from http://www.awid.org/publications/primers/factsissues2.pd

Attacks deprive 300,000 students of education. (2008, September 22). *IRIN News*. Retrieved September 23, 2008, from http://www.irinnews.org/Report.aspx?ReportId=80506

Bruni, F. (2004, February 1). Doctor in Italy tries to ease pain of an African tradition. *New York Times*, p. A3.

Child marriage worsens population pressure. (2009, March 16). *IRIN News*. Retrieved March 17, 2009, from http://www.irinnews.com/Report.aspx?ReportId=83505

Chun, H., & Gupta, M. D. (2009). Gender discrimination in sex selective abortions and its transition in South Korea. *Women's Studies International Forum, 32*, 89–97.

Cross-border FGM on the rise. (2008, October 17). *IRIN News*. Retrieved October 20, 2008, from http://www.irinnews.com/Report.aspx?ReportId=80988

Cutters turn razors on babies to evade FGM/C law. (2009, January 27). *IRIN News*. Retrieved January 28, 2009, from http://www.irinnews.com/Report.aspx?ReportId=82600

Dauer, S. (2001). Indivisible or invisible: Women's human rights in the public and private sphere. In M. Agosín (Ed.), *Women, gender and human rights: A global perspective* (pp. 65–82). New Brunswick, NJ: Rutgers University Press.

Daughters fetch high process as brides. (2007, July 17). *IRIN News*. Retrieved August 16, 2007, from http://www.irinnews.com/Report.aspx?ReportId=73272

Devraj, R. (2003). *A murderous arithmetic*. Retrieved August 26, 2006, from http://www.indiatogether.org/2003/jul/wom-girls.htm

Dial SOS circumcision and stop girls being cut. (2005, March 18). *IRIN News*. Retrieved April 17, 2009, from http://www.irinnews.com/Report.aspx?ReportId=53474

Early marriage adds to socioeconomic woes, NGOs say. (2008, November 26). *IRIN News*. Retrieved November 28, 2008, from http://www.irinnews.com/Report.aspx?ReportId=81667

Easton, P., Monkman, K., & Miles, R. (2003). Social policy from the bottom up: Abandoning FGC in sub-Saharan Africa. *Development in Practice, 13*(5), 445–458.

Ford, N. (2005). Communication for abandonment of female genital cutting: An approach based on human rights principles. *The International Journal of Children's Rights, 13*, 183–199.

Girl's death prompts search for new strategies to fight FGM. (2007, October 2). *IRIN News*. Retrieved September 27, 2007, from http://www.irinnews.com/Report.aspx?ReportId=74529

Government body moves to stem female genital mutilation. (2008, July 1). *IRIN News*. Retrieved July 1, 2008, from http://www.irinnews.com/Report.aspx?ReportId=79025

Guimbert, S., Miwa, K., & Nguyen, D. T. (2008). Back to school in Afghanistan: Determinants of school enrollment. *International Journal of Educational Development, 28*, 419–434.

Hayford, S. R. (2005). Conformity and change: Community effects on female genital cutting in Kenya. *Journal of Health and Social Behavior, 46*(2), 121–140.

International Center for Research on Women (ICRW). (2007). *How to end child marriage: Action strategies for prevention and protection*. Retrieved March 14, 2009, from http://www.icrw.org/docs/2007-childmarriagepolicy.pdf

Jha., P., Kumar, R., Vasa, P., Dhingra, N., Thiruchelvam, D., & Moineddin, R. (2006). Low male-to-female sex ratio of children born in India: National survey of 1.1 million households. *Lancet, 367*, 211–218.

Kassindja, F., & Bashir, L. M. (1999). *Do they hear you when you cry?* New York: Random House.

Kaur, G. (2006). *Foeticide journeys*. Retrieved August 26, 2006, from the India Together Web site: http://www.indiatogether.org/2006/aug/wom-usfoet.htm

LaFraniere, S. (2005, September 28). Nightmare for African women: Birthing injury and little help. *New York Times*. Retrieved September 28, 2005, from http://www.nytimes.com

Leidl, P. (2006). *Dying to give life: Maternal mortality in Afghanistan*. Retrieved August 26, 2006, from http://www.unfpa.org/news/news.cfm?ID=822&Language=1

Levine, R., Lloyd, C., Greene, M., & Grown, C. (2008). *Girls count: A global investment & action agenda*. Retrieved November 28, 2008, from http://www.icrw.org/docs/Girls_Count_a_Global_Investment_&_Action_Agenda.pdf

Merry, S. E. (2001). Women, violence, and the human rights system. In M. Agosín (Ed.), *Women, gender and human rights: A global perspective* (pp. 83–97). New Brunswick, NJ: Rutgers University Press.

Mikhail, S. L. B. (2002). Child marriage and child prostitution: Two forms of sexual exploitation. *Gender and Development, 10*(1), 43–49.

More parents saying no to FGM. (2008, September 11). *IRIN News*. Retrieved September 15, 2008, from http://www.irinnews.com/Report.aspx?ReportId=80290

Nishimura, M., Yamano, T., & Sasaoka, Y. (2008). Impacts of the universal primary education policy on educational attainment and private costs in rural Uganda. *International Journal of Educational Development, 28*, 161–175.

Origins of the violence in Swat Valley. (2009, February 26). *IRIN News*. Retrieved March 15, 2009, from http://www.irinnews.com/Report.aspx?ReportId=83105

Parrot, A., & Cummings, N. (2006). *Forsaken females: The global brutalization of women*. Lanham, MD: Rowman & Littlefield.

"Pleasure hospital" under construction for FGM/C victims. (2009, May 6). *IRIN News*. Retrieved May 6, 2009, from http://www.irinnews.com/Report.aspx?ReportId=84256

Ryan, W. A. (2006). *Fistula repair facility brings hope to the outcast*. Retrieved August 26, 2006, from http://www.unfpa.org/news/news.cfm?ID=818

Save the Children Denmark, Ministry of Education, & Ministry of Women's Affairs. (2008). *A study on violence against girls in primary schools and its impacts on girls' education in Ethiopia*. Retrieved October 7, 2008, from the UNGEI Web site: http://www.ungei.org/resources/files/Study_on_Violence_Against_schoolgfils_final.pdf

Sheth, S. S. (2006). Missing female births in India. *Lancet, 367,* 185–186.

Slackman, M. (2007, September 20). In Egypt, a rising push against genital cutting. *New York Times*. Retrieved September 20, 2007, from http://www.nytimes.com

Threat to legislation outlawing child marriage. (2009, February 23). *IRIN News*. Retrieved February 23, 2009, from http://www.irinnews.com/Report.aspx?ReportId=83081

Two thousand girls a year suffer genital mutilation. (2007, August 27). *IRIN News*. Retrieved August 27, 2007, from http://www.irinnews.com/Report.aspx?ReportId=73971

UNICEF. (1999). *The state of the world's children 1999: Education.* Retrieved September 8, 2006, from http://www.unicef.org/publications/files/pub_sowc99_en.pdf

UNICEF. (2004). *State of the world's children 2004*. Retrieved April 16, 2009, from http://www.unicef.org/sowc04/files/SOWC_O4_eng.pdf

UNICEF. (2005). *Changing a harmful social convention: Female genital mutilation/cutting.* Retrieved August 30, 2006, from http://www.unicef-icdc.org/publications/pdf/fgm-gb-2005.pdf

UNICEF. (2006). *State of the world's children 2006*. Retrieved June 21, 2006, from http://www.unicef.org/publications/index_30398.html

UNICEF. (2007). *A world fit for children statistical review*. Retrieved February 27, 2009, from http://www.unicef.org/publications/files/Progress_for_Children_No_6_revised.pdf

UNICEF. (2008). *Child marriage and the law: Legislative reform initiative paper series*. Retrieved February 27, 2009, from http://www.unicef.org/policyanalysis/files/Child_Marriage_and_the_Law(1).pdf

UNICEF. (2009). *Female genital cutting must stop*. Retrieved February 9, 2009, from http://www.unicef.org/media/media_47845.html

UNICEF. (n.d.). *Factsheet: Female genital mutilation/cutting.* Retrieved January 11, 2006, from http://www.unicef.org/protection/files/FGM.pdf

United Nations. (1995). *Platform for action*. Retrieved April 16, 2009, from http://www.un.org/womenwatch/daw/beijing/platform/girl.htm

United Nations. (2006). *Reservations to CEDAW*. Retrieved August 24, 2006, from http://www.un.org/womenwatch/daw/cedaw/reservations.htm

United Nations. (2007). *The girl child: Report of the Secretary General.* Retrieved February 28, 2008, from http://www2.ohchr.org/English/bodies/GA/62documents.htm

United Nations. (2009). *Convention on the Elimination of All Forms of Discrimination against Women*. Retrieved February 22, 2009, from http://treaties.un.org/Pages/ViewDetails.aspx?src=TREATY&id=326&chapter=4&lang=en

United Nations Population Fund [UNFPA]. (2006). *Fast facts: Fistula and reproductive health*. Retrieved August 26, 2006, from the Campaign to End Fistula Web site: http://www.endfistula.org/fast_facts.htm

United Nations Population Fund. (n.d.a). *Child marriage fact sheet.* Retrieved March 14, 2009, from http://www.unfpa.org/swp/2005/presskit/factsheets/facts_child_marriage.htm

United Nations Population Fund. (n.d.b). *Obstetric fistula in brief.* Retrieved March 14, 2009, from the Campaign to End Fistula Web site: http://www.endfistula.org/fistula_brief.htm

United Nations Population Fund. (n.d.c). *The campaign in brief.* Retrieved March 14, 2009, from the Campaign to End Fistula Web site: http://www.endfistula.org/campaign_brief.htm

United Nations Security Council. (2007). *Children and armed conflict: Report of the Secretary-General.* Retrieved February 23, 2008, from http://www.un.org/children/conflict/english/index.html

USAID. (2008). *Education from a gender equality perspective*. Retrieved October 16, 2008, from the UNGEI Web site: http://www.ungei.org/resources/files/Education_from_a_Gender_Equality_Perspective.pdf

von der Osten-Sacken, T., & Uwer, T. (2007). Is female genital mutilation an Islamic problem? *Middle East Quarterly, 14*(1), 29–36.

Widespread child marriage blamed for domestic violence. (2007, October 16). *IRIN News*. Retrieved October 17, 2007, from http://www.irinnews.com/Report.aspx?ReportId=74793

World Bank. (n.d.). *The Adolescent Girls Initiative*. Retrieved November 28, 2008, from http://go.worldbank.org/5PYHEZS360

World Health Organization. (2006). Female genital mutilation and obstetric outcome: WHO collaborative prospective study in six African countries. *Lancet, 367*, 1835–1841.

World Vision. (2008). *Before she's ready: 15 places girls marry by 15.* Retrieved March 14, 2009, from http://www.worldvision.org/resources.nsf/main/early-marriage.pdf/$file/early-marriage.pdf

Worth, R. F. (2008, June 29). Tiny voices defy fate of girls in Yemen. *New York Times*, p. A8.

Zhu, W. X., Lu., & Hesketh, T. (2009). China's excess males, sex selective abortion, and one child policy: Analysis of data form 2005 national inter-census survey. *BMJ, 338*. Retrieved April 16, 2009, from http://www.bmj.com/cgi/reprint/338/apr09_2/b1211.pdf

Conclusion

Homan, M. S. (2007). *Promoting community change: Making it happen in the real world* (4th ed.). Belmont, CA: Wadsworth/Thomson.

Mapp, S. (2008). *Human rights and social justice in a global perspective: An introduction to international social work*. New York: Oxford University Press.

Index